AF361413

UGO FOSCOLO'S TRAGIC VISION IN ITALY
AND ENGLAND

RACHEL A. WALSH

Ugo Foscolo's Tragic Vision in Italy and England

UNIVERSITY OF TORONTO PRESS
Toronto Buffalo London

ISBN 978-1-4426-4926-2

Printed on acid-free, 100% post-consumer recycled paper with vegetable-based inks.

Toronto Italian Studies

Library and Archives Canada Cataloguing in Publication

Walsh, Rachel A., 1975–, author
Ugo Foscolo's tragic vision in Italy and England/Rachel A. Walsh.

(Toronto Italian studies)
Includes bibliographical references and index.
ISBN 978-1-4426-4926-2 (bound)

1. Foscolo, Ugo, 1778–1827 – Criticism and interpretation.   2. Italian drama (Tragedy) – England.   I. Title.   II. Series: Toronto Italian studies

PQ4691.W24 2014   852'.6   C2014-905022-4

This book was published with the support of the Anna Maglione-Sie Endowment for Italian Culture at the University of Denver.

University of Toronto Press acknowledges the financial assistance to its publishing program of the Canada Council for the Arts and the Ontario Arts Council.

University of Toronto Press acknowledges the financial support of the Government of Canada through the Canada Book Fund for its publishing activities.

For Josh, Penny, Tad, and Lex

Contents

Acknowledgments

The subject of Foscolo the tragedian has been one of fascination for me for many years. I am deeply indebted to numerous individuals and institutions that have assisted me in various ways with this obsession. The financial assistance I received from the University of Denver's Faculty Research Fund, Internationalization Grants, Rosenberry Fund, and the Anna Maglione-Sie Endowment Faculty Research Travel Grants allowed me to conduct valuable research in Italy in 2009 and 2011. I was warmly welcomed and supported by the Biblioteca Nazionale Braidense and the Biblioteca Communale at Palazzo Sormani in Milan. The Biblioteca Nazionale Marciana and the Biblioteca d'Arte e Storia Veneziana del Civico Museo Correr were immensely helpful while I researched in Venice. I am extremely grateful for the University of Denver's Anna Maglione-Sie Endowment for Italian culture, which also provided funding for this book's publication costs.

Individuals, not just institutions, have been instrumental figures along the way. I am most indebted to Francesco Bruni of the Università Ca' Foscari di Venezia, whose steadfast counsel has been essential to this project, from when it was initially conceived many years ago in Chicago to my most recent trip to Venice. His astonishing intellect leaves me speechless, and he has provided me both erudite guidance and unrestricted access to the Ca' Foscari libraries and resources. I am also extremely grateful to Paolo Cherchi for his unparalleled wisdom, scholarly backing, and camaraderie over the years. He has been immensely generous with his time and support. I also must thank my dissertation adviser, Elissa Weaver, whose unfaltering direction pushed me to understand better what I was doing, and why I was doing it, when this project first began. She tirelessly follows my work with great care and impeccable thoroughness. Likewise, I have benefited greatly from professional guidance, encouragement, and invaluable advice from Armando Maggi and Rebecca West. My friendship with each of these scholars has deeply enriched my life and has inspired me to continue to revise and rethink my work.

I am forever grateful for the collective spirit of my colleagues, especially Suzanne Magnanini, who has served as a great mentor and friend here in Colorado. My enduring friendships with other alumni from Chicago, including Kristi Grimes, Nathalie Hester, Sally Hill, Peg Kern, Davide Papotti, and Courtney Quaintance, have provided me with much-needed social and intellectual relief over the years. I also am thankful for the support and amity of my University of Denver colleagues Alison Krögel and Li Li Peters. I would be remiss if I did not acknowledge my tremendous research assistant Desiree Patterson (BA Italian and Biology 2012). She was invaluable for this project and even found a curious fascination of her own for Urbano Lampredi.

Many Italianists have had the distinct pleasure of working with the University of Toronto Press in its Italian Studies series. I consider myself extremely fortunate to be one of them. I am also forever indebted to the late Ron Schoeffel, who closely guided me through the intricacies of publishing with a university press from this project's inception until his passing in the summer of 2013. It is one of the biggest regrets of my academic career that I never was able to celebrate my published manuscript with him. And yet, my work passed seamlessly and attentively into the hands of a new editor, Richard Ratzlaff, who provided a similarly invaluable – and refreshingly distinct – guiding hand. I am very grateful for his astute insights and enthusiastic support for my work. Together with the immensely valuable and constructive reports of several blind-reviewers, and John St James's meticulous copy-editing, my UTP experience could not have been more rewarding. This profound and exhaustive care directly assisted with the creation of the present volume.

Finally, I am humbled by the continuous love and support I receive from my family and friends. I am forever grateful for the generosity of the Foglizzo family, who welcomed me to Torino and into their home more than twenty years ago and who continue to support me whenever I travel to Italy. They were instrumental in helping me fall in love with all things Italian and their loving embrace is the primary reason why I do what I do today. And my deepest gratitude must go to my husband, Josh, for his thoughtful edits (even when he had his own deadlines to meet), and his steadfast belief in me. Not often does one find a spouse willing and able to move wherever and whenever for the other's career in the humanities. I am tremendously fortunate in this regard. My project never would have materialized without his efforts and support. Similarly, I will always be indebted to our children's "second mother," Cynthia, who lovingly cared for them while I finished this manuscript. Lastly, I thank my incomparable eight-year-old daughter, Penny, and my amazing four-year-old twin sons, Tad and Lex. I sacrificed too many hours and days with them, all for the figure of Foscolo.

Chronology of Ugo Foscolo's Life and Works

1778	6 February	Niccolò Foscolo is born on the Ionian island of Zakynthos to Andrea Foscolo and Diamanta Spathis.
1785		Family moves to Split, a Venetian colony on the Dalmatian Coast, where Andrea is appointed military hospital surgeon.
1788		Andrea dies.
1792		Family moves to Venice.
1794		Writes his first collection of poems – *Versi dell'adolescenza* – and dedicates them to his friend Costantino Naranzi.
1795		Begins to refer to himself as Ugo and writes the odes "La campagna," "A Dante," "La verità," and "La morte di ***."
1796	July	Retreats to the Euganean hills and begins work on his epistolary novel *Ultime lettere di Jacopo Ortis*.
	September	Returns to Venice and completes his *Piano di studi* and his first tragedy, *Tieste*. In this year, he also writes the poems "In morte del padre," "Il mio tempo," "In morte di Amaritte," "La croce," "Le rimembranze," "A Venezia," and "Al sole." The Repubblica Cispadana is formed at the end of this year. It includes Modena, Reggio Emilia, Bologna, and Ferrara.

1797	4 January	First tragedy, *Tieste*, debuts at the Teatro Sant'Angelo in Venice. The performance is replicated nine times.
	7 January	Giuseppe Compagnoni proposes the red, white, and green flag ultimately adopted by the Repubblica Cispadana.
	April	Leaves Venice for Bologna. The review "Notizie storico-critiche of Tieste" appears in volume 10 of Venice's *Teatro moderno applaudito*. The Repubblica Cispadana is absorbed into the larger Repubblica Cisalpina. The new entity comprises Lombardy, Cispadana, Massa, and Carrara.
	12 May	The First Coalition and Napoleon conquer Venice. Ludovico Manin, the last Doge, steps down.
	16–19 May	Returns to Venice.
	27 May	Co-authors "Per la istituzione d'un teatro civico."
	June	Participates in the Società di pubblica istruzione.
	27 October	Treaty of Campoformio is signed and Napoleon gives Venice to the Austrians. Foscolo retreats to Milan in October. In this year, he writes the poems "Sonetto," "In morte del padre," "La giustizia e la pietà," and "Ai novelli repubblicani" and begins work on "Bonaparte liberatore."
1798		A partial version of *Ultime lettere di Jacopo Ortis* is published in Bologna.
1799		Foscolo becomes a soldier for the republican army.
1800	June	Battle of Marengo. Foscolo is promoted to the rank of captain.
1802		Completes *Ultime lettere di Jacopo Ortis* and publishes it in Milan. He also writes his "Orazione a Bonaparte."
1803		Publishes his *Commento alla Chioma di Berenice* and his *Poesie*, a collection including "Alla

		sera," "A Zacinto," "In morte del fratello Giovanni," in Milan.
1804	May	Napoleon proclaims himself emperor and king of Italy.
1804–6		Foscolo is stationed in Valenciennes, France. He begins to work on translating Laurence Sterne's *A Sentimental Journey through France and Italy*. He is romantically linked to the mother (presumed to be Sophia Hamilton) of his only child, a daughter named Floriana, whom he would not meet until the final years of his life in England.
1806	March	Returns to Milan.
1807	April	Publishes his translation of the *Iliad* and his solemn poem *Dei sepolcri*.
1808	August	His first tragedy is staged at Milan's Teatro Carcano with the new title of *Atreo e Tieste*. It plays for three nights.
1809	22 January	As Chair of Eloquence at the University of Pavia, delivers his inaugural lecture, "Dell'origine e dell'ufficio della letteratura."
1810	4 April	Publishes "Sulla traduzione dell'*Odissea*" in the journal *Annali di scienze e lettere*.
	5 April	Publishes "Ragguaglio d'un'adunanza dell'Accademia de' Pitagorici" in the *Annali di scienze e lettere*.
	April	Begins writing "Ultimato di Ugo Foscolo nella guerra contro i ciarlatani, gl'impostori letterari ed i pedanti," "Il pasticcio settimanale per associazione," and "Sull'accademia de' pitagorici."
1811		Begins to work on his incomplete series of essays *I Frammenti sul Machiavelli*.
	5 May	Publishes the essay "Della poesia lirica" in the *Annali di scienze e lettere*.
	6 June	Publishes the essay "Memoria intorno ai druidi e ai bardi britanni" in *Annali di scienze e lettere*.
	7 July	Publishes the essay "Degli effetti della fame e della disperazione sull'uomo" and intends

		to publish the essay "Dello scopo di Gregorio VII" in the *Annali di scienze e lettere*, but censors prohibit its publication.
	9 December	His second tragedy, *Ajace*, debuts at Teatro alla Scala in Milan.
1812	Winter	Spends three months in Venice, where he visits with his mother for the last time before her death.
	17 August	Arrives in Florence, following a brief visit to Bologna. He finishes his translation of *A Sentimental Journey* and publishes it along with his humorous *Notizia intorno a Didimo Chierico* in Pisa in 1813.
1813	April	Resides at villa Bellosguardo and continues working on his poems, *Le Grazie*, and his third tragedy, *Ricciarda*.
	July	Leaves Florence for Milan.
	August	Visits Belgioioso and Como.
	September	Arrives in Bologna.
	17 September	*Ricciarda* debuts at the Teatro del Corso in Bologna.
1814	May	Napoleon is defeated at Leipzig and abdicates.
	September	The Congress of Vienna convenes to redraw the European map and establish the spheres of influence of Austria, England, France, and Russia. The work is finalized only in June 1815.
1815		Count K.L. Ficquelmont approaches Foscolo about developing a new journal in Milan. Foscolo accepts, and in February he writes his proposal "Parere sulla istituzione di un giornale letterario," which is approved by Vienna.
	30 March	Leaves Italy for Switzerland, never to return.
1816	1 January	Writes and privately publishes three copies of his *Vestigi della storia del sonetto italiano*. He also finishes and publishes his *Hypercalypseos* and another edition of the *Ultime lettere di*

	Jacopo Ortis during the first few months of 1816.
July	Applies for a visa to travel to England.
17 August	Leaves Switzerland and travels to England.
September	Arrives in London and immediately begins writing *Lettere scritte dall'Inghilterra* and what would become *Gazzettino del bel Mondo*, but never finishes the works.
1817	Publishes a new edition of *Ultime lettere di Jacopo Ortis* (John Murray).
1818	Writes his "Articles on Dante" and publishes them with the *Edinburgh Review*. He also writes his "Essay on the Present Literature of Italy" as an accompaniment to Byron's *Childe Harold's Pilgrimage*, canto the fourth (London: John Murray) and works on his "Writings on the Ionian Islands."
1819	Writes his article "Narrative and Romantic Poems of the Italians" for the *Quarterly Review*. Publishes his article "On Parga" in the *Edinburgh Review*.
1820	Publishes *Ricciarda* (John Murray).
1821	Writes the articles "Learned Ladies" (January), "An Account of the Revolution of Naples during the Years 1798, 1799" (January), and "On Hamlet" (April) for Thomas Campbell's *New Monthly Magazine*. Publishes his "Essays on Petrarch" in volume form this year and again in 1823. His only child, Floriana, comes to live with him after the death of her maternal grandmother.
1822	Writes his series of articles "Italian Poets" for the *New Monthly Magazine* and publishes "History of the Aeolic Digamma" in the *Quarterly Review*.
1823	Begins work on a series of lectures, later titled *Epoche della lingua Italiana*.
1824	Publishes two articles corresponding to the first two lectures, "Principles of Poetical Criticism as Applicable, More Especially

	to Italian Literature" and "Origin and Vicissitudes of the Italian Language" in the *European Review*. He also publishes "Italian Periodical Literature" with the *European Review* and the articles "Classical Tours" and "Antiquarians and Critics" for the *Retrospective Review*. He and Floriana are forced to leave his custom-designed home "Digamma Cottage" in Regent's Park due to overwhelming debt.
1825	Writes his "Discourse on the Text of the Divine Comedy" and "Historical Discourse on the Text of the Decameron."
1826	Begins to write the article "Della nuova scuola drammatica italiana." Publishes the articles "Boccaccio" and "The Women of Italy" in the *London Magazine*.
1827	Moves to the London suburb of Turnham Green. Publishes "Memoirs of Casanova" in the *Westminster Review* and "History of the Democratical Constitution of Venice" in the *Edinburgh Review*.
10 September	Dies following an operation for dropsy. He is buried in the Chiswick churchyard.
1871	Foscolo's remains are transported to Florence and reinterred at the church of Santa Croce.

UGO FOSCOLO'S TRAGIC VISION IN ITALY
AND ENGLAND

Ugo Foscolo's Tragic Vision

Ugo Foscolo (born on Zakynthos, 1778; died at Turnham Green, London, 1827), one of Italy's most celebrated figures, found himself at the home of his dear friend Giambattista Giovio (1748–1814) in Como at the end of August 1813.[1] He was fortunate to arrive in Como precisely when the town's newest architectural marvel, the Teatro Sociale, opened on Saturday, 28 August. Perhaps he was moved by the excitement of the opening, or even more likely, by the public reaction to the newest building in town. Whatever the case, Foscolo wrote a curious and seemingly random article about the architecture of the new theatre and the public reception of its construction. This piece, entitled "Sul nuovo teatro di Como," appears in issue number 30 of the *Giornale del Lario*.[2]

Foscolo focused his article on evaluating the *disegno intellettuale* (intellectual design) of the theatre's architect, Giuseppe Cusi. He defended Cusi's original design, or vision, of what he intended the theatre to become. There were other factors that played into the ultimate outcome, however. Extraneous circumstances, modifications, and even distortions of the original design influenced the finished product in the end. Foscolo proceeded to discuss each of these defects and he concluded from his observations that the architect and his talents should be judged more favourably based solely on the quality of his *disegno*, and not how it was actually implemented.

"Sul nuovo teatro di Como" has always been an oddity for Foscolo scholars. The article's subject matter seems on the surface to be a substantial departure from what literary scholars and historians would commonly associate with Foscolo, who is best known as a canonical novelist and poet – and not an expert in architectural design. Indeed, critics attempting to assign an all-encompassing label to the multifaceted intellectual usually classify him as Foscolo the Greek, the Italian, the exile, the poet, the critic, the Romantic, the neoclassicist, the patriot, and even Foscolo the lover. He certainly has never enjoyed the title of "architectural critic." This begs an important question – could there be a literary connection to this architectural work?

A good place to begin this inquiry is Foscolo's interest in the theatre. He had already written three neoclassical tragedies by the time his architectural article was published. His first tragedy, *Tieste*, debuted in Venice in January 1797, when Foscolo was only eighteen years old. The young author relied on his solid neoclassical training in Italian letters, adhering to Alfierian model in his debut on the tragic stage. Venetian audiences embraced his inaugural work, and it enjoyed a modest run of ten performances.

Foscolo did not return to the Italian tragic stage for another twelve years. When he did, critics and audiences alike did not warmly receive his most recent attempt. He may have been an established author and poet by this time, but that made no matter, at least in Milan, where the literary establishment rejected his poetics and approach to literary history. It did not help that Foscolo publically criticized the critical prowess of several members of the ruling literary elite in the pages of Milanese literary journals. This makes his decision to debut *Ajace* in Milan in December 1811 somewhat curious. And unfortunately for Foscolo, the debut ended in laughter – the worst possible ending for a tragedy – and several scathing reviews promptly followed. But Foscolo was not dissuaded. In fact he was as determined as ever to seek out success in the genre. His third and final attempt, *Ricciarda*, opened in Bologna in September 1813. Yet poor acting and downright unfortunate circumstances thwarted his final endeavour as well.

One persistent regret for Foscolo was that he never saw his intended tragic vision performed the way that he had envisioned. One could interpret, therefore, Foscolo's defence of the architect in "Sul nuovo teatro di Como" to be a metaphorical response for his own lack of success on the stage. An obvious parallel between the architect and a tragedian emerges: Foscolo presumably thought that just as an architect should bear little or no responsibility for the flawed implementation of his design, neither should a tragedian be held solely responsible for the stage production of his tragedies. That outcome depends on circumstances far beyond the tragedian's control, and people other than the tragedian are instrumental to this final production. The dramatist must continuously grapple with any number of obstacles – the censors, potentially inept actors, the Italian public, and the critics.

So why was succeeding as a tragedian so important for Foscolo? He achieved long-lasting renown as a poet and novelist, so it is hard to call his literary career a failure in retrospect. But it was not enough. Foscolo firmly believed that the tragedy was the highest form of literary accomplishment. He proclaimed this very idea even after his three failed attempts in an 1817 letter to his friend Silvio Pellico (1789–1854). He wrote, "One truthfully can say that a tragedy is the most beautiful product of human intelligence."[3] Compounding this yearning for poetic prestige was the opportunity for nearly instant celebrity status as a dramatist through the performance of the work. Put simply, tragedy gave Foscolo the potential to achieve simultaneously critical acclaim as well as popular fame from the masses.

Yet the masses did not grant Foscolo this long-sought fame. His neoclassical tragedies did not appeal to the ever-changing contemporary tastes and ideals of the long-eighteenth-century audiences, who instead ultimately found favour with the emerging Romantic tragedies. And scholars continue to neglect these works.[4] They generally consider Foscolo to be a failure as a tragedian – that is, if they even think about Foscolo's efforts in the genre at all. So, what then is the point of studying a particular author's literary failures? And how can this analysis contribute to defining a canonical author and his/her place in history? This book argues that these failures spark two profitable lines of inquiry – the theoretical and the biographical.

First and perhaps foremost, we are able to approach Foscolo's contemporary and future writings from a new perspective. His botched tragedies shaped his theoretical mindset when writing these works. From this angle, it becomes – or should become – clear that Foscolo did not limit his participation in the field of Italian tragedy to his tragedies and "Sul nuovo teatro di Como." Again and again, he unremittingly returned to the genre in both his letters and literary critical articles over a thirty-year period.

An exhaustive examination of Foscolo's subsequent writings on tragedy and theatre sheds further light on his active and extensive participation in and commitment to the field of literary journalism – participation that only flourished following his self-exile from Italy. Foscolo reviewed his own tragedies and those of other Italian dramatists, in addition to analysing Italian and European literary trends on the subject. He vigorously engaged with leading Italian and English intellectual figures in shaping Italian cultural identity on the pages of journals in Europe. Despite – or better, owing to – his exiled status, Foscolo was not isolated from Italian cultural debates. Quite the reverse, in fact.

Foscolo's failure in the genre of tragedy also allows us to reread his biography in an important new light. Today's reader can appreciate Foscolo's personal inner struggles and very public quarrels surrounding the composition, performance, and reviews of his three tragic works. The entirety of Foscolo's body of work demonstrates that for him the stage was more than just a forum to display his literary excellence – it was also a venue through which he could shape and influence the manner in which history would remember him. His efforts to live and breathe the tragedy in many ways blurred the line between writing about – and living – this tragic vision. A new narrative of Foscolo emerges through this tragic lens. It is a biography that hinges on the intersection of self-fashioning and fluctuating literary trends and the pivotal role that both political and literary conflict played in shaping the figure of Foscolo.

This book reassesses Foscolo's position in literary history as a tragedian, but it also describes the development of an Italian literary canon of the late eighteenth and early nineteenth centuries as created by the exiled author. *Ugo Foscolo's Tragic Vision in Italy and England* argues that the final period of Foscolo's life was intrinsically linked to his first, more creative period. It explains how Foscolo's artistic choices in his three tragedies came to influence his future literary-critical articles on the genre. Above all, this book's value resides in its unique literary-historical insights into the interpretation of a canonical, beloved, and – yes – tragic Italian literary figure.[5]

Ugo Foscolo's Tragic Vision in Italy and England provides this new interpretation of a canonical figure over five chapters. It presents the tragedies' compositions, debuts, and initial receptions and reviews, along with Foscolo's numerous literary-critical writings and epistolary reflections on the genre. Chapter 1 begins with a brief explanation of the status of the Italian tragedy during the eighteenth century. It sets the stage and presents the pertinent aspects of Foscolo's early education and his "relationships" with three extraordinarily influential figures in Italian culture and letters: Ludovico Antonio Muratori (1672–1750), Melchiorre Cesarotti (1730–1808), and Vittorio Alfieri (1749–1803). These eighteenth-century Italian intellectuals provided Foscolo with the necessary tools to compose his own tragedies and heavily influenced his subsequent literary-critical articles on the genre. The chapter continues with a discussion of Foscolo's neoclassical education. Even from the earliest points in his career, Foscolo apparently believed that the only way to achieve his desired success as a tragedian was to strictly adhere to the neoclassical principles espoused by his mentors.

The book continues chronologically with an examination of Foscolo's first contribution to the Italian tragic stage, *Tieste* (Venice, 1797). Chapter 2 explores the Italian reception of his first tragedy, concentrating on the historical context in which it was composed. It presents the tragedy's inaugural performance and reception through Foscolo's contemporaneous correspondence, the few accounts of the debut as told by Foscolo's biographers, and the first review of *Tieste*. The chapter explores Foscolo's own reaction to his tragedy and the level of influence he may or may not have had on *Tieste*'s ultimate reception.

Chapter 2 continues with an examination of the lengthy period of 1797–1809, in which Foscolo did not write any tragedies. Still, he did contribute to the development of the genre by creating and honing his own literary theories on the form and, most important in this period, function of Italian literature. Foscolo turned to the role of public educator and explored the ways in which tragedy had the power to educate and entertain the audience. His opinions not only influenced his own future compositions; they also had a significant impact on the Italian tragic tradition.

Chapter 3 presents an in-depth discussion of Foscolo's second tragedy, *Ajace* (Milan, 1811). It concentrates on the historical context in which it was composed and recounts the tragedy's disastrous opening night performance, including the negative reception of *Ajace* seen through Foscolo's contemporaneous correspondence and accounts of the debut as told by Foscolo's biographers. It presents for the first time a detailed discussion of each of the seven reviews that appeared in Milanese journals following the debut. This chapter addresses Foscolo's defensive explanations of what went wrong at each debut (e.g., bad acting, bad luck, intentional efforts at sabotage by a hostile Milanese literary community), and it ultimately concludes that *Ajace* would have failed under any circumstance for a much simpler and less nefarious reason – it was not very good.

But Foscolo refused to abandon his second tragedy. Instead, he played the role of the victim. Chapter 3 continues in the wake of the *Ajace* debacle and covers the period of 1812–13, when Foscolo vehemently defended his second tragedy. It explores how he stood by his artistic choices, maintaining that his second tragedy was not a failure, both in his correspondence and in the seemingly insignificant article "Sul nuovo teatro di Como" (1813). These writings emphasize Foscolo's theoretical convictions, and his unequivocal denial should be seen as a broad rejoinder to his hostile critics and perhaps even a pre-emptive defence of his then-upcoming third tragedy, *Ricciarda*.

Chapter 4 examines this third, and final, contribution by Foscolo to the Italian tragedy tradition, *Ricciarda* (Bologna, 1813), concentrating on the historical context in which it was composed. Unfortunately for Foscolo, *Ricciarda* fared no better on the Italian stage than his earlier attempts. The inevitable catastrophic conclusion that characterizes the tragic vision reared its ugly head once more. There was nothing that Foscolo could do, despite his best efforts to avoid such an ending. The chapter examines the tragedy's abysmal debut through Foscolo's contemporaneous correspondence, the accounts of the debut as told by his biographers, and its reception in Italian literary journals.

Chapter 4 continues by following the defeated Foscolo into exile in Switzerland and England, covering the period of 1815–20. It examines how Foscolo remained haunted by his failed attempts on the stage and focuses on his turn towards literary critical articles. In these essays Foscolo expressed his talents and justified his literary tastes. Chapter 4 presents his fierce desire to achieve the reputation of a pre-eminent Italian tragedian and critic in English literary circles. Through the collaboration of such figures as Lord Byron (1788–1824) and the preeminent publisher, John Murray (1778–1843), Foscolo ultimately saw a relatively significant amount of English success for his *Ricciarda*.

This narrative of Foscolo concludes in chapter 5 by exploring Foscolo's final reflections on the genre of tragedy and the emerging Romantic school. This chapter examines how Foscolo's career as a critic of tragedy, which focused primarily on the notion of the effective imitation of nature, notably contributed to the European discourse surrounding the Italian Classicists-Romantics literary debate. Foscolo never achieved membership as a tragedian in the annals of Italian literature, yet his criticisms of those who would (and the responses and defences that these criticisms provoked) provide a fascinating window into the development of the canon during a profoundly important period in Italian – and Italian literary – history.

The Epilogue illustrates the potential impact that this re-envisioning of one of Italy's most revered figures through the tragic lens will have on literary studies, and it offers suggestions for future inquiry. Finally, the appendix contains transcriptions of the seven initial reviews of Foscolo's second tragedy, *Ajace*. Giuseppe Nicoletti recently published Urbano Lampredi's (1761–1838) four articles on *Ajace* in the 2011 second volume of the appendix to the *Edizione nazionale delle opera di Ugo Foscolo*.[6] While he lists them as part of "la prima ricezione," or the first reception, and the table of contents states that they are from 1811–12, the versions he chose to include were actually revised by Lampredi and published in 1828. Unfortunately, there is no explanation of how or even if the reviews are different. I accordingly have compiled the variations between the two. No one has collected and published the *original* reviews together and the appendix should prove to be a valuable resource for today's reader interested in the initial reception of Foscolo's second tragedy. After all, it was to these original reviews, and not those published after his death, that Foscolo reacted and responded.

Ugo Foscolo's Tragic Vision in Italy and England presents an original and complete sequential portrait of Foscolo as a tragedian and tragic critic, distinctly placing him in a broader historical chronology. Yet this book does not complete the study of Foscolo's tragedies and literary criticism by any stretch. It is my intent to use this literary-historical methodology to shed light on a number of important and influential topics in a crucial period of Italian literary history. Foscolo's own tragic struggles on and off the stage provide an interesting biographical thread by which contemporary readers can better understand one of the most fascinating and challenging figures in Italian literary history. Frederick May aptly described the difficult nature and importance of Foscolo studies in his 1964 article "Calliroe e Ifianeo": "So much in his life and in his writings Foscolo deliberately made ambiguous or hid away altogether. It is impossible to see him plain, yet equally impossible not to find enrichment in the enhanced distancing which derives from research upon him."[7] These are fitting words to close this brief introduction. I now welcome the reader to explore the vast world of *Foscoliana* through tragedy.

Chapter One

Setting the Stage

Ugo Foscolo's place in the pantheon of Italian literature as a tragedian must be contextualized. It cannot be accurately presented or appreciated without an explanation of the leading Italian literary theories and practices almost a century prior to Foscolo's contributions. The literary scene at the turn of the eighteenth century was highly contentious, and Italian literature often found itself to be the object of ridicule and scorn. French intellectuals began harshly attacking Italian poets of the Seicento for their lacklustre eloquence, lavish descriptions, and extravagant conceits. Nicolas Boileau-Despréaux (1636–1711), René Rapin (1621–78), and Dominique Bouhours (1628–1702) led the way, attacking Italian's general "bad taste" and the absence of the leading classical ideals of truth, wit, and pure imitation of nature.[1] Their biggest complaint focused on Italians' erroneous imitation of nature, and their too-heavy reliance on imagination at the expense of truth. The majority of attacks were aimed directly at the Marinisti, followers of the exemplary Baroque poet Giambattista Marino (1569–1625). French critics sternly condemned the quality of both the Italian language and Italian literature from Dante to Tasso to their own contemporaries to demonstrate what should *not* be done when composing various literary genres.

These works triggered a deluge of responses from numerous Italian intellectuals. The most famous was orchestrated by Giovan-Gioseffo Orsi (1652–1733), a critic who retorted directly to Dominique Bouhours's criticisms with his 1703 *Considerazioni sopra un famoso Libro Franzese intitolato La Manière de bien penser Dans les Ouvrages d'esprit.*[2] Orsi's *Considerazioni* was a subjective collaboration of Italian intellectuals' responses to Bouhours's attacks.[3] The group attempted to defend Italian literature while preserving and restoring the reputations of Petrarch and Tasso. Italians also directly bolstered individual authors cited in the French criticisms, such as Ludovico Antonio Muratori's *La vita di A.M. Maggi* (1700) and Giusto Fontanini's *'L'Aminta' di Torquato Tasso difeso e illustrato da Giusto Fontanini* (1701).

Formal academies produced a number of treatises designed to promote Italy's literary reputation and inspire a return to *buon gusto* among Italian authors. The *Arcadi*, members of the Academy of Arcadians in Rome, led the charge. Their *custode generale*, Giovan Mario Crescimbeni (1663–1728), put forth the highly influential treatise on what constitutes beautiful poetry, *La bellezza della volgar poesia* (1700, 1712, and 1731). Crescimbeni meticulously unpacked the virtues of poetry from antiquity to the present in an attempt to respond to French criticisms and to refashion Italian literary-cultural identity. He also penned a very direct and telling essay, *Osservazioni generali su la francese letteratura*, on the Academy's reaction to the French in 1697.[4] The Academy of Arcadians' proto-national responses were not limited to the city of Rome. Members came from throughout the peninsula and by 1726 forty colonies had been founded in various Italian cities.[5] Arcadians' efforts succeeded in sparking peninsula-wide discussions of how to reshape and renew Italian culture, while contributing to and ultimately influencing the fields of literary criticism and literary history throughout Europe. This example alone underscores how Italians were not going to sit idly by and play the part of the victim in this exchange.

French criticisms were complemented by the great success of French tragedies in the period. The works of Pierre Corneille (1606–84) and Jean Racine (1639–99) – although substantially different – were models for aspiring tragedians of what the literary genre should be. Both Corneille and Racine followed strict guidelines when composing their tragedies. They carefully observed the three classical unities of action, time, and place derived from Aristotle's *Poetics* (the plot must have a logical consistency and must be completed within a span of twenty-four hours in a single location). Their tragedies were composed entirely in rhyming couplets of twelve-syllable alexandrines, and they followed other clearly defined rules. Violent events could only occur offstage. The vocabulary was limited, with frequently repeated poetic phrases, which refrained from expressing any vulgarity. Corneille's tragedies centred on affairs of state and featured noble characters, who were never depicted as vile. Although Aristotle wrote that *katharsis* should be the goal of tragedy, for Corneille this was only an ideal.[6] He upheld the moral codes of the period, which insisted that plays must not show evil being rewarded or nobility being degraded. Racine's tragedies – inspired by Greek myths and the tragedians Euripides, Sophocles, and Seneca – condensed their plot into a tight set of passionate and duty-bound conflicts between a few noble characters, and concentrated on these characters' unfulfilled desires and hatreds. No one at the time challenged the French domination in the genre of classical tragedy, and their pre-eminent place in the seventeenth- and eighteenth-century literary hierarchy is still undisputed.

Seventeenth-century Italians stand in stark contrast to this French triumph. They enjoyed great success in the field of melodrama, but their presence on the tragic stage was uninspiring. Two exceptions stood out from the mediocrity: Scipione Maffei (1675–1755) and his 1714 *Merope* and Antonio Conti (1677–1749) with his 1726 *Giulio Cesare*. Both of these works are examples of *tragedia a lieto fine* – or tragedy with a happy ending. Enrico Mattioda justly explains how audiences found this sense of justice, or happy ending, appealing.[7] But these works ultimately sacrificed the requisite tragic gravitas for this sense of optimism. To make matters more difficult, there was the question of Italian tragic verse. There simply wasn't one. Pier Jacopo Martello (1665–1727) was instrumental in the quest to find a uniquely Italian version. His *verso martelliano* and opened the door for the iconic Alfierian *versi sciolti* that would appear at the end of the eighteenth century. So, the efforts of these early pioneers were not failures by any stretch. They just were not enough to challenge the French domination in the genre.

Nonetheless, the field of critical tragedy studies in Italy experienced a boom at the turn of the eighteenth century, with intellectuals seemingly producing more writings about tragedy and its perfect composition in the Italian context than actual tragedies themselves.[8] Although several of these authors indirectly responded to French criticisms, they were more interested in discussing the varying styles of recitation from country to country in general terms. Gian Vincenzo Gravina (1664–1718), Antonio Conti, Pietro Calepio (1693–1762), and Giuseppe Gorini Corio (1702–66) in particular offered theories on tragedy. They noted at times the stylistic differences between certain countries, but they also simultaneously avoided direct discussion of French critics and the substance of their criticism.[9] These intellectuals, who dictated the form and function of the ideal Italian tragedy, may have viewed the re-establishment of Italy's place of prominence in European letters as a matter of national pride, but they also put forth myriad differing – and oftentimes diametrically opposed – theories on what constituted the most fundamental characteristics of tragedy.

It is no secret that eighteenth-century Italian tragedy, like other genres, experienced a significant transformation. Theorists and tragedians sought to move the genre away from the previous century. But questions remained as to what the new Italian tragedy should be. Enrico Mattioda began his two-volume edition *Tragedie del Settecento* with a sixty-three-page introduction subtitled, fittingly, "Questioni,"[10] which led the reader through the intricate and often thorny process of monumental change. He examined how tragedians were faced with addressing the fraught relationship between authors and actors during the period. This included discourse surrounding recitation and the seemingly impossible task of finding a suitable Italian verse for the tragic stage.[11] Mattioda then discussed the relationship between the author and the spectator. Eighteenth-century authors and scholars thought long and hard on the function of theatre and its role in shaping the moral convictions of the audience. The introduction continues with lengthy inquiries into aesthetics and passions – ranging from the presence of religious morals on stage, to courtly norms regarding representations of violence on stage, to the limits of the spectator's imagination.[12] Mattioda further remarked on the shifts in tragedy's subject matter during the century from the mythological to the historical. This naturally raised the question of what history would be retold and to what aim?[13] The vast array of questions surrounding tragedy during this period illustrates the complexity of the genre in Italy during the period.

What did Italian authors then make of these queries? For the purpose of this book, three essential – and perhaps all-encompassing – questions arise when an aspiring tragedian, such as Foscolo, first steps out on the dramatist's stage – *What* are the required components of a good tragedy? *Why* would one write tragedies? And *how* precisely should one go about writing them? For Foscolo, the answers to these questions lay in the monumental treatises and essays of three prominent literary figures of eighteenth-century Italy: Ludovico Antonio Muratori, Melchiorre Cesarotti, and Vittorio Alfieri. The aspiring tragedian turned to Muratori to answer the *what*, to Cesarotti to answer the *why*, and to Alfieri to answer the *how*. Indeed, the works of these three men would prove to be instrumental in shaping the historical, theoretical, and compositional practices of Foscolo the tragedian.

Muratori was perhaps the most prominent Italian historian of his time, having written or edited numerous histories of Italian literature, including *Della perfetta poesia italiana* (written 1702–3, published 1706), *Rerum Italicarum scriptores*, 28 volumes, (1723–51), and *Antiquitates Italicae medii aevii*, 6 volumes (1738–42). He served as the archivist and librarian of the house of Este's library from 1700 until his death in 1750. Muratori was a member of the Academy of Arcadians, with the pseudonym Leucoto Gateate. He responded to French criticisms with his four-book treatise *Della perfetta poesia italiana*, which became an influential guide book for aspiring Italian poets.[14] Books 1, 2, and 3 contain Muratori's theoretical reflections on poetry, while book 4 is an anthology of Italian poetry containing brief critical remarks based on the other books' reflections.

Muratori tackled head-on the French ideal of the pure imitation of nature. In *Della perfetta poesia italiana*, Muratori recognized that poetry is the product neither of pure imagination nor of a strict adherence to the truth. Instead, it is a delicate mix of both fantasy and fact. In chapter 7 of book 1, Muratori defined the two components of poetry as *materia* (the factual source of the literary work) and *maniera* (the manner in which a poet imitates this source). He argued that a poet must prudently combine the authentic foundation of his chosen *favola* (story) with the manner in which he tells it. For Muratori, a poet following the proper method could produce what the new, modern Italian poetry should be.

Muratori's principles were fundamental for aspiring poets, like Foscolo. The historian predominately focused his treatise on lyric poetry, yet he also defined the principal literary concepts that were central to dramatic discourse of the eighteenth century, such as the notions of truth, verisimilitude, and fantasy, among others.[15] In chapter 7 of book 1, Muratori discussed the notion of the sublime, arguing that the poet's foremost objective is to guide the reader to a pleasurable, transcendent moment. He relied heavily on what were then considered the writings of the philosopher Longinus (ca. 213–73 AD), defining the concept of the sublime as referring to something "new, rare, extraordinary and marvelous, that in orations, and especially in verses, provokes amazement, suddenly kidnaps us, and delights, and either gently or by force, moves the emotions inside of us."[16] Muratori further explained the manner in which a poet creates this sublime moment in chapter 8. He stressed that the poet must not only imitate nature, but he also must attempt to do better and perfect it.[17] When a poet undertakes this task, he must simultaneously maintain a sense of verisimilitude, which can be accomplished by simply looking to nature itself. Muratori cautioned, however, that the poet needs to reveal the beauties of nature by using inventive elements from his own imagination.[18] According to Muratori, a poet needed to ground his story on some aspect of "absolute" truth and then embellish, or add onto, this truth with elements that are plausible, even if they did not actually occur.[19] In sum, he believed that a poet must, above all else, convey this possible, probable, and believable truth, *il verisimile*, to readers in order to suspend reality temporarily and create any sound and serious pleasure. In chapter 10 of book 1, Muratori continued his thoughts on combining truth and imagination and discussed the poet's duty to use both facts and fantasy in order to guarantee his audience's favourable reception.[20]

Muratori succeeded not only by providing thorough definitions of key literary concepts such as *il verisimile*, but also by setting forth his guidelines for how (i.e.., by and for whom) these concepts should be used in a literary work.[21] *Della perfetta poesia* became a standard text for Italian intellectuals immediately following its publication. It provided a specific response to a critique of a particular era that is very traditional, historical, and classical in structure and tone. Muratori's exploration of the subjective nature of beautiful poetry further demonstrated it to be an aesthetically modern work. *Della perfetta poesia* was well received in Italy, and became one of the most influential Italian literary histories during the eighteenth century. Its influence and renown lasted well into the nineteenth century.

Intellectuals throughout Europe continued to discuss and debate the very same key terms and concepts that Muratori defined. Indeed, the question of what were the required elements of a good tragedy was one of the "hot topics" of the century. With the publication of his *Lettres philosophiques* (1734) and "Dissertation sur la tragédie ancienne et moderne" (1748), Voltaire (François-Marie Arouet, 1694–1778) contributed to the tragedy discourse in response to the Italian Antonio Conti's use of Shakespeare as a possible model for tragedy. Voltaire responded by expressing his negative opinions on the English playwright. Shakespeare, who later became an icon for the Romantic movement, was praised by Voltaire for combining the natural and the sublime. Yet the French playwright also considered the Bard to be ignorant of the rules of drama put forth by Aristotle, and so labelled him a barbarian.

In addition to the French and Italian views on the tragedy, German intellectuals also contributed to the discourse in the late eighteenth century. Gotthold Ephraim Lessing (1729–81) was perhaps the most influential German contributor to the field with his 1766 *Der Laokoon* and 1767–9 *Hamburgische Dramaturgie*. Contrary to Corneille and Voltaire's "théâtre classique" (strictly observing the three unities), Lessing promoted an idealized tragedy – a theatre of the Greeks and Shakespeare.

Eighteenth-century European authors also focused on the aims of literature (i.e., *why* one would write tragedy). The role of the poet took centre stage during the Enlightenment. This period's discussions of verisimilitude were rooted firmly in Horace's *Epistle to the Pisones* (more commonly known as his *Ars poetica*), as well as on the important notion that a poet must educate as well as entertain his audience.[22] The didactic function of the tragedy was paramount. Tragedians were concerned with more than just providing spectators with a pleasurable experience. They also focused on shaping the moral convictions of the audience in order to inspire proper behaviour among a nation's citizens.

The moral implications of theatre famously came to the forefront in 1758 with the publication of Jean-Jacques Rousseau's *Lettre à M. d'Alembert sur les spectacles*. Rousseau was concerned with how Geneva should regulate theatre and with the very broad notion of how theatre regulates our lives, as David Marshall aptly pointed out in "Rousseau and the State of Theater."[23] For Rousseau, theatre is a fall from the state of nature. As an instrument for instruction, the exchange between actors and spectators that occurs during a performance represents "the more dangerous theater that society has become."[24] Thus, a moral imperative emerged and theatre was thrust into discourses surrounding the making of the modern citizen.

European theorists and philosophers jumped at the chance to grapple with this issue, including the Italian intellectual Melchiorre Cesarotti. The University of Padova professor was renowned throughout Italian literary circles for his 1763 and 1772 translations of the poetry of Ossian (*Poesie di Ossian*).[25] Cesarotti was the most influential literary authority in north-eastern Italy in the late eighteenth century, and he mentored numerous aspiring Italian literary scholars, including Foscolo. Cesarotti expressed his theories on tragedy in his 1762 "Ragionamento sopra il diletto della tragedia."[26] This essay attempted to answer the question of why one would write tragedies.

Cesarotti discussed the didactic function of literature in his essay. A follower of the Locke-inspired school of Sensism, Cesarotti also devoted a significant portion of "Ragionamento" to exploring the spectator's emotions while viewing a performance. He built upon Horace's premise that a successful poet will awaken a sense of aesthetic pleasure (*diletto*) in his audience while educating the spectators. Cesarotti centred his "Ragionamento" on his examination of a tragedian's ability to impart moral instruction to his audience during a performance by stimulating different sensations and emotions within the spectator. He fundamentally argued that the education of the audience is a necessary consequence of the sensations that a tragedian is able to invoke through the actions on stage.

Cesarotti began his essay by speculating as to why audiences attend the theatre to watch tragedies. He summarized the previous theories on spectator response put forth by Jean-Baptiste Dubos (1670–1742) in his 1719 *Réflexions critiques sur la poésie et la peinture*, Bernard le Bovier de Fontanelle (1657–1757), in his 1685 *Réflexions sur la poétique*, and David Hume (1711–76) in his 1753–4 "Of Tragedy."[27] Cesarotti paid particular attention to the spectator's sensations of pleasure and pain experienced during a performance. He then turned to outlining the "proper" manner in which a tragedian should compose – and receive praise for – his works. It had become customary during the late eighteenth century for the tragedian to take the stage and accept and acknowledge the audience's praise. Cesarotti rejected this growing theatrical tradition and argued that such an action, as well as any other through which the poet makes his presence known with distracting and superfluous language (i.e., pompous descriptions and comparisons), was not suited to the fundamental goals of a tragedy. Cesarotti instead believed that this conduct only served to interrupt the illusion of the work and distracted the audience from the sublime moment. The tragedian thus should hope to produce a spectacle that leaves the audience completely entranced – and silent. He must do whatever is necessary to maintain this silence and must remain invisible.[28]

Cesarotti continued his essay by elaborating on what he viewed was the most crucial role of the modern tragedian – shaping the moral convictions of his audience. He felt that the tragedian should invoke sensations firmly grounded in pain and terror in the audience that, in turn, would educate the spectators. Cesarotti then turned to a discussion on spectator response. How would a spectator respond to various tragic scenarios portrayed on the stage? And what might he learn from them? According to Cesarotti, the three emotions of compassion, terror, and horror normally permeate a tragedy. He defined them as follows:

> Compassion is a pain mitigated by morality, by a terrible misfortune, obtained by an interesting character because of some imperfection of which we believe ourselves capable ... Terror is a violent fear, but mitigated by

morality, by which the spirit concentrates on itself until it protects itself against the idea of an awful evil that could pull itself on top of it for some fault or defect … Horror is a thrill of the soul attempting to repel the sight or idea of a terrible fact from itself in which the excess of evil is not tempered by any good, nor offset by morality.[29]

Cesarotti believed that the manner in which a tragedian represents these emotions necessarily was intrinsically linked to the degree of aesthetic pleasure (*il diletto*) and moral instruction (*l'istruzione morale*) a spectator would experience from the work. He argued that the tragedian must avoid staging horrific scenes at all costs, given that they serve no didactic purpose and only elicit a sense of pure disgust from the audience. Returning to Aristotle, Cesarotti continued with an elaboration on Aristotle's notion of *katharsis*.[30] He concluded by explaining that "the representation of other people's misfortunes becomes a mirror of our own dangers, and the interest that I felt in other people's evils, reawakens the most intrinsic evil that I feel in myself."[31] This was the goal. It was the very essence and desired outcome for a tragedy.

While it might have been beneficial for a young, emerging tragedian to study the theoretical writings of Muratori and Cesarotti, in order for a new Italian theatre to truly emerge, this new author also would require actual examples of tragedies. It came as a great relief when, after nearly a century of treatises and failed attempts, Vittorio Alfieri emerged as the ideal, modern, Italian tragedian.[32] Alfieri had written twenty tragedies by 1786.[33] He was so successful that the term "Alfierian" became synonymous in Italy with the term "neoclassicist" (follower of both the ancients and French neoclassical theatre) during the late eighteenth and early nineteenth centuries. The Alfierian school of tragedy quickly spread throughout Italy and gained widespread recognition across Europe.

Alfieri contributed to the renown of his own theories on tragedy. He published "Parere sulle tragedie," a self-analysis of his tragedies and compositional style, which contains extensive discussions on exactly how he composed each of his tragedies in 1789.[34] Alfieri claimed to have examined his own works with a strictly unbiased eye, arguing that this was possible because although he gave his best efforts in the works themselves, he acknowledged his more obvious shortcomings.[35] In addition to a close analysis of each work, Alfieri offered an overview of the thematic components found in his tragedies:

invention, scenario, and style.[36] Alfieri used "Parere" to catalogue the common characteristics that defined his works, including the good and not-so-good.

This second section of "Parere," concerning scenario, was easily the most useful for an aspiring tragedian modelling his tragedies closely after Alfieri's works. Alfieri began by distinguishing himself from other tragedians. Referring to himself in the third person, he was quick to note that he did not build upon any previous versions of his chosen subject matter; instead, he stripped each story down to its barest essentials, and began anew.[37] Alfieri made three important points. He explained that because he completely rebuilt each story, the intensity of each verse requires the audience's fullest attention. Yet he believed that the need for absolute and unbroken concentration by the audience actually detracted from the overall success of each work.[38] In order for a spectator to fully appreciate and comprehend his tragedies, he or she must view the work on more than one occasion.

Alfieri acknowledged that although he often violated the unity of place, and occasionally that of time, he strictly followed the unity of action in all his tragedies. Indeed, he argued that this advancement of a tragedy's action was the most important "rule" to follow.[39] He saw his main objective as a tragedian as to guide the action forward, building momentum with each act so that the audience gradually becomes enraptured with the spectacle.[40] He explained that each of his creative decisions was based solely on whether he thought the particular choice was necessary to advance the action of the play.

However, Alfieri discussed how this growing intensity oftentimes is hindered by secondary characters who contribute virtually nothing to the play's plot.[41] Thus, he believed that the best way for a tragedian to ensure that the action would progress unabated was to limit the cast to only four characters. This was exceedingly difficult, of course.[42] "Parere" explains that if additional characters are necessary for an accurate portrayal of the story, each and every one of these characters must have a defined purpose – according to Alfieri, he never created a superfluous character in any of his works, even though he frequently used more than four main characters. The tragedian emphasized that secondary characters should not be introduced if they serve no purpose in the development of the tragedy's action. Along these lines, he claimed that his secondary characters never divulged or exposed any major plot points of the tragedy; in his opinion, only major characters should be responsible for such revelations.[43]

Alfieri then addressed the issue of how to maintain a sense of verisimilitude on stage. He recounted that he attempted to avoid narrating what would be obvious to the spectator. The Astian stated that he never narrated what could have been acted, while still remaining faithful to the verisimilar nature of the work. Thus, he used his primary characters to set forth the necessary action when narration was necessary.[44] He believed that the earlier Italian tragedians' use of large numbers of characters and inclusion of the customary chorus between each act disrupted the work's dramatic action. Alfieri consequently reduced the number of characters and eliminated the choruses entirely.

"Parere" continues with a detailed discussion of the structure of the tragedies. Alfieri acknowledged the main perceived defect of his works – that they were relatively uniform and, for the most part, similarly structured. The tragedian concisely described the basic composition as follows: Act 1 was extremely short; for the most part, the protagonist would not enter the stage until the second act; there would be abundant dialogue and not a lot of action in the first four acts; act 5 was also very brief, but extremely fast-paced; and for the most part, the final act would contain all the actions in the tragedy, with the dying characters speaking extremely succinctly.[45] Alfieri used a single brief paragraph to inform his public of precisely what he considered to be the major characteristics of his own tragedies, and it ultimately served as a guide for aspiring young writers, including Vincenzo Monti, Ippolito Pindemonte, and Ugo Foscolo.[46]

Let's return for a moment to the three questions presented earlier. *What* are the required components of a good tragedy? *Why* would one write tragedies? And *how* precisely should one go about writing them? An aspiring tragedian such as Foscolo could easily find the answers to these questions in the writings of Muratori, Cesarotti, and Alfieri. And he did.

The following chapters will demonstrate how Foscolo relied on the works of Alfieri and Cesarotti for guidance when writing his tragedies. At the opening performances of his *Tieste*, *Ajace*, and *Ricciarda*, he closely adhered to Cesarotti's teachings on how a tragedian should comport himself. He looked to Muratori for guidance in building on this eighteenth-century foundation in his own literary criticism, and explained his own opinions on the poet, the historian, and the notion of verisimilitude. Foscolo used his critical writing to defend his artistic choices (and those of other Alfierians) when challenged in his later years by the new literary movement Romanticism. Indeed, Foscolo would rely on these eighteenth-century influences throughout his career as an author and critic of tragedy.

Foscolo's Early Formation

Niccolò Ugo Foscolo was born on 6 February 1778 on the Ionian island of Zakynthos, which was under Venetian rule at the time. He was the oldest of four children born to a father of Venetian decent, Andrea Foscolo, and a Greek mother, Diamanta Spathis. His siblings were sister Rubina and two brothers who both committed suicide: Gian Dionisio (a.k.a. Giovanni) and Costantino Giovanni (a.k.a. Giulio). Andrea was a doctor, and in 1784 he was appointed military hospital surgeon in Split, a Venetian colony on the Dalmatian coast. Niccolò and the rest of the family joined Andrea the following year. It was here that Foscolo began his formal schooling under the direction of Francesco Gianuzzi.

Andrea passed away in 1788, and following a brief separation, Foscolo joined his mother in Venice in 1792. He was educated at San Cipriano in Murano. His first and perhaps most influential teacher was Angelo Dalmistro (1754–1839), a staunch classicist who translated selections by Alexander Pope and Thomas Gray and directed the periodical *L'anno poetico* from 1793 to 1800. Dalmistro revered both the classics and contemporary Italian neoclassical literature, and he provided all his students, including Foscolo, with a solid basis of canonical classical literature and the early great Italian writers. Dalmistro was a member of the Academy of Arcadians, which believed that Italian intellectuals must look to their past in order to appreciate fully – and contribute to – the present. Foscolo eventually excelled as a student of Italian neoclassicism under this tutelage.

Foscolo's education was not purely theoretical. He composed a collection of poems in 1794, which he dedicated to his friend Costantino Naranzi. Several influential figures of Venetian literary society noticed the young author's talents as a poet and scholar, and they quickly became his literary mentors and guides.[47] One of these notable influences, the Biblioteca Marciana's librarian and erudite philologist Jacopo Morelli (1745–1819), introduced Foscolo to perhaps Venice's most prominent woman, Isabella Teotochi Marin (1760–1836). Like Foscolo, she was born on a Greek isle, Corfù. Teotochi arrived in Venice and married Carlo Antonio Marin in 1776. She established a modest salon in Venice in 1781 that eventually became one of the period's most influential regional gathering places.[48] The participants included such prominent

Italian intellectuals as Melchiorre Cesarotti, Ippolito Pindemonte (1753–1828), Paolo Costa (1771–1836), Saverio Bettinelli (1718–1808), and Aurelio de' Giorgi Bertola (1753–98).[49] Foscolo met Teotochi some time in 1794 or 1795, when she and her husband had separated and were in the process of annulling their marriage. Foscolo and Teotochi immediately took to each other, and he became a regular participant at her salon. Any romantic infatuation that Foscolo may have harboured for Teotochi was short-lived, however, as on 28 May 1796, Isabella secretly married Giuseppe Albrizzi. Nonetheless, the amicable relationship between Foscolo and Teotochi lasted for decades.

This friendship proved to be immensely useful, and it allowed Foscolo to make many advantageous professional connections. His participation in the Teotochi salon permitted him to write to the single most influential literary figure of the region, Cesarotti. Foscolo introduced himself in a 28 September 1795 letter, and he expressed his admiration for the prominent author and scholar and his hope of forging a lasting relationship with him. The aspiring poet also asked if Cesarotti would be willing to read and critique two poems that he was writing, "Il Genio" and "La Verità."[50] Cesarotti acceded to Foscolo's request, and Foscolo soon after began referring to Cesarotti as his literary mentor, father, and even his angel.[51] Cesarotti assisted in Foscolo's scholarly development from this point forward, just as he had done for numerous other aspiring poets.

Foscolo not only made the necessary professional acquaintances with figures such as Dalmistro, Morelli, Teotochi, and Cesarotti during his early years of study, but he also took great care to lay the groundwork for his future as a scholar. Foscolo composed his *Piano di studi*, which is both a record of his early literary and cultural formation, and an outline of his plan for future studies.[52] The 1796 outline was nothing less than a chronicle of the young author's interpretation of Italian literary history. Foscolo turned to another important Venetian intellectual, Andrea Rubbi (1738–1817) and his *Parnaso degli italiani* (1784–91) as his literary model.[53] The *Parnaso* is an enormous collection of fifty-six volumes, containing literary works that Andrea Rubbi considered to be the most important in the Italian literary canon.

Foscolo's interest in Italian literary history was inspired by the notion that an intellectual had the capacity to shape a collective identity with a literary history. Muratori's *Della perfetta poesia italiana* was of particular interest, and the eighteenth-century historian served as a neoclassical inspiration for Foscolo from the outset of his career. Foscolo, in a letter of 10 December 1794 to his Brescian friend Gaetano Fornasini, indicates that he had already read *Della perfetta poesia italiana*. He remarked that he frequently used Muratori's treatise when composing his early poetry.[54]

Muratori's idea of Italian literary history shaped Foscolo's conception of Italian literature in the 1796 *Piano di studi*.[55] Here he chronicled his more ambitious and original projects, including plans to annotate the works of Petrarch ("Annotazioni a gran parte del Petrarca") and Muratori ("Annotazioni alla *Poesia perfetta* del Muratori"). This effort shows how the young Foscolo, at only seventeen, was beginning to grapple with and work out his own concept of the Italian literary canon. Foscolo never got around to writing his "Annotazioni alla *Poesia perfetta* del Muratori," but he nonetheless referred to the pre-eminent historian and his letters and writings throughout his career. He clearly valued Muratori's meticulous historical accounts of Italian literature.

The second section of Foscolo's *Piano di studi* lists the literary works that he had already composed, those on which he had just begun to work, and those he intended to compose in the future. Foscolo announced his intention in this section to annotate the works of Petrarch and Muratori. He was preoccupied with understanding Italian literary history and literary criticism, and under the title "Prose originali" Foscolo listed additional projects that he planned to pursue, including an examination of the pastoral genre ("Parallelo fra il *Pastor Fido* e *l'Aminta*") and a philosophical history of poetry from the twelfth to the nineteenth century ("Storia Filosofica della Poesia dal secolo duodecimo sino al decimo-nono; opera ideata soltanto ma da comporsi dopo qualche anno").

Piano di studi demonstrates that Foscolo had become at least moderately interested in theatre before 1796. He listed Metastasio as a dramatist in the outline and included four tragedians under the heading "Tragici." Foscolo expressed his plan to read Vittorio Alfieri, as well as the works of Sophocles, Shakespeare, and Voltaire. Foscolo's conspicuous inclusion of only one Italian, Alfieri, warrants some attention. Where was Vincenzo Monti (1754–1828)?[56] Foscolo also omitted the dramatists Alessandro Pepoli (1757–96) and Giovanni Pindemonte (1751–1812), whose plays were staged throughout Venice during this same period.[57] Although Foscolo witnessed their successes first-hand, neither dramatist strictly followed the Alfierian model. Pepoli's and Pindemonte's works are examples of yet another shift in the genre towards the end of the century. Foscolo was privy to these tentative rebellious steps, and he was also quite aware that his mentor, Cesarotti, was also moving away from the Alfierian model. These developments made it apparent that by 1796 Foscolo was entering into an environment ripe for new literary contributions in the realm of the tragedy.

Venice was just the city in which to make his debut. Venetian theatres had enjoyed immense success before Foscolo's arrival. The Teatro La Fenice, the largest theatre in the city and one of the most important dramatic venues in all of Europe, opened with a performance of Pepoli's drama *I giuochi d'Agrigento* on 16 May 1792. There were seven other prominent theatres with continuous activity: San Cassiano, San Moisè, San Luca, San Samuele, Sant'Angelo, San Giovanni Grisostomo, and San Benedetto.[58] The Venetian theatres did not limit their audience to certain classes. As the historian Franca Baricelli has explained, "The theatre in Venice was open to the paying public from its origins in the sixteenth century; less affluent spectators could purchase inexpensive seats high up in the gallery and gondoliers enjoyed free admission as members of the *claque*."[59] Venetian theatre therefore did not just represent and serve the aristocracy.

This broad Venetian audience also influenced a playwright's level of renown and was especially attractive to emerging authors. The stage offered these authors the possibility of immediate success *and* popularity. Put simply, they had a much greater chance for recognition and renown as playwrights than in any other literary sphere. A contemporary lyric poet relied primarily on a literate public who had access to his publications to advertise his name and talents. But a play's inherent performative nature allowed an audience to instantaneously judge his prowess. This judgment oftentimes then spread quickly by word of mouth throughout the city, acting companies, and playhouses. A playwright's failure or success was virtually instantaneous.

Foscolo was enticed by the prospect of theatrical renown. His unimpeachable education, the intellectual guidance of Cesarotti, and the promotion of Isabella Teotochi Albrizzi's prestigious literary salon caused him to jump at the opportunity to try his hand at writing tragedy. His motives for doing so have long been apparent to critics. Indeed, as early as 1835, Mary Shelley remarked in her biography of Foscolo that he had "resolved to follow in the steps of Alfieri, and to acquire fame as a tragedian."[60] But the tragic stage in Italy was an inherently contentious arena, and so Foscolo's success was far from certain. Foscolo entered the fray in 1797 with his first tragedy, *Tieste*. He continued to write tragedies and essays on the form and function of the genre throughout the rest of his life.

Chapter Two

Debut, Acclaim, and Instruction

Foscolo's appreciation of classical literature and his desire to contribute to the field of Italian tragedy can be traced back to the earliest stages of his career. On 30 October 1795, the aspiring seventeen-year-old author explained to Cesarotti how he dared to retell the very same story that Crébillon and the great Voltaire had once recounted – that of Thyestes.[1] The aspiring tragedian left no record of his progress towards completing his first tragedy aside from this initial letter to Cesarotti. He listed *Tieste* in the second section of his 1796 *Piano di studi*, however, so it appears that he had completed his first work by that date.[2] Foscolo referred to the breakneck pace of his composition of *Tieste* several years later in a 6 February 1811 letter to his family. He was writing his second tragedy, *Ajace*, at this time, and he lamented that "the time of having written one act per day (like when I wrote *Tieste*), is passed, along with the enthusiasm and courage of my youth."[3] Yet despite these few indicators, we cannot date Foscolo's completion of *Tieste* with any precision.

Tieste is a sound snapshot of the young Foscolo's literary and cultural formation, much like his *Piano di studi*. He adhered to the subject matter put forth in the works of Crébillon and Voltaire to some degree, but he mainly looked to the newly established Italian tradition for ideas about the tragedy's form. The Alfierian model that Foscolo had studied was especially suited for his new work. Alfieri recommended in his essay "Parere sulle tragedie" that the ideal tragedy should have only four characters, but he simultaneously cautioned that this severe limitation might present an extremely challenging task to any tragedian.[4] Foscolo eagerly accepted this challenge; to him, the exercise tested his poetic prowess.

Tieste consists of five acts and 1401 lines of unrhymed hendecasyllabic verse. It respects the three classical unities: the tragedy is set exclusively in the region of Argo, and the one main action entirely takes place over the course of twenty-four hours, with the first two acts set during the day, the third and fourth acts at night, and the fifth at the following daybreak. *Tieste*'s four speaking characters are Atreo (the king of Argos), Tieste (Atreo's brother), Erope (who conceived a son with her lover, Tieste, but was forced to marry Atreo), and Ippodamia (mother of Atreo and Tieste). It also includes a number of silent characters: the illegitimate son of Tieste and Erope, and Atreo's guards (appropriately named *fanciuletto* and *guardie*). Foscolo dedicated much of the tragedy to the development of the two female characters, Ippodamia and Erope.

Foscolo's version begins when Tieste, who had been exiled for five years by Atreo for adultery, returns to his brother's kingdom under a mistaken belief that Erope has been condemned to death. He finally learns upon his arrival that their affair produced a son. Tieste tries but fails to kill Atreo, who retaliates by sending his brother to prison with Erope. Atreo pretends to listen to the pleadings of his mother (Ippodamia), and he offers Tieste freedom in exchange for permanent exile. Atreo asks Tieste to drink from the family cup to seal the deal; Tieste agrees without hesitation. Unbeknownst to Tieste and Erope, however, the cup contains the blood of their murdered illegitimate son. Tieste lifts the cup to his mouth and only then realizes what it contains. He is stunned and horrified and again attempts to kill his brother, but during these efforts he is surrounded by guards and inflicts a fatal wound upon himself, finally dying in his mother's arms. The tragedy concludes with Atreo proclaiming his vindication. He announces that he will wait for divine power to decide his own fate at death.

Foscolo relied heavily on the work of his predecessors when composing his *Tieste*. The subject matter as presented in the original version by Seneca inspired the prolific eighteenth-century French authors Crébillon and Voltaire to produce their own adaptations. Crébillon's *Atrée et Thyeste*, in rhymed verse (1513 lines), was first performed on 14 March 1707. The tragedy has eight main characters and respects the unities of time, place, and action. For the most part, Crébillon remained faithful to Seneca's original telling of the story.[5] Voltaire's version, *Les Pélopides, ou Atrée et Thyeste*, was written in 1771, but it was not performed.[6] It is more concise than Crébillon's version, consisting of only 1116 lines (in rhymed verse) and only seven speaking characters. While *Les Pélopides* also follows the three unities strictly, as P.J. Davis notes in his book *Seneca: Thyestes*, Voltaire's account "constitutes the most radically rewritten version of the myth," with the inclusion of the female characters of Aerope and Hippodamie.[7] Foscolo's reliance on Voltaire's version is especially noteworthy given its altered storyline.

Foscolo sought to avoid being labelled unoriginal, and he constructed his own account of the tale. His use of the Alfierian model may have been a foregone conclusion, but the manner in which Foscolo used *Tieste* as a vehicle to showcase his knowledge of other Italian authors was anything but obvious. Foscolo revealed his intention to retell the tale of Thyestes in his letter to Cesarotti, and went on to acknowledge the previous versions of the story and describe the manner in which he intended to approach it, beginning with "only four characters." Foscolo characterized Crébillon's *Atrée et Thyeste* as "too intricate," and Voltaire's *Les Pélopides, ou Atrée et Thyeste* as "not terrible enough," demonstrating that he not only had studied the modern versions of the story of Thyestes, but also that he had formed his own critical opinions of both versions.[8] Foscolo explained how he would be content if *Tieste* moved the rest of the public, the *ignari*, to tears, even if he could not find favour with the critics.

Foscolo's characterization of a portion of his audience as *ignari*, or ignorant, is notable. It illustrates the young author's negativity towards the Venetian audiences of the period, which valued the showy spectacles of Pepoli and Pindemonte more than the literary quality of the tragedies of Alfieri. Notwithstanding these criticisms, however, Foscolo seems to have believed that even the *ignari* could be shaped and moulded as an audience. Foscolo intended to compose a tragedy according to the compositional parameters set forth by Alfieri in his "Parere sulle tragedie." Yet this scholarly exercise also tested his knowledge of Cesarotti's theories set forth in "Ragionamento sopra il diletto della tragedia" regarding the manner in which tragedies can provide moral instruction to an uneducated audience. Cesarotti affirmed that a drama should inspire the spectator to feel compassion and terror, and it should simultaneously provide moral instruction.[9] Foscolo also took to heart this notion that a tragedian had both the power and obligation to educate and delight his audience.

Foscolo did not intend for his first tragedy solely to reflect Cesarotti's theoretical principles, however. He had a genuine interest in the Italian literary trends of the late eighteenth century and he was acutely aware that his two primary Italian models, Cesarotti and Alfieri, did not see eye to eye on certain aspects of a tragedy. Indeed, the Venetian school (including Pepoli and Pindemonte) and Paduan (Cesarottian) school were attempting to distance themselves from the Alfierian model at the precise time that Foscolo was composing his tragedy. Cesarotti and his students acknowledged that Alfieri's tragedies were a substantial step towards the long-awaited archetype of a national tragedy, but they still criticized the Astian's unnecessarily bitter and severe language and expressed a desire for tragedians to develop a softer and more lyrical verse based on the French tradition.[10]

But on whose writing would Foscolo model this new, softer style? He had indicated only one other potential Italian exemplar in his *Piano di studi:* Metastasio. The extraordinarily successful dramatist held a prominent place in the literary and cultural formation of the young Foscolo. Maria Maddalena Lombardi adroitly explained, in her "Scheda introduttiva" of *Tieste,* that Foscolo's characters of Erope and Tieste are indecisive and more lyrical – they are essentially Metastasian, not Alfierian.[11] I would take this analysis one step further and posit that Foscolo's imitation of both these models can be interpreted as clear evidence of his attempt to follow the Cesarottian desire to lighten the Alfierian tragedy.

Softer verse aside, Foscolo intended his audience to be overcome with tears and filled with terror. It would be his way of improving on Crébillon's and Voltaire's versions. He informed Cesarotti of his plans in a 30 October 1795 letter, in which he speculated at length on his goal of using his verse to inspire the audience to succumb to tears and terror.[12] It is no surprise that Foscolo outlined his plans to his mentor. Cesarotti had after all meticulously outlined his definitions of the three emotions most often invoked by a tragedy – compassion, terror, and horror – in his "Ragionamento sopra il diletto della tragedia."[13] Foscolo took the opportunity with *Tieste* to demonstrate his firm knowledge of the European theatrical tradition, including Cesarottian theories.

Tieste's act 5, scene 3 demonstrates Foscolo's attempts to negotiate these three emotions. Foscolo aimed for the second, terror, in his version. In this scene Tieste realizes that the family cup is filled with his illegitimate son's blood. Foscolo recognized that Seneca's *Thyestes,* in which the protagonist not only drinks his children's blood, but also consumes their flesh, evoked a horror too great in his spectators.

Conversely, Voltaire's version lies at the opposite end of the spectrum. He significantly minimized the horror for its courtly audiences. In *Les Pélopides*, Thyeste is presented with the family cup of blood, but he does not lift it to his mouth. Instead, Mégare, who announces that the child has been taken from the guards, interrupts him. This leads to Atrée's admission that the cup contains the blood of Thyeste's son, and Thyeste's cannibalism is avoided.[14]

Foscolo's version is not as horrific as Seneca's. But it is more terrifying than Voltaire's. While Erope is pleading for her son to be brought to her, Atreo leads everyone to believe that the guards will fetch the boy after giving Tieste the cup:

ATREO: Un sacro
          Innanzi ai numi giuramento stringa
          Nostra amistà.
 EROPE: Mio figlio!
ATREO: (*Alla guardia*)   Emneo la tazza,
          E il fanciuletto. (*La Guardia reca una tazza*) – Ecco la tazza: giura (*A
          Tieste*)
EROPE: Ov'è mio figlio?
ATREO: Il figliol tuo verratti.
          Gli augusti giuri non tardar. – (*Alla Guardia*) Gli porgi
          Il nappo; va': guida il fanciul. (*La Guardia porge la tazza a Tieste, e
          parte*).[15]

Tieste has no reason to mistrust his brother at this point, and he takes the cup and pledges peace: "In faccia i numi io giuro pace; io ferma/ Amistà giuro."[16] Only at the very last moment, as the cup nears Tieste's lips, does he realize that it is filled with blood:

EROPE: Il figlio mio …
TIESTE: (*Accostando la tazza alle labbra*)   Che bevo?
          Sangue! … (*Getta la tazza*)
ATREO: Felloni! è questo il figliuol vostro: (*Mostrando il sangue, che è sparso
          in terra*)
          Del misfatto godete.[17]

With his emphasis on Erope's repeated and desperate pleadings for her son and Tieste's blind trust of Atreo, Foscolo intended for his audience to be overcome with tears and filled with terror. He effectively sought to terrify his audience, offering yet another interpretation of the story of Thyestes.

While he communicated his initial plans for *Tieste* to Cesarotti, Foscolo did not show his mentor the finished product. This omission was not in character for the young author; he previously had shown

Cesarotti his early poems at every step of the compositional process. Cesarotti was nonplussed with this turn of events. He wrote to Tommaso Olivi on 25 November 1796 and expressed his displeasure with Foscolo for not asking for advice from those with whom he had a close relationship before *Tieste*'s debut. Cesarotti acknowledged that Foscolo had shown him an earlier draft of *Tieste* in which "there was much to correct" and that he had not seen subsequent versions of the work.[18] Plinio Carli argued in his notes to the critical edition of Foscolo's letters that Foscolo perhaps was reluctant to show the final version of his tragedy to Cesarotti because he was confident of the success of his work.[19] Carli speculated that Foscolo did not want to hear any cautionary criticisms, and thus he elected not to provide his mentor with a copy of the completed tragedy before opening night.[20]

But perhaps Foscolo skirted Cesarotti's review in order to avoid any tension between the two. Although he included more lyrical, or Metastasian, characters in accordance with Cesarotti's prescription to soften the Alfierian model, Foscolo's fundamental choice to align *Tieste* so closely with the Alfierian school was an explicit departure from his mentor's general compositional philosophy. Foscolo surely was cognizant of the rift between the Alfierian and Cesarottian schools, and he most likely feared that Cesarotti would view his first tragedy as being too Alfierian. Foscolo therefore likely declined to allow Cesarotti to review the finished tragedy in order to avoid offending his mentor.

Critics tend to evaluate *Tieste* on its substantive literary merits. But this approach frequently neglects the substantially influential biographical factors that coloured Foscolo's compositional choices. In terms of his first tragedy, Foscolo's intellectual foundation and the development of his familiarity with the theatrical tradition and theories stand at centre stage. The ultimate question when evaluating *Tieste*'s success on Foscolo's terms is whether or not he effectively demonstrated his wide-ranging knowledge of the Latin, French, and, most importantly, Italian traditions. Foscolo simultaneously tried to (a) follow Cesarotti's theoretical goals of a tragedy, (b) imitate Metastasio's voice, and (c) employ Alfieri's structure when composing *Tieste*. His absorption of various elements from each of these three Italian authorities neatly illustrates his scholarly training, and indeed provides the formative underpinnings for Foscolo to develop his further theories on the genre. Ultimately, *Tieste* unmistakably embodies the variable state of Italian tragedy at the end of the eighteenth century.

The Performance and Review of *Tieste*

Venetian censors approved *Tieste* for staging on 28 December 1796, and it opened on 4 January 1797 at the Teatro Sant'Angelo. *Tieste* "was a great triumph," according to Foscolo's 1842 biography by the Venetian author Luigi Carrer.[21] Two factors played a significant part in *Tieste*'s immediate success: (1) the cast of performers, especially the young and talented Anna Fiorilli Pellandi (1772–1841), playing Erope; and (2) the conspicuous absence of any critics in the audience. Indeed, *Tieste*'s opening night audience consisted mostly of Foscolo's closest friends and admirers.

Pellandi was the most important actress in early-nineteenth-century Italy. It was not customary for an actress of her status to blindly accept a role in a piece by a relatively unknown author, such as Foscolo. Nicola Mangini explained that it was Fiorilli Pellandi's and Foscolo's mutual friend, Cesarotti, who secured her performance in *Tieste*.[22] The composition of the audience was influenced, in part, by the time of year *Tieste* opened – Carnival. Venetians would typically attend parties and other social Carnival events, and many of those who chose theatre opted to see comedies instead of tragedies. In addition, the newest work of the well-known playwright Giovanni Pindemonte, entitled *Donna Caritea, regina di Spagna*, which opened in Venice the same evening as Foscolo's *Tieste*, drew a large share of those Venetians who chose theatre that night, leaving only those with some special interest in Foscolo or *Tieste* to attend its performance.

Two reviews appeared almost immediately following *Tieste*'s debut, on 7 January and 14 January 1797. Both reviews were published anonymously in the *Gazzetta Urbana Veneta*. The reviews praise Foscolo for his great success on stage. The first one went so far as to say, "Its [*Tieste*'s] young author was raised up to the stars by applause; his genius promises new honours to the Italian tragic theatre and his name is repeated everywhere with admiration and praise."[23] Both reviews comment on the terrifying subject matter, the use of only four principal characters and the overwhelmingly positive reception from the Venetian public.[24]

More than a month after *Tieste*'s debut, Foscolo wrote (in the third person) to his mentor, Cesarotti, and dramatically described his first tragedy's good fortune on the stage: "My father – One saw *Tieste*; one fell silent, one cried. There is the praise that I give to the eighteen-year-old Foscolo."[25] *Tieste* continued to enjoy a favourable reception in the press. The *Giornale dei Teatri* reported that *Tieste*, the "fortunate tragedy," was performed another nine times to popular acclaim.[26] Having read the initial positive reviews, and cognizant of *Tieste*'s ten-night run at Sant'Angelo, the Venetian public regarded the tragedy and its young author as great successes.

Yet the warm reception did not stop Foscolo from questioning the public's acclaim for *Tieste*. This self-doubt was perhaps warranted. Foscolo was well aware that his first tragedy did not have an exceptional run at the Sant'Angelo. Indeed, the ten-day duration of *Tieste*'s tenure on stage did not necessarily mean that it was an unqualified success. A successful drama during this period would typically run for more than twenty-five performances, and thus, *Tieste* was neither a failure nor a great triumph.[27] Furthermore, perhaps in an effort to act the part of a modest and promising young tragedian, Foscolo adopted a self-deprecating stance and rejected the positive reviews of his *Tieste*, immediately voicing his desire to improve upon it.

The perceived success of *Tieste* also can be attributed to the historical circumstances surrounding the tragedy. Foscolo's audience was ready for a story about liberty and freedom. Contemporary Venetians had grown weary with the existing government, the Republic of Venice (*La Serenissima*), which had existed since the late seventh century. They found Tieste's plight against the tyrant Atreo inspiring. Foscolo, however, was primarily concerned with his art and not the political overtones of the work, and he did not hide his disinterest in public opinion. Foscolo further lamented his displeasure with the public's positive reception of his first tragedy in his letter to Cesarotti. He remarked how "the author" was "not an expert in any field, and even less so" in the realm of tragedy. Despite the fact that the author was happy that the audience found favour with "the style, with the simplicity, and most of all with the great passions and energies" of the work, one crucial fact remained. In his view, *Tieste* failed to properly manage and depict passion.[28]

Foscolo was dissatisfied with the lack of criticism his tragedy received, and he remarked in his letter to Cesarotti that he intended to become a self-critic.[29] He composed numerous literary-critical observations soon after *Tieste*'s opening. With his letter, Foscolo included a collection of observations, or "Osservazioni," on his first tragedy and the opening night performance. He presumably intended the "Osservazioni" to be published, though unfortunately they have since been lost. Foscolo sought Cesarotti's views on *Tieste*, requesting that he "judge it with the utmost severity."[30] A miffed Cesarotti responded on

10 February 1797, explaining in his letter how he was "surprised, mortified and almost irritated" to hear of the applause *Tieste* received from others and not personally from Foscolo. Cesarotti continued with a warning for Foscolo not to become "drunk from the applause," since his work did need revising.[31] He nonetheless discerned that, with revisions, the "Osservazioni" "will be publishable."[32] Cesarotti also requested a copy of *Tieste* in his letter so that he might better evaluate Foscolo's reflections with the "interest of a father and with the severity of a critic."[33] His mentor's response seemed to indicate that Foscolo's primary intent in publishing his "Osservazioni" was to further guide the Italian public in interpreting the work.

It is impossible to know the precise content of Foscolo's lost critique. Yet the first published edition and analysis of *Tieste* is available. The Milanese editor Antonio Fortunato Stella (1757–1833) oversaw the production of volume 10 of *Teatro moderno applaudito*, a supplement of the *Giornale dei Teatri*, in Venice in April 1797. Foscolo's *Tieste* is the first of four plays published in this volume, followed by *I falsi galantuomini* (a comedy by Camillo Federici, a.k.a. Giovanni Battista Viassolo, 1749–1802), *Don Gusmano* (a tragic-comedy by Giuseppe M. Foppa, 1760–1845), and *Il sonnambulo* (a farce by Francesco Albergati, Capacelli, 1728–1804). Immediately following each play was a literary-critical article, entitled "Notizie storico-critiche," offering the public a literary-critical analysis of each drama. These "Notizie" were published anonymously and written in the journalistic first-person plural, as was the custom of the day. They purported to represent the collective voice of the journal, with an identical tone and uniform format.

"Notizie storico-critiche sul 'Tieste'" is a puzzling work. First, the author of the article is unknown. It seems clear that Foscolo played some role in its publication, but to what extent remains unclear. Guido Bézzola discussed the conflicting conclusions of many critics on the topic in his introduction to volume 2 of the *Edizione nazionale delle opere di Ugo Foscolo*, which recounted the gist of this scholarly discussion. Bézzola observed that Domenico Bianchini and Giovanni Mestica had concluded that the "Notizie" was merely a revised edition of Foscolo's own "Osservazioni," which he had submitted to Cesarotti for review; in contrast, G.A. Martinetti and Francesco Viglione had concluded that the "Notizie" was not, in fact, Foscolo's work.[34] Furthermore, since Foscolo was not a contributor to the journal, it is highly unlikely that he actually primarily authored the work. This does not rule out the likelihood, however, that Foscolo had some significant involvement in the article's production.

This last suspicion is supported by several pieces of evidence. To begin with, the editor Stella intended to publish the volume several months before its eventual printing in April 1797, yet an ill Foscolo delayed the publication process. The "Notizie" itself explains how Foscolo's illness and his desire to review the work, and in various places correct it, did not permit its publication until April.[35] That explanation for the delay strongly suggests that Foscolo was privy to Stella's decision to include his tragedy and the accompanying "Notizie." This likely interaction between the two men implies that Foscolo was in an opportune position to contribute to the "Notizie."[36] Moreover, two elements of the article – the overwhelming emphasis on Foscolo's young age and the recognition of the theatre-going public's power to make or break a piece – are conspicuously similar to the sentiments in Foscolo's private letters written before publication of the "Notizie."[37]

The generally positive review in the body of the "Notizie" is most interesting given its similarities to the young author's own opinion of his first tragedy expressed in his letters. The article praises Foscolo's first attempt on the stage, providing a synopsis of three earlier representations of the story of Tieste: Seneca's *Thyestes*, Crébillon's *Atrée et Thyeste*, and Voltaire's *Les Pélopides, ou Atrée et Thyeste*. The anonymous critic follows this literary history by highlighting the similarities between Voltaire's and Foscolo's versions, stating that "it is without a doubt Voltaire's version, more than any other, [that] served as the model for our author."[38] The "Notizie" compares the plot of Foscolo's *Tieste* to Voltaire's *Les Pélopides*, emphasizing the former's more severe tone. It calls Foscolo's verse harsh and sees this as the expression of the young tragedian's meticulous study of Alfieri. The anonymous author heaped praise upon Foscolo and his tragedy, and unmistakably placed the young Italian tragedian in the company of Seneca, Crébillon, Voltaire, and Italy's own Alfieri.

This focus on the youth of the author of *Tieste* was a theme that ran throughout Foscolo's discussion of his work. He used his age as both a sword and a shield to promote and defend his tragedy. This is by no means a negative criticism of the tragedian. Foscolo astutely felt that the popular success of *Tieste* was only enhanced by his young age, yet, at the same time, any shortcomings were excused by that same youth. This sentiment is perhaps best expressed in Foscolo's 30 October 1795 letter to Cesarotti, in which Foscolo voiced his concern about how his mentor would view his literary endeavour.[39] Foscolo continued to emphasize his age in his letter to Cesarotti following the debut of *Tieste*. This can be seen in his third-person account to the Paduan of the tragedy's success, calling himself "the eighteen-year-old Foscolo."[40] When he asked his mentor to read and judge his "Osservazioni" in this letter, Foscolo once again emphasized his youth, stating that he was simply "a youth who desired to prepare himself with this his first labour the esteem and the contempt of men."[41] Foscolo feared failure in the eyes of his mentor and thus implicitly provided Cesarotti with a ready-made excuse for the potential shortcomings of *Tieste* before he even reviewed it. This pre-emptive strategy was ideal for Foscolo – any negative criticism automatically would be undercut, and the emphasis on his young age also would demonstrate the potential for improvement in any future literary endeavours.[42]

The anonymous author of the "Notizie" similarly emphasized Foscolo's youth in the few paragraphs dedicated to the author. For example, the article begins at the outset by referring to Foscolo's *Tieste* as "the inaugural work of a young man who had not yet turned nineteen."[43] This sentiment echoes what is found in Foscolo's private letters, and it effectively excused any flaws in the work simply because Foscolo was so young, allowing critics to ultimately look favourably on his inaugural contribution to the Italian theatrical tradition.

The notes accompanying the "Notizie" appear to be more critical of the young tragedian and less flattering than the main text. This difference in tone between the notes and the body of the text suggests that perhaps the "Notizie" was written by multiple authors. The body of the text closely aligns with Foscolo's opinions of his first tragedy, while the notes serve as a critical counterpoint to the body. The criticisms included in the notes comment on the text and on Foscolo. The author took issue with the title of *Tieste*, believing that *Erope* would have been more suitable.[44] There is also a specific criticism of Foscolo's composition that pointedly highlights the erroneous length of one of his verses.[45] The notes also explain how the thinly veiled political allusions seem ill suited for the tragedy and ultimately "cool down one of the most heated tragic situations."[46] And while the body of the text excuses and even exalts Foscolo's young age, the notes find fault with this youth. They make it quite clear that Foscolo would not have even been allowed to produce such a work in Greece during the time of Aristophanes, since it was "prohibited for poets to produce anything on the stage before the age of thirty, or according to others, forty."[47]

Overall, and despite the relatively negative tone of the notes, the review seems to have had Foscolo's best interests in mind. Foscolo intended his first tragedy to be much more than simple entertainment for Venetians during Carnival – he wanted his audience to appreciate his study of the Italian theatrical tradition. For the young playwright, *Tieste* largely was an exercise in composing a tragedy according to neoclassical norms. Foscolo's literary ambitions were lofty, and he desired nothing less than an audience capable of understanding and appreciating them.

Foscolo's adherence to certain compositional methods of Alfieri was not his only homage to the great tragedian. It would hardly be an exaggeration to say that Foscolo even mimicked Alfieri's behaviour. The Astian also had publicly disowned his first tragedy, *Cleopatra, una tragedia*. The work debuted in Turin on 16 June 1775, and was a great success. But Alfieri did not listen to the public acclaim, and he immediately concentrated on avoiding the artistic mistakes that he felt he made in *Cleopatra* when composing his next tragedy, *Filippo*. Alfieri's 1789 "Parere sulle tragedie" even goes so far as to acknowledge only nineteen tragedies, omitting his first work, *Cleopatra*.[48] Foscolo similarly was uneasy with both the favourable public reception of *Tieste* and the quality of the work itself until his death. He refused in 1802 to acknowledge explicitly two of his early compositions – his first tragedy and his ode "Bonaparte liberatore" – claiming that they were simply youthful compositions, and not worthy of study.[49] So in this way, too, he followed Alfieri's lead.

Yet despite Foscolo's desire to discount his first tragedy, *Tieste* did return to the stage following its 1797 Venetian run. The reprise occurred in the summer of 1808 at Milan's Teatro Carcano under a new name, *Atreo e Tieste*. The great Anna Fiorilli Pelandi returned in her role as Erope and the performance ran for three nights.[50] Indeed, 5 August was hailed as an evening in honour of Pelandi at the theatre.[51] Her performances in Milan that summer earned her a privileged place in the press. The *Corriere Milanese* touted her beauty, virtuosity, and ability to move any audience in a 4 August article (entitled "Teatro Carcano").[52] The anonymous author even went so far as to proclaim that Pelandi held the title of premier actress in all of Italy.[53]

Very little additional information about the Milanese version remains. We do know from a letter written by Ugo Brunetti that Foscolo significantly modified *Tieste* for the Milanese performance, including rewriting what Brunetti deemed a "long and frivolous scene between Erope and Ippodamia."[54] Brunetti was most likely referring to act 3, scene 1, when the two women banter back and forth for seventy-two verses. In any event, the Milanese script has been lost.[55] The announcement presented in the *Raccolta foscoliana Acchiappati* describes the opening and subsequent two performances as great successes.[56] Yet, Foscolo was not even in attendance. The tragedian had retreated to the Como home of his close friend Giambattista Giovio, away from the unrelenting summer heat. Foscolo only mentions the Milanese performance months later in a letter to Vincenzo Monti.[57] He was apparently unimpressed with that version of his tragedy and went so far as to proclaim publicly that his *Tieste* was undeserving of public praise, and that it warranted whistles from the audience. Still, if he had received the whistles, Foscolo explained, "perhaps I might never have written or read ever again."[58] Foscolo reiterated this opinion of *Tieste* in England late in his life. In 1818, he wrote, "The courage and the youth of the author enabled him to triumph over his rivals, and his *Thyestes* received more applause than perhaps it deserved."[59]

Public Education and the Theatre

Foscolo continued to contribute to the Italian tragedy tradition immediately following the Venetian debut of *Tieste* in 1797. But he would not begin to write another tragedy for another eleven years. He turned his focus to educating the public on theatrical theory. He essentially picked up where Cesarotti had left off in the development of his own ideas on literature expressed in his didactic works. Specifically, Foscolo's often overlooked manifesto "Per la istituzione d'un teatro civico" (1797) and the discussions that this work produced within the Society for Public Education (Società di pubblica istruzione) are concrete evidence of the author's convictions about literature's function in a modern Italian society and the manner in which literature can be used to educate one's audience.[60]

Venetian politics presented the young author with the opportunity to demonstrate the theatre's potential to serve as a useful tool in the education of a society. Napoleon's forces kidnapped the doge, Ludovico Manin (1726–1802), and forced him to resign as chief magistrate and leader after conquering Venice on 12 May 1797. Foscolo had left the region and was residing in Bologna at the time, but he first heard about Venice's change in government in a letter from Almorò Fedrigo, dated 13 May 1797.[61] Foscolo was ecstatic, believing that Venetian independence would soon follow a brief French occupation.[62] Once the French troops settled into Venice, the *maggior consiglio* founded a provisional democratic municipality, or *Municipalità*. The French brought a new temporary government to the city, and strengthened Italian Jacobinism.[63]

The French officials filled the streets with Jacobin propaganda, hoping to persuade Venetians that the occupation was just and that they were, in fact, the liberators, not the oppressors, of the city. In an effort to seem less tyrannical than the previous rulers, the temporary municipality decided to form a special task force made up of Italian intellectuals, whose sole purpose would be to educate the public on the new government. The municipality was founded upon the dogma "Education is that which forms man and the citizen," and it did its part in emphasizing the importance of the citizen, or *cittadino*, and the friend, or *amico*.[64] It comprised nine committees, the most visible of which was the Committee of Public Health. It was this group that decreed the creation of a Committee of Public Education, *Comitato di pubblica istruzione*, to carry out the fundamental goal of education on 27 May 1797.[65] The express charge of this new committee was to "instruct the People, and to excite in it that energy on which its salvation depends, and that subordination to the Laws and to the established Authorities that form the essential base of the true democratic Liberty and Equality."[66]

The newly formed committee organized public gatherings and held closed-door sessions of six societies – on censorship, education, correspondence, charity, economy, and on hall inspection.[67] The committee as a whole published both their public documents and the minutes from their closed meetings so as to present, as their manifesto says, a sense of transparency and to foster a feeling of mutual trust between the citizens and this branch of the government.[68] On the very same day that it was formed, 27 May 1797, the Society of Public Education immediately proclaimed that use of the "vain titles of Marquis, Count, Cavalier, Excellence, Most Illustrius" was forbidden and that instead they should be replaced by those titles that inspire love for one's country, such as the "sacred names of *Citizen* and *Friend*."[69] There was a presumed equality of membership that invited participation from all Venetians, not just a select few. The Society of Public Education included representative participants from all social classes and genders. It oversaw the dissemination of the propaganda and instructed the public on the new regime, highlighting the differences between the new and the old government. The society's discussion topics included, among various issues, the characteristics of a true and false patriot, definitions of the various forms of tyranny, and the function of public education with regard to the government.[70]

Foscolo wrote to the Municipalità of Reggio Emilia on 16 May 1797 to announce that he was leaving Bologna and returning to Venice to join his compatriots, who were celebrating the city's liberation. He rejoiced, "I fly! I go to shed the first free tears, and to speak to my fellow citizens who for so long suffered their chains."[71] Immediately upon his return to Venice, however, Foscolo fell ill and was unable for a month to participate in the city's political activities. Once he regained his strength, Foscolo wrote a letter to the society on 18 June 1797, asking to participate in the group and pledging his fidelity to their cause.[72] Members of the society read Foscolo's letter aloud at their next meeting, and granted him immediate admission.[73] Foscolo served the Municipalità both as recording secretary and as a member of the Society of Public Education.[74] Foscolo's name appears frequently among the pages of the minutes.[75] But it was his work – and the committee's – before July that focused on revising the form and function of Venice's theatres.

The civic function of the theatre that became a focus for Foscolo and the society was not an original concept in the late eighteenth century.[76] Indeed, Horace had addressed the topic centuries earlier with his *Epistle to the Pisones*, or *Ars poetica*.[77] The society and Foscolo relied on Cesarotti's more empowering 1762 "Ragionamento sopra il diletto della tragedia," which affirmed that the playwright possessed the power to mould the moral convictions of his public. Venetian theatres were the perfect forum for such endeavours. Mario Marcazzan has explained in his article "La letteratura e il teatro" how in Venice the theatre was "not only a reflection of life and customs, but actually *Venetian* life and customs themselves" (author's emphasis).[78] The blurring of the boundaries between stage and reality was not necessarily a positive attribute. Indeed, it can be spun in a very Rousseauian and negative fashion. Yet the potential for improving one's society far outweighed any of the dangers of possibly inspiring less-than-desirable moral behaviour. Foscolo, along with fellow members of his committee on education, chose to use the popular and influential forum of the theatre to unveil the ideals of the new regime and to educate the Venetian public.

Although the society, like Cesarotti, essentially considered the primary function of a playwright to be the moral education (*l'istruzione morale*) of the public, the term "moral education" had assumed a new meaning in the last few years of the eighteenth century. "Morality" for Cesarotti in 1762 was centred on the general qualities of a person's behaviour – whether it was good or bad – and on how one's behaviour affected the society in which he or she lived. This concept was linked to a person's sense of civic responsibility, which was a notion that

Giuseppe Parini famously brought to light in 1759 with his ode "La salubrità dell'aria." Accordingly, Cesarotti instructed tragedians to consider how one's behaviour affected the society in which one lived. By 1797, however, the society equated "morality" with a political, or more precisely nationalist, conscience, believing that the playwright's goal should be to inspire a citizen to consider himself or herself as not just a member of society, but more important, as a member of *Italian* society. This connection between education and a citizen's patriotism was highlighted on 23 May 1797, when Niccolò Corner emphasized the primary role of public teachers in inspiring moral character and social virtues, especially including love for one's country.[79]

The society subsequently wrote about theatre's role in this moral education. Foscolo and seven other citizen-members (*cittadini*) of the society published the short manifesto "Per la istituzione d'un teatro civico,"[80] which is included in the first volume of the ten-volume *Raccolta di carte pubbliche, istruzioni, legislazioni e del nuovo governo democratico* (1797).[81] Critics are not certain if Foscolo was the primary author of this piece; however, according to Giovanni Gambarin in his introduction to the national edition of the work, the fact that Foscolo's name appears first on the closing list of *cittadini* makes it quite likely that he was indeed the largest contributor to the manifesto.[82] There is no date on "Per la istituzione," but the documents preceding and following the declaration suggest that it was published between 25 and 28 May 1797.[83]

What is most curious about "Per la istituzione" is that it appears to be precisely from a period in late May when Foscolo had yet to be officially admitted to the society. In fact, Foscolo professed to be extremely ill during this time. There is no epistolary or biographical evidence that he discussed the composition of "Per la istituzione" with any other members of the society. Furthermore, the authoritative accounts of Foscolo's Venetian tenure do not mention the manifesto. Adriano Augusto Michieli's 1904 seminal account of Foscolo in Venice and Manlio Pastore Stocchi's 1986 version neglect to mention the manifesto whatsoever.[84] Consequently, the reader is still left wondering how and why Foscolo's name appeared first on the list.

This peculiar chronology aside, "Per la istituzione" is worthy of study when one examines Foscolo's theories on tragedy, if only to serve as an example of the then-prevalent opinions of the period on the form and function of theatre in society. The manifesto takes the form of a letter to the citizens of Venice. It introduces them to the members of the society of public instruction and discusses the idea of a new Venetian theatre.[85] The manifesto's opening paragraph describes how the eight signing authors were able to express their ideas freely, and in turn produce works for the public good, without any restrictions by government censors: "Now regaining new life, free and unleashed from the barbarian chains of prejudice, and only subjects to those far more gentile, of honour and humanity, of duty and the Law we can freely give space to our thoughts, ponder our ideas, and render our studies useful."[86] "Per la istituzione" argues that this very didactic function of theatrical works would be useful to the new government. In this light, it argues, the theatre is the best venue through which to educate the public on any topic, especially matters of government. The manifesto proposes that the collective talent of Venice's playwrights would be used best to create a civic theatre, *un teatro civico*, designed to cultivate a sense of civic duty in every Venetian citizen, regardless of his or her economic class:

> We propose a Civic Theatre. We will dedicate ourselves to declamation, to music and to composing in order to educate the Public, leaving up to our genius the choice of whether we will have some endowment; requiring some temporary funding, it will be very small, and under the title of a simple loan. Everything that would be collected beyond what is spent will be distributed to the poor.[87]

"Per la istituzione" closes with a list of promises made by the authors. They explained not only the manner in which they vowed to make their works more important for the nation, but also how they would guide the public through the transition from the old regime to the new.

Men were not the only active participants in this new regime. The *cittadini* also commented on the important role of women in this education process, and on how their female compatriots needed to follow their example. They charged their readers to "animate our fellow female citizens to follow our example."[88] The specific emphasis of "Per la istituzione" on female participation in the new society was not unheard of at this time. Women began to hold integral roles in Italian society as educators during the eighteenth century. In her 2002 book *The Century of Women: Representations of Women in Eighteenth-Century Italian Public Discourse*, Rebecca Messbarger explained how male intellectuals were re-evaluating the role of women during the *Settecento*. Messbarger discussed the works of three prominent figures of the period, Pierdomenico Soresi, Melchiorre Delfico, and Saverio Bettinelli: "Among *illuministi*, women were reconceived in terms of the Enlightenment project as 'citizens,' as 'the soul of society,' and as 'the linchpin of public happiness.'"[89] She continues: "Redesignated 'the cradle of [modern] deportment and reason,' the home now represented a primary training ground for an enlightened citizenry."[90] Lastly, "Mothers, as 'the most worthy educators of every man,' practically facilitated this training and the consequent well-being of the modern state."[91]

The Napoleonic regime knew fully well that one of the most effective ways of spreading the message of the new government was through education, with women playing an integral part in this process. They were the primary educators within the family unit and were responsible for the moral upbringing of their children. It is apparent that Foscolo and his colleagues were acutely aware of this important role of women (their *Concittadine*) as educators during this period in Venice. A significant number of the society's meetings centred on the education of women and their function in educating fellow citizens. They actively used "Per la istituzione" to enlist women to assist with the formation of this new society.[92]

The desired civic theatre materialized at the end of May 1797. The fact that it actually was constructed is notable, since very few of the municipality's proposed projects were actually undertaken. The nearly immediate institution of the civic theatre was assisted by a female citizen, Virginia Chigi Grimani, whose family owned the large and popular theatre in San Giovanni Grisostomo (today's Teatro Malibran). She approved the use of the theatre for this new purpose. For nearly three months (10 July–1 October 1797), Venetians, including Foscolo, were entertained and educated while attending seventeen different plays.[93] Foscolo was so inspired by the idea of the Venetian civic theatre that he actually attempted to write a tragedy intended to be staged for the cause – *Timocrate*.[94] Yet, while he was not short on patriotic passions, the actual tragedy never materialized. Any and all drafts or sketches of *Timocrate* unfortunately do not exist.

Foscolo lived and breathed the role of public educator. He did not feel that it was enough to simply write works that would inspire the public to love their country and embrace ideal moral principles. It was also necessary to *live* the role of the patriot and be a moral example. An author's character should be considered in any evaluation, no matter how exceptional his or her works. Foscolo publically proclaimed this conviction on 22 September in a meeting of the society. The group was discussing who should be seen as the emblematic figure of an Italian patriot; Vittorio Alfieri's name, of course, rose to the top. Foscolo proclaimed that Alfieri was a "great man" and a "great Republican Writer, and worthy of imitation and praise. Italy would be happy if all the tragedians equalled him!"[95]

Yet Foscolo surprisingly objected to Alfieri's glorification as a patriot. He explained how, in contrast to his iconic poetic representations of tyranny versus liberty, Alfieri conspicuously failed to fight against the tyrannical French aristocracy when residing in France. Foscolo pointed out that Alfieri retreated "to the shadow of neutrality" by leaving France for Florence, rather than actively participating in the revolution.[96] He praised Alfieri's work as a tragedian and poet, but Foscolo was relentless and steadfast in his opinion that Alfieri's character did not serve as a model for the society or an Italian patriot. He proclaimed, "Perhaps I will not be heard; but I will have proclaimed the truth. Alfieri is silent! Alfieri speaks only to cast reproaches on Italy. Alfieri, therefore, is not entitled to the esteem of the patriots."[97] In the end, Foscolo was a follower of the Alfierian tragedy, but showed no interest in emulating the Astian's moral behaviour.

The municipality continued to emphasize the necessity of shaping the morality of its citizens. On 27 October 1797, the Committee of Public Education also published detailed instructions for playwrights. The article "Ai cittadini autori teatrali rappresentazioni, capi comici ed impresari di opere" outlined the contemplated role of playwrights in contributing to the *teatro civico*.[98] In it, the committee implored Venetian playwrights, who were "still young children in the career of liberty," to use their artistic works to educate the public. They aspired to a theatre that would ultimately "arrive at the highest perfection," becoming "a school of moral custom."[99]

Members of the society eagerly awaited the ultimate liberation of Venice from foreign occupation, but these hopes were soon dashed. On 17 October 1797, Napoleon ceded the city to the Austrian government in the Treaty of Campo Formio. The dreams of Foscolo and his compatriots were ruined by the very person – Napoleon – whom they believed would ultimately free Venice. Shortly after this disappointment, on 9 November 1797, Foscolo's participation as a member of the municipality ended when he left for Bologna.[100] Nonetheless, his work for the society on the core function of a playwright and patriot, however short lived, undoubtedly contributed to his development as a theatrical scholar and theorist, influencing his future tragedies and literary-critical works.

Fourteen years separated Foscolo's participation in the society and the debut of his second tragedy, *Ajace*. He turned to producing his more renowned literary works during this period. Foscolo began by internalizing his immense disappointment in Napoleon. The feeling of political betrayal and disillusion is palpable in the pages of his semi-autobiographical *Ultime Lettere di Jacopo Ortis*. The epistolary novel, reminiscent of Goethe's *The Sorrows of Young Werther* (1774), recounts the story of the troubled figure of Ortis, his unrequited love for Teresa, his exile from Venice, and his final tragic decision to commit suicide. Foscolo's novel was an instant success. He also wrote several emotionally charged poems during this period, such as the nostalgic sonnet about his native land "A Zacinto" and the mournful sonnet about the suicide of his younger brother "In morte del fratello Giovanni." He published two odes and twelve sonnets in Milan in 1803 in a collection entitled *Poesie*. Foscolo would continue to incorporate autobiographical elements in his writings throughout the remainder of his career.

In addition to writing, Foscolo also actively participated in the republican army. He was promoted to the rank of captain in June 1800 and found himself travelling throughout the north of Italy, and ultimately was stationed in Valenciennes, France, in 1804–5. It is here that he was romantically linked to the mother (presumed to be Sophia Hamilton) of his only child, a daughter named Floriana, whom he would not meet until the final years of his life in England. Foscolo also turned his creative eye to translation and began to translate Laurence Sterne's *A Sentimental Journey through France and Italy* and Homer's *Iliad*, books 1 and 3.

Foscolo returned to Milan in March 1806, where he continued to make a name for himself in literary circles. In April 1807, he published his *Esperimento di traduzione dell'Iliade di Omero* and one of his most renowned works, the solemn poem *Dei sepolcri*. Following the 1806 Italian application of Napoleon's Edict of Saint-Cloud (originally decreed in 1804), the moral and religious questions of whether or not graves should be marked, and for what purpose, sparked intellectual debate. Foscolo's *Dei sepolcri* was a literary call to arms for all Italians to embrace their great ancestors, using the forum of the graveyard to inspire national pride and unity. If *Ultime lettere* was his claim to fame in prose, then *Dei sepolcri* sealed his position as one of Italy's greatest poets.[101]

Foscolo reprised his role of public educator on 18 March 1808, when the government named him to the coveted position of professor of eloquence at the University of Pavia. He spent several months preparing for his new teaching position, yet he ultimately was disappointed when the government cancelled the appointments of several professorships, including his own, on 15 November 1808. Foscolo was permitted to teach a few classes during the next year, however, and on 22 January gave his opening lecture, "Dell'origine e dell'ufficio della letteratura," in which he proposed that the key function of literature was to contribute to the development of a nation.[102]

Subsequent critics have focused their attention on the similarities between the theories Foscolo expressed in *Dell'origine* on the connection between a society's literature and its history, and those expressed by Giambattista Vico (1668–1744) in his *Scienza nuova* (first edition 1725, second edition 1730, and third edition 1744). Vico viewed poetry as a free creative act of the imagination. He believed that it could present a version of national history that might be decidedly different from that of historical documents, but which nonetheless should be considered crucial to understanding the past. Foscolo's ideas in his *Dell'origine* echoed Vico's, yet he went beyond the latter's understanding of the inseparable relationship between the literary arts and the people's sense of nationalism and added to the discussion. The nationalist tone assumed by Foscolo in *Dell'origine* marked an apparent return to the theme of his Venetian manifesto, "Per la istituzione d'un teatro civico," twelve years earlier. According to Foscolo's 1809 lecture, literature should inspire a sense of national awareness, especially during a time of foreign occupation.[103]

Foscolo urged his colleagues to highlight the spirit of the Italian people in their works in order to make a significant contribution to Italian history. By doing so, Foscolo argued, future generations of Italians could learn about their history, at least in part through literature. He commended the efforts of Gerolamo Tiraboschi (1731–94), Francesco S. Quadrio (1695–1756), Giovan Mario Crescimbeni, and Ludovico Antonio Muratori for their histories, which catalogue the names and dates of important literary figures and their seminal works.[104] Foscolo lamented, however, the absence of a single true history of Italian literature illustrating the overarching spirit and passions of the long-eighteenth century. He encouraged Italians to reject then-current literary norms, which were dictated by an elite few, urging them to strive to better represent the spirit of the Italian people in their literary works. Foscolo believed that literature should present the history of the past and "paint the opinions, habits and appearances" of a modern audience.[105] Put simply, he fundamentally bemoaned that Italy's history was being told mostly by foreigners, and he called on his broad audience – Italian literary society as a whole – to provide a literary history of the era.[106]

The subject of Foscolo's opening lecture at the University of Pavia at first blush appears to be significantly removed from his work on the Italian stage. Yet Foscolo's general thoughts on Italian literature, as set forth in his talk, directly reflect the views he held of his role as a theatrical scholar and playwright. Theatre was a representation of life for Foscolo, and it provided a concrete example of how literature could shape a society's national identity. In the coming months, Foscolo himself would begin to grapple with writing a new tragedy. His precepts on literature presented in Pavia, coupled with the very real and hostile reactions by the Milanese literary elite, would directly affect the writing and reception of this new work. Foscolo's lessons in Pavia and on the Italian stage were no longer separated by a seemingly vast distance.

Chapter Three

The Rise and Fall of *Ajace*

Foscolo returned to composing tragedies following his brief tenure at the University of Pavia. He agreed to write a new work on 18 July 1809 for Salvatore Fabbrichesi (1760–1827), director of the Compagnia dei Commedianti ordinari di S.M.I. e R.[1] Foscolo initially selected the Ovidian fable of Byblis and Caunus (*Metamorphoses*, 9, 441–665) as his subject, but he was slow to compose any verses. He abandoned the idea when his friend Antonio Gasparinetti decided to base his new tragedy on the same tale. Foscolo also toyed with the idea of composing a tragedy on Oedipus, but once again, he lacked the necessary inspiration or motivation to begin this project in earnest.[2] All that remains of Foscolo's *Edippo* today is a sparse prose outline for three acts.[3] Foscolo ultimately settled on the story of Ajax, taken from the lost epic poem alluded to in Homer's *Odyssey*.[4] He turned to Sophocles, one of the four major tragedians listed in his 1796 *Piano di studi*, for inspiration.

This was not the first time that Foscolo considered the subject of Ajax. He referred to the warrior years earlier in his famous 1807 poem *Dei sepolcri*.[5] But Foscolo's familiarity with the subject matter did not make writing any easier. He remarked in a letter to Ugo Brunetti that he finally began writing on 2 February 1811.[6] Almost two years after he initially promised Fabbrichesi a completed tragedy, Foscolo informed his own family that he was working very slowly.[7] He repeatedly lamented *Ajace*'s compositional difficulties during the next eight months. Foscolo was determined to honour his agreement with Fabbrichesi, however, and he finally completed the tragedy on 12 October 1811.[8]

Foscolo's *Ajace* consists of five acts and 1902 lines of unrhymed hendecasyllabic verse. Six speaking characters inhabit the tragedy, which is set in the Greek military camp below the walls of Troy. Foscolo faithfully follows the unity of time, setting the tragedy over a precise twenty-four-hour period, from dawn to dawn. This version of the story commences in the immediate aftermath of the death of the warrior Achille. Ulisse plots against the Greek hero Ajace for control of the troops of the recently deceased Achille. He begins by planting a seed of doubt in King Agamennone regarding Ajace's allegiance. Ulisse notes that his rival sided against the king at a recent gathering, and he observes that Ajace's half-brother Teucro had a Trojan mother and that Ajace's wife was a Trojan slave. A mistrusting Agamennone does not respond to the masses' demand that Ajace be awarded the troops and instead decrees that he alone has the power to make such a decision. Ulisse continues his scheming and sends Teucro and his troops away. He tells Teucro that he and Ajace will join him later, and in the same breath he spreads the rumour that Teucro has fled.

The priest Calcante arrives and advocates for Ajace by warning Agamennone that he should be most wary of Ulisse. Ajace attempts to make his own case with the king, but Agamennone is consumed by solitude, self-hatred, and indecision, and he accuses Ajace of being power-hungry. The Greek kings announce their intent to support Ajace, but Ulisse again intervenes, stirring up enough trouble that the kings decide to leave the decision up to the captive Trojan princes. Agamennone believes the rumour that Teucro has fled, and he takes Ajace's son as a hostage. A despondent Ajace is convinced that everyone, including his brother Teucro, has betrayed him, and he mortally wounds himself. Teucro convinces Ajace of his love and fidelity as his brother lies dying, yet he also informs him that Ulisse has just assumed control of Achille's troops. Foscolo returns to his theme of the dangers of power (previously included in *Tieste*) when Agamennone speaks the final verses of the tragedy and laments the high moral price required by its pursuit.

Generally speaking, Foscolo's second tragedy follows the Alfierian model. For example, the characters of Agamennone and Ajace represent the traditional "tyranny versus liberty" theme, a central fixture of the Alfierian tragedy, and the protagonist does not enter the action until the second act. Yet Foscolo departed from this model in several instances. To begin with, the tragedy is extremely long, and by straying from a main event and focusing on various episodes of the Trojan wars in copious monologues, Foscolo did not follow the classical unity of action. Furthermore, Alfieri stipulated in "Parere sulle tragedie" that the final act of a tragedy should be the shortest, with the most action and spectacular effects.[9] In contrast, in Foscolo's *Ajace*, the final act is the longest, 419 lines, and is virtually devoid of any significant action except for the tediously slow death of Ajace. Alfieri also would have objected to the many lines Foscolo gave to his secondary characters. For example, in act 2, scene 1, Foscolo assigned ninety-eight of the one hundred and fifty-four lines to a secondary character, the priest Calcante, and only fifty-six to the main character, Agamennone.[10]

Twentieth-century critics chiefly viewed *Ajace* as a failure. Mario Fubini noted very little resemblance between the prototypical Alfierian tyrant and the liberator figures of Agamennone and Ajace in his 1978 book *Ugo Foscolo*.[11] Similarly, Eugenio Donadoni was quick to dismiss Foscolo's second tragedy as lacking in intrinsic force and characterized the work as neither lyrical (like the works of Metastasio) nor melodramatic.[12] Giorgio Pullini compared Foscolo's *Ajace* to another tragedy of the period, Vincenzo Monti's *Caio Gracco* (1789–90), in his 1982 book *Teatro italiano dell'Ottocento*. Pullini explained how *Ajace* is similar to Monti's third tragedy with its disregard for Alfierian concision and its abundant number of stories being told offstage. He described Foscolo's characters as "one-dimensional" in their stoic greatness, and claimed that Tecmessa is the most alive character in the work.[13] Roberto Alonge also highlighted Foscolo's lack of Alfierian qualities in his 1978 book *Struttura e ideologia nel teatro italiano fra '500 e '900*, labelling the work a tragedy without action. For Alonge, Foscolo's protagonist merely talks for four acts, and then dies in the fifth.[14]

Yet recent scholars have adopted a modern revisionist criticism of Foscolo's second tragedy. There is something important about the work – but what? For Andrea Ciccarelli, the inaction of Ajace was a deliberate artistic choice of Foscolo's and rather than being viewed as a primary flaw of the work, we should read it as innovative.[15] For Maria Maddalena Lombardi the verbosity of *Ajace* was also intentional. She posits in her "Scheda introduttiva" that Foscolo may have meant to pay homage to the tale's original author, Homer, by combining the severe Alfierian verse with the robust Homeric verse.[16]

Lombardi describes the style and metre of *Ajace* as similar to Foscolo's recent translation of Homer, *Esperimento di traduzione della Iliade di Omero*.[17] Foscolo explored the world of translation and the various ways in which a translator presented a translation in this work. He published his translation of the first canto of the *Iliad* alongside Cesarotti's prose translation and Monti's translation and offered critical commentary in 1807. Foscolo was preoccupied with developing a translation that conveyed not only a faithful rendition of Homer's verse, but also the authentic spirit of Homeric poetry. He would continue to work on this translation for the rest of his life.

Therefore, according to Lombardi, it is only logical that four years later Foscolo would return to his translation while writing his second tragedy. She remarks on how numerous verses in *Ajace* include a double accent on the sixth and seventh syllables, affecting a particularly vigorous and serious rhythm. Lombardi aptly notes that this is typical of Foscolo as translator of Homer.[18] Her extensive notes even highlight examples of linguistic similarities between Foscolo's *Ajace* and his *Esperimento*. For example, in act 1, scene 3, verse 21, "*Lungo il lito del mar* trascorre a torme" (italics mine) can be compared with verse 41 of the *Esperimento*, "*E muto al lito* andò *del mar* fremente."[19] Likewise, verse 93, "*Sotto il brando d'Ettorre*, Ajace apparve" echoes verses 277–8 of *Esperimento*, "Quando cadrà gran messe di trafitti | *Sotto il brando d'Ettorre*."[20] Moreover, verses 153–4, "Ajace figlio d'Oïleo che in petto | *Non* ha *virtú che di corrucci e sangue*," sound similar to verses 203–4 of *Esperimento*, "chè in petto | *Non t'è virtú che di corrucci e sangue*."[21]

But what does Lombardi's philological evidence really tell us? Linguistic similarities often abound when authors choose to write on a similar subject matter. In the case of *Ajace*, I would argue that Foscolo's return to Homer, and by extension his four-year-old translation of the first canto of the *Iliad*, had everything to do with then current events. Specifically, Foscolo's troubling struggle with the Milanese establishment essentially was bleeding into his second tragedy.

It is no secret that Foscolo was considered "Public Enemy Number 1" in the eyes of the establishment following his inaugural lecture in Pavia. He had encouraged Italians to reject then current literary norms dictated by an elite few, and urged them to strive to better represent the spirit of the Italian people in their literary works. Foscolo irritated prominent figures like Vincenzo Monti, Francesco Pezzi (1781–1831), Luigi Lamberti (1759–1813), and Urbano Lampredi. The tension escalated when Foscolo published his 1810 article in the journal *Annali di scienze e lettere* entitled "Sulla traduzione dell'*Odissea*," which effectively insulted the competency of Vincenzo Monti as author and translator.[22] Foscolo's subsequent essay "Ragguaglio d'un'adunanza dell'Accademia de' Pitagorici" aggravated matters by expressing his displeasure with the absurd and unwarranted importance literary journals gave to mathematicians and scientists.[23] Foscolo even labelled the mathematician Lampredi and his followers the "Accademia de' Pitagorici," and questioned why they were permitted to review and comment on literature, a subject on which they presumably knew very little.

These articles predictably infuriated Lampredi, and, as was the custom of the day, he publicly responded to Foscolo in a 15 May 1810 article published in the literary journal *Corriere Milanese*. Lampredi accused Foscolo of unjustly and inaccurately reproaching him and Monti, along with others in their intellectual circle.[24] Foscolo, in turn, immediately retaliated with a harshly worded article, "Ultimato di Ugo Foscolo nella guerra contro i ciarlatani, gl'impostori letterari ed i pedanti" (begun in 1810, incomplete), claiming victimhood and labelling Lampredi the "King of the league of literary charlatans."[25] Lampredi, along with Monti and Lamberti, founded a new literary journal *Il Poligrafo* (7 April 1811–27 March 1814), largely in an effort to respond to the views of Foscolo and the *Annali di scienze e lettere* on literary matters.[26] Literary battles unfolded on the pages of Lampredi's *Il Poligrafo* and the *Annali*.[27] Each author focused his response on one or two points from the most recent insulting commentary; the participants considered it especially persuasive or compelling for one man to use his antagonist's own language against him when responding to a key point.

Ajace, therefore, appeared precisely at a time when Foscolo was warring with the Milanese elite. His choice to portray the story of Ajax brings to mind both his past success (*Dei sepolcri*) and current struggles (the ongoing literary blood feud over translation and literary criticism). Foscolo actually assumes the role of tragic hero in this period, aligning himself with the character of Ajax, fighting against what he viewed as his enemies' unwarranted and unjust oppression. He purposefully wrote in a Homeric style that is, on the one hand, verbose and often tedious, but, on the other hand, surprisingly telling when viewed in this light. If we place more emphasis on *Ajace*'s historical value – as an artefact capable of illustrating Foscolo's biographical, cultural, and political realities – then the tragedy becomes, as Thomas Peterson recently remarked, "a masterwork essential to any genuine understanding of Foscolo."[28] *Ajace* appears at the centre of Foscolo's lifelong career in the realm of tragedy, spanning from 1797 to 1827. Its opening performance at the end of 1811 marks almost exactly the middle of this thirty-year career, and the tragedy materializes during a period of intense adversity that would forever plague Foscolo. In this light, *Ajace* can be seen as the focal point of Foscolo's life.

The Performance of *Ajace*

The life-defining conflict between Foscolo and Lampredi culminated with the opening performance of *Ajace*. It opened at the Teatro alla Scala on 9 December 1811 to an audience comprising both Foscolo's friends and his literary enemies.[29] The Compagnia Reale, directed by

Salvatore Fabbrichesi, performed the tragedy with a distinguished cast, including the extraordinary actress of the period Anna Fiorilli Pellandi playing Ajace's wife, Tecmessa.[30] The performance began without incident and provoked polite applause. However, during the intermission between the second and third acts, one of Foscolo's enemies posted the following epigram at the theatre's entrance and circulated it throughout the audience:

> Here lies dead the furious Ajax.
> Rest in peace …
>
> [Qui estinto giace il furibondo Ajace.
> Requiescat in pace …][31]

Foscolo was understandably shaken that his tragedy was effectively entombed before the inaugural performance was even half over.

And the worst was yet to come. The audience seems to have been uninfluenced by the epigram and erupted in thunderous applause, and called for Foscolo to take the stage during the third act and acknowledge their praise, as was the customary practice of the time. Yet he was nowhere to be found. Foscolo refused to give the audience what they wanted and left the theatre without accepting or acknowledging their accolades.[32] Scholars have proposed a number of explanations for the snub. Perhaps Foscolo did not want to appear on stage for fear of suffering further humiliation from his enemies. Another possible explanation rests with Foscolo's goal of acting the part of the "respectable" tragedian and his accompanying desire for the audience to maintain its focus on the tragedy. This conjecture alludes to the teachings of Cesarotti's 1762 "Ragionamento sopra il diletto della tragedia," in which Cesarotti explains that in order to maintain the verisimilar nature of the tragedy, a tragedian must have a silent and attentive audience. He strongly objected to the author taking the stage or making his presence known during the tragedy's performance.[33] In this light, Foscolo may have viewed the applause and requests for him to take the stage as unwelcome distractions.

The actors performed the final two acts of the tragedy to minimal applause. The epigram and Foscolo's snub were not the only incidents tempering the audience's reception. Most notably, the audience broke out in laughter during the penultimate scene of the fifth act, when Fabbrichesi, playing Teucro, recited the lines:

Oh Salaminians, o poor
Strong ones, o wretched ones who remain,
Who is left for you now?

[… O Salamini, o soli
Di tanti forti, o sciagurati avanzi,
Chi più vi resta omai?][34]

Foscolo meant for the words "Salamini" to refer to the people of the Greek island of Salamis, Ajace's birthplace. According to Giuseppe Pecchio's 1830 biography, however, the term had an unfortunate double meaning – "salamini" were also little sausages made in Lombardy.[35] Foscolo's phrase "sciagurati avanzi," or "wretched leftovers," also invoked images of food. The audience was reminded of a mundane aspect of daily life instead of being drawn into this serious and poignant moment in the tragedy, and the performance ended in laughter.[36] The debacle of *Ajace* persisted long after opening night. Foscolo was memorialized as the "King of little sausages" ("re dei salamini") following the inaugural performance.[37]

The Censors

The remainder of *Ajace*'s tenure on the Milanese stage was hardly more successful. The viceroy Eugène de Beauharnais (Napoleon's stepson, 1781–1824) was suspicious of the purportedly anti-Napoleonic message hidden within Foscolo's *Ajace*. Conventional wisdom held that the ambitious and omnipotent Agamennone represented Napoleon, Ajace was the general Jean-Victor Moreau (1763–1813), Calcante was Pope Pius VII (1742–1823), and Ulisse was the minister of police, Joseph Fouché (1759–1820). Foscolo protested in his 1818 "Essay on the Present Literature of Italy" that these sorts of political allusions were far from his mind, and subsequent critics and biographers have accepted his explanation on its face. Yet this *post hoc* justification was unsuccessful in convincing the French censors. The viceroy was not amused, and suspended performances of the tragedy for fifteen days so that the work could be scrutinized by the censors.[38] Foscolo attempted to defend himself by insisting in a letter that he "could not possibly have had the daft intention of agitating a public that venerates the founder of the Kingdom of Italy."[39] Nonetheless political censors upheld the suspension of the performance indefinitely and banned the publication of the tragedy in Milan.

Yet occupying government censors were not solely (or even largely) to blame, despite Foscolo's later claims. He declined to assume any modicum of responsibility for his second tragedy's failure following the disastrous opening. Foscolo instead attributed *Ajace*'s negative reception solely to the actors' abysmal performances and the epigram posted by his spiteful literary enemies. But these rationalizations are unconvincing. *Ajace* suffered from numerous problems on its face, such as its excessive length, and Foscolo was no doubt aware of them long before opening night. Indeed, almost two months before *Ajace*'s debut, Foscolo admitted in a 15 October 1811 letter to Giuseppe Grassi that he had received various suggestions as to how he might edit and rework his second tragedy to improve its reception. Foscolo explained that he had read the tragedy to a "few young men," who "all judged that the first act was perhaps worse than the others." They even suggested that Foscolo should shorten the act, but he flatly refused, writing, "How can it be done? One cannot take away even half of one verse without unravelling the entire tragedy; and I am so dead from that work, that I would choose to write an entirely new tragedy from scratch rather than have to rake over the scenes of this one."[40] As far as Foscolo was concerned, he had finished the tragedy, and it was too late to change anything.

Ironically, the "young men" seem to have been right about *Ajace*. Their critique of the tragedy neatly corresponds to the audience's reception of the tragedy on opening night. There was very little applause after the first two acts; the final two acts generally were considered to be pathetic; and the tragedy, on the whole, was overlong. Foscolo was well aware of *Ajace*'s shortcomings; he was just unwilling to address them. Foscolo therefore must assume the lion's share of the blame for the negative reception of *Ajace*.

Reviewing the Reviews

Yet Foscolo's ongoing conflict with the Milanese literary establishment treated the tragedy worse than the censors. The reviews of *Ajace* influenced its reception and effectively buried *Ajace* for all eternity. Foscolo was powerless to avoid the catastrophic reviews of his second tragedy.

Ajace's reviews appeared in four different Milanese literary journals – *Corriere Milanese*, *Corriere delle Dame*, *Giornale Italiano*, and *Il Poligrafo*. French censorship affected the tragedy in more indirect ways as well. Milan's occupying French government decreed on 27 November 1811 that only eight literary journals were permitted to publish political news. This censorship is relevant to Foscolo's second tragedy because the four journals containing reviews of *Ajace* were included among the sanctioned eight.[41] All four enjoyed an increased readership following the limitation on political reports. The first three were the most widely read, according to Carlo Capra. The *Corriere Milanese* had 3000 subscribers, the *Giornale Italiano* had nearly that many, and the *Corriere delle Dame* had 700.[42] *Il Poligrafo* was one of the minor journals with no more than 200–300 subscriptions.

Some of the reviews focused solely on the public reception of *Ajace*, rather than the tragedy itself. The first review was one of these. It appeared immediately after the opening night in the *Corriere Milanese*. Critics and historians attribute this article to the periodical's director, Francesco Pezzi.[43] There was no love lost between Foscolo and Pezzi, who was one of the ringleaders in the whole kerfuffle between the supporters of Monti, who published in the *Corriere Milanese*, the *Giornale Italiano*, and *Il Poligrafo*, and the supporters of Foscolo, who wrote for the *Annali di scienze e lettere*. Yet Pezzi refrained from evaluating Foscolo's prowess as a tragedian in his review. On the contrary, the review is primarily an account of the public reaction to and reception of the opening performance, not an evaluation of the tragedian himself.

Pezzi pulled few punches in his review. The 198-word article appeared in the journal the morning after *Ajace*'s botched debut under the section entitled "NOTIZIE INTERNE: Regno d'Italia." Pezzi informed the reader that there was to be a second performance of the tragedy that evening. It is a more-or-less factual account written from the third-person, omniscient point of view. He began by acknowledging the incredibly large audience that filled the theatre, noting that several spectators were turned away after La Scala was filled to capacity. Pezzi then explained that the audience was silent, and listened attentively during the performance. The remainder of the review focuses on the amount of applause generated. Pezzi first discussed how the audience applauded sporadically for "certain worthy verses."[44] This is the only praise for *Ajace* in Pezzi's review. He continued by explaining that at the end of the performance, the spectators were exhausted from the tragedy's verbosity, and did not applaud. Pezzi recounted that after two minutes the audience finally reacted and there were "some indiscrete and even unjust whistles mixed in with the applause. But these last ones were victorious."[45]

Other reviews expanded on their criticisms to include the substance of Foscolo's work. An anonymous author published a review of *Ajace* on the front page of Milan's *Corriere delle Dame*, on 14 December – one day after the viceroy's suspension of the tragedy.[46] The husband-and-wife duo of Giuseppe and Carolina Arienti Lattanzi had founded the journal in 1804, and the eight-page weekly periodical catered to a primarily female audience.[47] It is unclear if Carolina or Giuseppe wrote the 345-word review of *Ajace*, which appeared under the heading "R. Teatro Della Scala" on the first two pages of the journal. One piece of evidence that hints at Carolina is the fact that she signed the notice to subscribers that preceded the review. In any event, the review was written from the first-person-singular point of view, and it is a mixed evaluation that contains both positive accolades for the accomplished poet as well as pointed critical questions about several of Foscolo's artistic choices. It broadly praises Foscolo by highlighting his literary prowess, proclaiming him to be one "to whom no one denied veracity of intelligence and dignity of style."[48] However, the author also noted that Foscolo did not receive the applause and praise generally expected to accompany the work of such an esteemed author.[49]

The review proceeds to question Foscolo's choice of a more *favoloso* subject rather than something *storico*. It also expresses reservations about Foscolo's portrayal of characters, remarking on the lack of *gravitas* of Ulisse and Calcante, and comparing the former to a comic troublemaker and the latter to an optical telegraph.[50] The reviewer asked a more fundamental question: Why did Foscolo choose to have Ajace kill himself? These dubious artistic choices resulted in the audience's poor reception of a work that (perhaps) had the makings of another literary masterpiece. The review ends with another mention of Foscolo's literary excellence, stating, "My naive warnings do not detract from the poetic merit of Mr Foscolo, both for the elocution as well as the lines and images to which he gave new and enlightening wisdom in this tragedy."[51] Above all, this review goes even further out of its way to avoid overly harsh criticism. The reviewer certainly questioned several elements of Foscolo's tragedy, but he or she consciously avoided condemning Foscolo the poet.

The same cannot be said for the third review. It appeared in the second-most-read journal in Milan, the *Giornale Italiano*, which was founded by Vincenzo Cuoco in 1804 with the goal of contributing to the formation of "the public spirit of a nation."[52] The *Giornale Italiano*, along with the *Corriere Milanese*, showcased the writings of many of Foscolo's literary enemies, including Monti, Lampredi, and Lamberti. A section entitled "Varietà" contains the review of *Ajace*. Like many reviews of the period, it was written by an anonymous author, who is identified only with the initials "A.C." It is much longer than the previous two reviews, at 1189 words, and is written from the first-person-plural point of view, often using the "we." The review contains several of the same literary suggestions and concerns that the earlier review of the *Corriere delle Dame* had expressed.

The review begins by recounting the enormous public anticipation for Foscolo's second tragedy, and quickly concludes that the work did not come close to meeting these heightened expectations.[53] It offers a number of recommendations and warnings as to what Foscolo should do in his future career as a tragedian, which as the review states, Foscolo "seems intent on pursuing."[54] It first complains about the lack of action and sheer number of lines, observing that these faults prevent *Ajace* from ever stirring or moving the spectator, "which of course, is the only goal of tragic poetry."[55] The review explains how following the performance the hearts of the public were unfortunately left "cold or indifferent" from the tragedy's lack of inspiring poetry.[56] The review finds the excessive wordiness of Ajace's soliloquy and his lengthy death scene to be inappropriate and in need of editing.[57] It concludes that Foscolo misrepresented the well-known historical characters, especially Ulisse and Agamennone. The review bluntly states that the former "is no longer the wise son of Laertes, but a vile flatterer" and that the latter's political ambition appears to be "modelled more on the precepts of Machiavelli and Hobbes than on the archetype that is presented by Homer."[58] But the chief flaw cited is similar to that mentioned in the *Corriere Delle Dame* review – Foscolo's choice to write about a mythological or fantastic story instead of one that is more historical. The author recommended that Foscolo select more suitable and historically grounded subjects for future works,[59] and concluded that Foscolo's selection of a more mythical subject matter negatively affected the public's reception of *Ajace*. The review is generally negative, but it is not overly sensational, like those that were to appear in the coming weeks.

The conventional-wisdom retelling of *Ajace*'s reception is much less generous to Foscolo's tragedy than these three generally negative but restrained reviews display. The popular account focuses on four memorable – and harshly negative – reviews published on 15, 22, and 29 December 1811 and 5 January 1812 in the small literary journal *Il Poligrafo*. Each article shifts from the first-person singular to the first-person plural and back again numerous times. The anonymous author, who signed each review with the letter "A," has been identified as

Urbano Lampredi, a long-time literary "enemy" of Foscolo. It should be no surprise in light of the animosity between the two men that Lampredi was ecstatic when the inaugural performance of *Ajace* ended in laughter. He set to writing the reviews that became the commonly accepted version of *Ajace*'s reception. They do not contain even the slightest hint of praise. Their criticism and tone are unabashedly negative, and in many instances they turn downright nasty.

Lampredi began his first article by attributing the negative public opinion directly to *Ajace*'s poorly designed text. He argued that Foscolo failed to drive the action and ultimately ruined the moment of verisimilitude by allowing the spectator to hear only the poet and not the characters; thus, "the illusion is broken, the action slowed even more, and the spectator becomes disengaged and terribly bored; then, in the end, he truly has no idea why Ajace killed himself."[60] The only aim of this series of articles must have been to humiliate Foscolo. Lampredi even declared that *Il Poligrafo* was committed to exposing Foscolo's flaws and offering suggestions on how to accurately portray the story of Ajax. He wrote:

> The inconveniences and the mistakes of this Tragedy will show themselves in a clear light when we examine the characteristics, be they false or grotesque, that U.F. gave to Homer's heroes. In fact, it has been said that this is not a fit subject for tragic action. We hope to be able to show the contrary, underlining a design through which, in our eyes, one can make a good tragedy out of Ajax. We will put it before the eyes of our readers and the public in the next *Poligrafo*. It seems to us that, after having seen how one should not make this tragedy, we were able to imagine how one should make it.[61]

Lampredi's most insistent and effective criticism was repeatedly aimed at Foscolo's design for *Ajace*. There are seemingly innocuous phrases such as "let us look at the design and economy of the tragedy of Mr U. F. and at the characteristics of his characters."[62] But Lampredi quickly condemned Foscolo's *disegno*, beginning with the episodic nature of the tragedy. He questioned, "Now I ask, with this design of bizarre, disconnected scenes, can he make a real and good tragedy?"[63] Lampredi again reiterated that Foscolo's *disegno* was "poorly conceived."[64]

Lampredi further characterized the *disegno* as a monster or disaster on numerous occasions. For example, the opening phrase of the second review states, "We have already demonstrated that the tragedy *Ajace* is a real monster with regard to the design."[65] He insulted Foscolo's prowess as a poet, asserting that this flaw can be attributed to the author's "ignorance or inconsideration of the good concepts of art."[66] Lampredi described the qualities of the main characters as equally monstrous later in the same article.[67] And he insists that this too, must be attributed to Foscolo's unfamiliarity with the concepts of art. Lampredi quipped: "And from this side still some study of the art would have benefitted the author, to teach him that the characteristics of famous heroes must represent either the history, or the traditions, steadily painted by more reputable authors.."[68] Lampredi scoffed at Foscolo's depiction of the title character and even asked, rhetorically, an imagined figure of Ajax:

> Tell me I repeat, would you have recognized yourself, if you had come to see the new tragedy, entitled with your great name? Oh my! Oh my! You would have certainly renewed the slaughter of the lambs and the flagellation of the billy goat, and you would have killed yourself a second time, seeing yourself depicted in such a strange caricature, and represented on the one hand like a furious man who flies into rage without motive, and on the other hand like a shy novice, who, aware of his deficiencies, throbs and trembles in the presence of the high-priest Calcante?[69]

Lampredi even went so far as to compare Foscolo's entire cast of characters to a comical brigade of caricatures best suited to the *commedia dell'arte*, and not worthy of the elite genre of tragedy.[70]

Lampredi used this same terminology in his third review. He expressly included Foscolo's *disegno* in a list of *Ajace*'s flaws, proclaiming that the text was deficient "with regard to the design, to the action, to the numerous adventures, to the characters, to the lack of exposition in the beginning, and the absence of any and all good moral endings in the conclusion."[71] He even insinuated that Foscolo's work was a bad composition through and through, with no redeeming qualities: "Few and rare defects will never destroy the value of a composition that is truly good in the essential parts; but a composition bad in its entirety will always be bad in spite of any beauty that shines within it."[72] Lampredi maintained that *Ajace* fell into the latter category.

Lampredi's own design for his series of reviews was incomplete. He failed to make good on his promise to show how one should properly stage the story of Ajax. He actually acknowledged in the final article that he would set to working on an effective *disegno* for the story of *Ajace*, despite the fact that many believed that the "subject is not suited for tragedy."[73] Lampredi apparently was less interested in completing his initial task and more interested in assailing his literary nemesis, and never actually undertook that task. He concluded his entire series by insinuating not only that Foscolo lacked poetic prowess, but also that he was ignorant of what constitutes the essential principles of art, incapable of discernment, and among other things, wanting in good taste.[74]

Ajace did not return to the Italian stage until 1816 in Florence, after Foscolo had left Italy. He was residing in Switzerland at the time, and was greatly relieved that five years had passed and the literary conflict between himself and Lampredi had dissipated so that it could no longer colour the public's perception of his work. Foscolo believed that the Italian public, at long last, would be able to understand fully and appreciate his literary effort. These aspirations were misplaced; in a letter to the prominent Florentine Quirina Mocenni Magiotti (1781–1847), dated 7 February 1816, Foscolo recounted how "poor *Ajace*" was met with a multitude of Florentine whistles.[75] Foscolo yet again rationalized *Ajace*'s failure by blaming outside individuals or external factors – in this case, the acting company and the Italian public itself, which he believed lacked the necessary political passion to fully appreciate his work.[76] Following almost eighteen years of Napoleonic rule, the Congress of Vienna redistributed the Italian states in 1815 to various occupying governments, with the majority of the Italian peninsula falling under the control of another foreign power, the Austrian Empire.[77] Foscolo argued that this made Italians complacent and subservient, when they should have been fighting, like Ajace, for control of what was rightfully theirs.

Foscolo concluded his letter by arguing that only a few spectators accurately understood and appreciated his efforts as a tragedian.[78] He conceded that *Ajace* indeed needed revision, yet he still asserted that his efforts as a tragedian were largely misinterpreted and misunderstood by the Italian public through no fault of his own. Foscolo suggested that Italians were demoralized by yet another occupying government, and that they were incapable of comprehending the tragedy's poetic genius. Foscolo saw himself, again, as a victim. He played up his own role as the tragic hero who suffers terribly at a level disproportionate to his culpability. *Ajace*'s failure irrevocably scarred Foscolo, dissuading him from ever publishing the work. Ironically, none other than Urbano Lampredi published it in 1828 – almost one year after Foscolo's death.

He included revised versions of the infamous four articles initially published in 1811–12 in *Il Poligrafo* as a critical commentary for posterity.

Foscolo was incensed with Lampredi's 1811–12 reviews. He turned to working on his translation of Sterne's *A Sentimental Journey* in 1812 immediately following his Milanese debacle. But the bitterness of failure was too much for Foscolo to handle. He began to write incessantly about the role of the critic and the injustices that were inherent in the contemporary literary journal scene. His displeasure and intense desire to vindicate both his artistic choices for *Ajace* and his own reputation as a tragedian endured for many years. He refused above all to let Lampredi and his colleagues have the last word on *Ajace*, and mainly focused on rebutting Lampredi's specific complaints that he was "ignorant or inconsiderate" of the concepts of art and that his characters, and the general design of the entire work, were a "monstrosity." Foscolo's perhaps indirect – but nonetheless unmistakable – response was lodged in two venues: (1) a letter to his friend Silvio Pellico from 23 February 1813,[79] and (2) the often overlooked architectural article "Sul nuovo teatro di Como," from August 1813.[80]

Discordia armonica

Silvio Pellico wrote to his dear friend Foscolo in early 1813 seeking professional advice. Pellico asked him to review his recently completed tragedy, *Laodamia* (1813). This was not a unique request, since the two men often exchanged literary ideas. Foscolo replied with a kind letter that counselled Pellico in general terms on the manner in which tragedies should be composed. Foscolo's counsel was not only amicable – it also was collegial and informational and provided Pellico with a series of professional suggestions to improve his tragedy. Foscolo began by describing his very positive initial emotional reaction to the first scene of *Laodamia*. He confessed that he was moved to tears, and Foscolo complimented Pellico's creation of the main character, Laodamia, and her "profound truth of passion."[81] Foscolo pledged to be brutally honest in his critique of Pellico's work, and proceeded to identify certain items that a tragedian must fully understand when composing his or her work, including how to formulate the main characters, as well as the passions that those characters experience and the overarching action of the tragedy.

Foscolo approached his role as adviser by focusing on how a trage-dian should create unique characters and select the proper subject mat-ter for them. His choice of *Ajace* as a model was perhaps a curious one, given its utter failure on the stage. Yet Foscolo argued that it was ap-propriate, proclaiming, "I can speak with more foundation about my intentions" in the work.[82] This further demonstrated Foscolo's stub-born belief that *Ajace*, despite its unfavourable reception, was an excel-lent composition. He asserted that "there will come a day when that tragedy [*Ajace*] will live in the heart and in the mouth of many who resemble you [Pellico], and who have love of virtue, of true glory and of country."[83]

The fact that Foscolo would presume to undertake the role of master tragedian, notwithstanding his lack of success in the genre, is curious to say the least. Pellico did not invite him to use *Ajace* as a model, but he did ask Foscolo for advice. The letter, therefore, illustrates Foscolo's personal decision to tout his second tragedy, despite its poor recep-tion by both critics and the public alike. It also directly responded to Lampredi's chief complaints that Foscolo had created a laughable cast of characters, not suited for the genre of tragedy, and that he profound-ly lacked any knowledge of good concepts of art.

Foscolo began his advice to Pellico with a discussion on how to create appropriate characters that are endowed with admirable qualities. He asserted that these qualities should be based on "human nature" and not fortune, and should give the character legitimacy and make him or her "more believable" to the spectator.[84] He elaborated further on this point, stating that "the author must gather these characters from the everyday experience of the world and from histories, and add beauty, grandeur and ideal deformity to reality, just as the best painters and sculptors do."[85] Foscolo cautioned that these characters also must be completely original, and that we cannot find a model that is similar to them in real life – thus creating something new, marvellous, and sub-lime.[86] Echoing the eighteenth-century discussions of *il verosimile*, Foscolo emphasized the importance of balancing reality with fantasy. He expanded on this notion, suggesting that another important ele-ment of a tragedy rests with the spectator's understanding of the "*truth of the passions, and this is the truth that one recognizes most easily, which forces us to feel before we reason.*"[87] Foscolo's lengthy and nu-anced discussion of the intricate concepts of art can be seen as a not-so-subtle rejoinder to Lampredi's insinuation that Foscolo was ignorant of such principles.

Foscolo continued defending his prowess as a tragedian, launching into a detailed discussion of what he called harmonious discord (*discordia armonica*).[88] The concept is commonly referred to as *discordia concors*, or the unity achieved by combining conflicting elements.[89] This poetic device allows an author to highlight a particular characteristic by embodying it in two seemingly different characters, thus allowing the audience to see how the characteristic manifests itself in multiple examples with which they may be familiar. The various exhibitions of certain attributes are more akin to how they are exhibited in the real world, and the audience (theoretically) should find the characters more believable.

Foscolo elaborated on *discordia concors*, informing Pellico that a dramatist needs to invent characters that contrast with one another in such a palpable manner that the audience feels this difference. He counselled: "And as for the characters, common sense always leans to composing them with a certain harmonic discord, in such a way that from the contrast between the various characters follows that harmony that one sees – actually one feels more than sees – in the composition of a historical painting of a distinguished master."[90] Foscolo continued by describing how he attempted to express this harmony in the characters of *Ajace.* He first discussed the very different ways in which his characters Ajace and Agamennone both desire glory but went about achieving this goal in very different ways, thus effectively creating a sense of harmony and, at the same time, discord, in the work.[91] Foscolo asserted that while Ajace and Ulisse are only absolute extremes (the liberator and the tyrant, respectively), Ulisse both resembles and contrasts with the tragedy's other characters. For example, Ulisse and Calcante possess contrasting spirits, yet they are fundamentally similar because both seek Ajace's ruin above all else. Ulisse and Agamennone likewise exhibit analogous violent tendencies, but they differ in their approach to achieving their desires.[92]

Foscolo refrained from using *Ajace* as an example when he instructed Pellico on how to formulate the action of his play. He, like Alfieri, regarded simple and straightforward action to be perhaps the most important element of a tragedy, because this sort of easy-to-follow action better involves the audience in the work. Conversely, "a more complex action makes it less believable for the audience."[93] His counsel unfortunately would have been undercut with any mention of *Ajace*. Foscolo was well aware that he had veered off on numerous tangents and created a confusing and hard-to-follow tragedy. Astutely, he abandoned his *Ajace* here and opted to speak more generally about the desired characteristics a tragedian should include in his or her work.

Or did he? Foscolo concluded this discussion with a two-prong assertion about the fate of a tragedy. He asserted the tragedian should aspire to a well-written tragedy, with aptly developed characters (who create the desired sensation of harmonious discord) and a well-developed action. If both these goals are achieved, then the tragedy is "the most beautiful product of human intelligence."[94] Foscolo continued by defending a tragedy that has a poorly designed action, but well-designed characters. He maintained that this is an "imperfect" tragedy, but nonetheless "always great and useful and pleasant, because it represents individual persons paired with truth from models in nature, and adorned with the divinity of fantasy."[95] This can be interpreted as a tacit admission that although his *Ajace*, decidedly lacking in one main action, was indeed flawed, it was, at the same time, still a valuable work full of skilfully designed characters.

This defensive rationalization of the validity of a tragedy is reminiscent of Lampredi's ultimate conclusion in his fourth article on *Ajace*. Lampredi dismissed Foscolo's second tragedy, writing (as set forth above), "Few and rare defects will never destroy the value of a composition that is truly good in the essential parts; but a composition bad in its entirety will always be bad in spite of any beauty that shines within it."[96]

Foscolo adopted Lampredi's views. He answered this attack with his own assertion – *Ajace* was not completely bad. Foscolo challenged the insistence of Lampredi and others that a tragedy must be founded on a more historical subject instead of a fantastic or mythical one. He explained to Pellico that a tragedy that adheres too much to history and only focuses on the action, thus neglecting the characters, makes a tragedy "always a miserable thing; from which, if the characters are vulgar souls, the action, as extraordinary and great as it may be, remains beholden to the very history that suggested it to the poet, and it actually becomes less credible."[97] According to Foscolo, the worst reaction to a tragedy would be if the audience found it unbelievable. He insinuated that his *Ajace* could not fall into this category, thus continuing to defend his competence as a tragedian.

"Sul nuovo teatro di Como"

Foscolo continued to attempt to bolster his reputation as a tragedian, and at the end of August 1813, did so in an unusual and unsuspecting venue. He found himself a guest of Prince Alberico XII Barbiano in Belgioioso. His visit ended abruptly and unfortunately with the death of his host following an "apoplectic attack" on Saturday, 21 August. Foscolo retreated to the home of his dear friend Giambattista Giovio in Como.[98] It is here that Foscolo witnessed the opening of the Teatro Sociale on 28 August and wrote his architectural article "Sul nuovo teatro di Como" for the *Giornale del Lario*.[99]

As I mentioned in the introduction, Foscolo scholars generally do not know what to make of "Sul nuovo teatro di Como," and almost all of them ignore the article. Luigi Fassò offered little information about the article in his 1933 introduction to the only extant edition of the article, and he certainly did not propose any reason for why Foscolo might have decided to dabble in the new and unfamiliar subject of theatrical architecture. Fassò merely includes the article in the volume *Prose politiche e letterarie 1811–1816* under the generic section "Scritti vari."[100] But after close examination of the article, I believe that there is compelling evidence to suggest that "Sul nuovo teatro di Como" is more significant than previously thought. By looking at this as yet another response to Lampredi and a defence of his failed *Ajace*, I think that today's reader can view Foscolo's article as a logical and perhaps even ingenious undertaking.

Foscolo was in attendance when the theatre opened on Saturday evening, 28 August 1813 with performances of Antonio Fonseca Portugal's (Marcos António Portugal, 1762–1830) *Adriano in Siria* (1813) and Giuseppe Mosca's (1772–1839) *I pretendenti delusi* (1811). Yet his article in the *Giornale del Lario* from that very same morning does not mention the impending theatrical performances or their theatrical texts, both of which were subjects closer to Foscolo's expertise than that of the architectural discussion actually presented in the article. It is similarly curious that Foscolo did not mention "Sul nuovo teatro di Como," its composition, or even his stay in Como, in his contemporaneous correspondence. Instead, he simply explained in a letter to his dear friend Quirina Mocenni Magiotti from Monday, 30 August 1813 that he had returned to Milan after having spent longer than he initially anticipated in the Lake District.[101]

Foscolo did not write about his travels until they were complete. In volume 17 of the *Edizione nazionale*, Plinio Carli included a 16 August letter from Foscolo to Giuseppe Grassi, as well as an undated letter to Ugo Brunetti, in which Foscolo stated that he was in Milan until 18 August, followed by the letter to Mocenni Magiotti on 30 August.[102] Foscolo referred to his visit to the region in a 2 September letter to

Giuseppe Grassi, but he mentioned little more about his journey.[103] It was only two days later, in a letter to the Countess of Albany (Louise of Stolberg-Gedern, 1752–1824), that Foscolo proffered details of his trip, including the tragic circumstances surrounding Prince Alberico's death. He also specifically mentioned the opening of the Teatro Sociale and explained how the premiere festivities were delayed for eight days.[104]

"Sul nuovo teatro di Como" was a reaction to an article previously published in the same journal at the end of July. The earlier article had only praise for the new building, and Foscolo intended to offer a more objective review. He used "Sul nuovo teatro di Como" to critique the various architectural aspects of the new structure – both the positive and negative – and attempted to offer the reader a comprehensive and balanced presentation of the building. He began by calling attention to the critical shortcomings of contemporary critics, and cited their (relatively) abusive analysis of the defects of a work, as well as their insistence on holding the artists accountable to vague and unrealistic abstract principles, as their chief concern and their primary disgrace. He vowed, in contrast, to evaluate the structure in a more honest fashion. Foscolo acknowledged that in each work there are extenuating circumstances, obstacles, and complicated situations that arise during creation that interfere with the artist's original vision. Foscolo also conceded that these extenuating circumstances are relatively minor in comparison to the artist's original *disegno intellettuale* (intellectual plan), but they should be taken into consideration during any evaluation.[105] His repeated emphasis on this all-important aspect implied that he had actually examined Giuseppe Cusi's original architectural plans for the theatre. Later, in "Sul nuovo teatro di Como," he even went so far as to claim that he had reviewed these original plans.[106] Whether this claim is true is unknown. Foscolo nevertheless again and again invoked the term *disegno* – six times in the fifteen paragraphs that make up the article.

This focus on *disegno* is, of course, unsurprising, given the architectural subject matter. Nor is this the only instance in which it is ambiguous whether Foscolo's odd terminology should be attributed to an overarching purpose or to the architectural theme. Foscolo also repeatedly used the terms *difetti* or *difetto* (defects or defect), employing them on four separate occasions to describe various perceived flaws, or defects, of the design that have the potential to inspire a disapproving reaction among critics and the public. He also used such similar expressions as *le colpe, questi errori, la deformità*, and *gravissimi inconvenienti* to express the negative aspects of the Teatro Sociale's construction.

The main *difetto*, according to Foscolo, rested with the architect's decision to not specifically erect a structure that is easily recognizable as a theatre. The building's outside appearance is generic, and it is situated adjacent to a building that is used for a multitude of public events.[107] Foscolo even remarked that the theatre looked like it could be a seminary dormitory.[108] This diversion away from the noble initial intent of the project – that of creating a recognizable, prestigious theatre – might very well have contributed to the not-so-perfect outcome of the building. Foscolo then inquired if the architect should be held responsible for all of these *difetti*, asking, "Are these and the other defects only the fault of the architect?"[109] His answer? Of course not. The general thrust of Foscolo's article focuses on the analysis of various defects of the theatre, and his assigning the appropriate blame to the rightful culpable parties – be it the architect, in the case of a faulty design, or the craftsmen tasked with carrying out this design.

Foscolo's empathy for the architect resounds throughout "Sul nuovo teatro di Como." He shifted the blame for the theatre's reception to poor fortune, along with other factors far beyond the architect's control.[110] Foscolo pointed out that the columns as actually constructed ruined the architect's design, and he further noted that the recent chiselling of the stone partially hid the bronze tint that would have darkened with time.[111] Likewise, the lamentable impatience of the workers carrying out the *disegno* persuaded them to plaster the columns with a paint that was more black than bronze, thus obscuring the marble. Foscolo concluded that the end result of this compromise unfortunately departed from the original *disegno* and was ultimately loathsome, smacking of an ill-timed and wretched imitation.[112] He repeatedly emphasized the difference between Cusi's original plans and the finished theatre, even remarking at one point that the finished product does not come close to reflecting the architect's abstract vision.[113] For example, the architect intended for additional columns in an amphitheatre of sorts to be in the Doric style, and yet, thanks to the incompetent craftsmen carrying out the architectural plans, they were actually Ionic, which caused the amphitheatre to appear disproportionate.[114] Foscolo concluded from these observations that the architect and his talents should be judged more favourably based solely on the quality of his *disegno*, and not on how it was actually implemented.

The author largely exonerated the architect from culpability for many of the construction shortcomings, yet he countered by highlighting a negative aspect of the theatre's structure for which the architect should take responsibility: the three doors of the main façade which were not proportionate in width and height.[115] He also listed several other *difetti* for which the architect must accept the lion's share of the blame – from the inclusion of a short second floor for dressing rooms with small, square windows that give the appearance of cheap rental housing, to the absence of entrances with columns or arcs leading to the two sprawling terraces.[116]

Foscolo balanced these criticisms with praise for the architect's successes, including for the design of the curve in the theatre, which provides every seat in the house with an excellent view of the stage.[117] Foscolo also commended the architect for separating the front stage and the first private boxes – *palchi a proscenio* – with the orchestra section. He explained how the *palchi a proscenio* were a common feature in many theatres of the period that often interrupted the audience's suspension of disbelief during a performance. He lamented, for example, how this architectural design allows the spectator to view both the fictional princess reciting about love and a private box with an actual aristocratic lady who is in the process of making love to her *cicisbeo*, or dandy.[118] Foscolo believed that Cusi was well advised in electing to separate the stage from the spectator when designing the theatre. On the whole, Foscolo was reasonably balanced in his critique of Cusi and his *disegno*, and certainly attempted to make good on his promise to be objective and comprehensive and include the defects along with his praise.

But why did Foscolo even enter the field of architectural criticism in the first place? I proffer that his defence of the architect in "Sul nuovo teatro di Como" was a metaphor for his own lack of success on the stage – a general response to his hostile critics, and perhaps even a pre-emptive defence of his then-upcoming third tragedy, *Ricciarda*. Foscolo's main objective in his 1813 article was to distinguish between critiquing a designer's work and the actual execution of that design as a finished product. An obvious parallel between these views and his thoughts on tragedy emerges. Foscolo presumably would argue that just as an architect should bear little or no responsibility for the flawed implementation of his design, neither should a tragedian be held solely responsible for the stage production of his tragedies – that outcome depends on circumstances far beyond his or her control, and a number of people other than the tragedian are instrumental to this final production. The dramatist must continuously grapple with the *riguardi, circostanze*, and *ostacoli* of the censors, potentially inept actors, the Italian public, and the critics.

This hypothesis certainly makes intuitive sense, though its generality and breadth admittedly make it essentially unprovable. There is also an alternate potential explanation for "Sul nuovo teatro di Como," however. The article might also have been intended by Foscolo to be not just a broad defence of himself as a tragedian, but also a specific response to his harshest and most vitriolic critic, Lampredi. This theory is especially attractive because of an obvious linguistic connection between Lampredi's criticisms and the terminology Foscolo used in "Sul nuovo teatro di Como" that provides compelling support for it.

The key to uncovering this aspect of Foscolo's motive when writing "Sul nuovo teatro di Como" lies with his heavy emphasis on the term *disegno*. While the similarly widely used term *difetto* and its synonyms are commonplace in both architectural and literary reviews, the term *disegno* is not frequently used in the literary sphere. Indeed, Foscolo does not appear to have used this terminology in any of his literary critical works. So why does it takes such a place of prominence in "Sul nuovo teatro di Como"? The answer perhaps can be found in Lampredi's four scathing reviews of *Ajace*, which, as noted earlier in this chapter, explicitly dwell on the perceived failure of Foscolo's *disegno* and the significant *difetti* in the work.

"Sul nuovo teatro di Como" was Foscolo's attempt at co-opting Lampredi's *disegno* terminology, responding to a vexing period in his life, if only to pave the way for his future theatrical endeavours. Foscolo refuted Lampredi's critical approach to *Ajace*, which relied on public opinion about the opening performance with regard to the *disegno*, and emphasized that it is a critic's responsibility to separate the performance (and consequently, public opinion about it) from the text (or *disegno*) when evaluating the work. "Sul nuovo teatro di Como" not only defends the architect of the new theatre, but Foscolo as a tragedian – both retrospectively for his *disegno* of the failed *Ajace*, and pre-emptively for his future *disegno* of what he had hoped to be his redemptive success on the stage, *Ricciarda*. In fact, precisely when this article was published, Foscolo was leaving for Bologna to begin work with the struggling production company that ultimately performed his final dramatic work. This last tragedy was also a failure, as discussed in chapter 4 – yet according to the pre-emptive defence espoused in "Sul nuovo teatro di Como," any potential *difetti* that might be revealed at its opening would be forgivable, because his *disegno* was sound.

The linguistic connection between Lampredi's attack on Foscolo's *disegno* and Foscolo's metaphorical defence of it in "Sul nuovo teatro di

Como" may be the only direct evidence that Foscolo's odd architectural review was intended to be a response to his antagonists, but it hardly is the sole support for this theory. "Sul nuovo teatro di Como" is in the form of a letter, presumably to Giovio, and signed by one of Foscolo's numerous pseudonyms, Didimo Chierico. Foscolo's choice to sign his article with this notorious name is also telling. At the time of "Sul nuovo teatro di Como," Foscolo had recently introduced Italian audiences to the figure of Didimo as the translator of Sterne's *A Sentimental Journey through France and Italy*. Often hailed as the alter ego to Jacopo Ortis, Didimo appears mature, reserved, and capable of composed, wise critical irony that is in contrast to what Foscolo would refer to as the inadequate, insulting, and oftentimes incomplete work performed by many critics of the period.[119]

Foscolo was fully self-conscious of his own active and ongoing participation in these literary wars, or *eunuchomachia*, and for several years he focused a large part of his attention on defending himself against his enemies. He even explicitly commented on this phenomenon, remarking in his cleverly constructed satire *Hypercalypseos* that Didimo Chierico had found a book on the very subject of *eunuchomachia*.[120] Foscolo began working on his literary response to his quarrel with Lampredi in 1812 and the work was eventually published in Switzerland in 1816.

Hypercalypseos is not the only evidence of Foscolo's continued preoccupation with defending himself against unjust criticisms. Even though the culmination of the Lampredi-Foscolo conflict – the debacle of *Ajace*'s opening night and the subsequent scathing reviews by Lampredi – transpired a year and a half before the composition of "Sul nuovo teatro di Como," Foscolo never put the whole ordeal behind him. Indeed, he revisited and reiterated his disdain for Lampredi in a poem within a letter to Leopoldo Cicognara on 15 June 1813, only two months before publishing his article on the Teatro Sociale.[121] This background and context suggests that Foscolo purposely used the pseudonym Didimo Chierico to subtly refer in "Sul nuovo teatro di Como" to the practice of *eunuchomachia* – which had consumed so much of his life as of late – and Lampredi's attacks in *Il Poligrafo*. This practice certainly would continue to colour his future efforts in the realm of tragedy.

Chapter Four

Ricciarda in Italy and in England

Foscolo wrote to Isabella Teotochi Albrizzi on 29 July 1812 to announce his plans for a new tragedy. He explained that he had already begun his new work with much fervour and it was "all about love." He also lamented that he needed to set it aside because he had "a thousand things" in his heart, "but absolutely nothing" in his brain.[1] Indeed, the change of subject and setting did not make writing the new tragedy any easier for Foscolo. He began writing in September 1812, but was repeatedly interrupted with unforeseen delays and health problems. Foscolo wrote to Cornelia Rossi Martinetti on 14 September explaining how he needed to leave his translation of *A Sentimental Journey* and focus on his tragedy. He lamented, "My poor *Ricciarda*, who was the most beautiful, most in love, and most unfortunate among the princesses, waits for me."[2] Foscolo wrote to Sigismondo Trechi a few weeks later and explained at length his incessant respiratory problems. He bemoaned his failure to complete the third tragedy, exclaiming, "God only knows! When will I be able to see the end of it?"[3] Foscolo was hoping that *Ricciarda* would be ready to debut at the latest in December, potentially on the anniversary of the ill-fated *Ajace*. He expressed this hope to Silvio Pellico in a letter of 4 October. Foscolo intended *Ricciarda* to be a success and hoped that it would not fall prey to "the censors and the quarrels" that his second tragedy did.[4]

But Foscolo could not meet his own deadline. He suspended work on *Ricciarda* to concentrate on the never-completed series of poems *Le Grazie* in the late fall of 1812. He finally finished *Ricciarda* nearly eight months later, on 7 June 1813. Andrea Calbo (Andrea Kalvos) was also born in Zakynthos and served as Foscolo's copyist. He noted on the complete manuscript of *Ricciarda* at the Biblioteca Vaticana in the Raccolta Ferrajoli that the work was begun the morning of 1 May and completed the evening of 6 June. But Foscolo changed the date of 6 June to the morning of 7 June in the final version.[5] Foscolo again wrote to Teotochi Albrizzi on 8 June 1813 and discussed his work. He explained that the plot of *Ricciarda* was based not on an ancient myth, but instead originated from a relatively modern love story. He also mentioned that he used love to soften the work's elements of terror and to complete the action.[6]

Ricciarda is a relatively short work, consisting of five acts and only 1296 unrhymed hendecasyllabic lines. There are a number of silent characters (*i guerrieri*), four main speaking characters (Guelfo, Ricciarda, Averardo, and Guido), and one secondary speaking character (Averardo's squire, Corrado). The tragedy takes place during the Middle Ages in the underground burial room of the palace of Salerno, with the tomb of the mother of Ricciarda, the protagonist, in the foreground.[7] Once again, Foscolo respected the unity of time: act 1 begins one hour before sunrise and ends at dawn; act 2 is set between noon and one; act 3 between 3:00 p.m. and 4:00 p.m.; the action of act 4 takes place between sunset and evening; and act 5 is set during the night, ending two hours before dawn.

Foscolo's tragedy is centred on the tension between rivalry and love. The rivalry is between two stepbrothers: Guelfo, the tyrant of Salerno, and Averardo, the son of their mutual father's second wife. Before the beginning of the action, the elder brother, Guelfo, has usurped the inheritance of the younger, Averardo. The two have been engaged in an armed conflict for thirty years, with the pope supporting Guelfo, and the emperor supporting Averardo. The tragedy focuses on Averardo's attempt to reclaim his legitimate rights in Salerno. Corrado helps Averardo gain access to the castle of Salerno – his main goal is to reach and kill Guelfo, who is hiding in the basement. Foscolo contrasts the hatred between the stepbrothers with a love story between Guido, the son of Averardo, and Ricciarda, the daughter of Guelfo. The finale occurs during an invasion by Averardo's troops, when Guelfo suspects that Guido is also hiding in the basement and calls for him to show himself. Guido ignores Guelfo's entreaties, and Guelfo pretends to kill Ricciarda in a ruse to lure out Guido. Guido emerges to protect his beloved, and Guelfo fatally wounds him. Guelfo is then overcome with murderous rage and fatally stabs his daughter. He is distraught and commits suicide.

Passions, including rage, jealousy, and – most important – love, dominate the tragedy. Foscolo believed that if a tragedy was to tell a love story, this emotion, in all its forms, should drive all the action in the work. He employed the thematic umbrella of love to achieve his desired goal of harmonious discord (*discordia armonica*) between his characters in *Ricciarda*. Specifically, the characters of Ricciarda, Averardo, and Guelfo all represent individuals struggling with two irreconcilable forms of love: Guelfo (the prototypical Alfierian tyrant) struggles between his love for his daughter and his love of power;[8] Averardo (the prototypical Alfierian liberator) is forced to decide between his love for his son and his love of his *patria*; and finally, Ricciarda is torn between her love for Guido and her father.

Ricciarda actually is more classically Alfierian than *Ajace* – the dialogue is concise, there are fewer soliloquies, and its one main action is simple and straightforward. Moreover, Foscolo drew upon Alfierian subject matter when depicting *Ricciarda*'s familial conflict. For example, Alfieri's famous tragedy *Mirra* (1784) was an influential example for Foscolo's *Ricciarda*, with its father-daughter conflict and incestuous undertones. As Giorgio Pullini explained, "Guelfo loves his daughter Ricciarda too intensely, he is jealous, and by denying her to Guido, son of Averardo, he thinks about punishing Averardo as well, but in reality, he satisfies above all his own will to exclusively possess the affection of his daughter."[9] Roberto Alonge also discussed the familial relationship, writing, "The tragedy is, therefore, a tragedy of a morbid father–daughter relationship and of the impossibility of ever breaking it. And all the action is nothing more than a continuous process of abdication of Ricciarda's will to that of the father."[10] Alonge aptly pointed out that Ricciarda's final words in the tragedy are not for her love, Guido, but for her father: "Perdona … al padre … mio" (act 5, line 219).

The father–daughter relationship also should be read from the tyrant's point of view. From this perspective, the celebrated 1782 Alfierian tragedy *Saul* serves as an obvious model. Saul, the eponymous tyrant, oscillates between love for his daughter Micol and jealousy of her husband David. Foscolo's Guelfo similarly struggles with his love for Ricciarda and his overwhelming hatred for his step-brother, Averardo. Guido Di Pino has argued, however, that Foscolo does not actually replicate Alfieri's love-hate relationship between Saul and Micol in *Ricciarda*; instead, he contends, Foscolo demonstrated his originality by having Ricciarda's father, Guelfo, alternate between the more delicate emotions of tenderness, or *tenerezza*, and fury, or *furore*, for his daughter.[11]

Foscolo turned to other Italian literary classics for inspiration for his characters. In act 2, scene 3, Foscolo gives the father of Guelfo and Averardo the name of Tancredi.[12] This name, along with the tragedy's medieval setting and its story of a daughter's forbidden love, evokes the Italian tale from Giovanni Boccaccio's *Decameron* – the story of Tancredi and Ghismonda.[13] Foscolo's use of the name also calls to mind another famous European literary work, Voltaire's acclaimed 1760 tragedy, *Tancrède*.[14] Although Foscolo's medieval tale in *Ricciarda* is not indebted to Boccaccio and Voltaire, his use of the name Tancredi should easily be seen as an attempt to ground his work in the well-established European literary tradition.[15]

Ricciarda's subject matter is the clear result of Foscolo's interest in Italian history. In his 1810–11 incomplete article "Frammenti su Machiavelli" and his 1811 article "Dello scopo di Gregorio VII," Foscolo examined the early politics of Italy and its representation in Italian literature.[16] He also forged several relationships with important scholarly figures and studied their works relating to medieval Italy. One such figure, Giovanni Battista Gigola (1769–1841), was a close friend of Foscolo and a prominent Brescian artist. Gigola completed a collection of mini-illustrations depicting various episodes of Boccaccio's *Decameron* in 1811. Maria Maddalena Lombardi has explained how Foscolo's description of Ricciarda's costume closely corresponds with many of the *troubadour* figures depicted in Gigola's *Decameron* illustrations.[17]

Ricciarda's focus on Italian history also is closely connected to what several critics have called the "pre-risorgimental" patriotic tone found in Foscolo's third tragedy.[18] Other critics have even gone so far as to label Foscolo's innovative character development "Romantic."[19] Yet although it may be easy for present-day critics to apply these anachronistic labels to Foscolo's *Ricciarda*, the terms did not exist when he was composing his third tragedy. It is perhaps more useful to view Foscolo's compositional choices as the result of his lifelong desire to become a great Italian tragedian. After all, Alfieri approached the subject of the Italian Middle Ages with his 1781 tragedy *Rosmunda*, and Giovanni Rucellai did the same in the sixteenth century.[20] It is true that Foscolo adhered to the neoclassical premise that authors should look to the past in order to appreciate and contribute to the present, but he also incorporated elements that he hoped would appeal to an Italian audience. Above all, Foscolo was currying favour with a contemporary Italian public. He hoped that if he chose a subject from Italian history and used a purer Italian verse, then his tragedy would be more appealing to his audiences. Eugenio Donadoni, among others, echoed this observation in his seminal 1910 book *Ugo Foscolo: Pensatore, critico, poeta*, suggesting that Foscolo's decision to base his third tragedy on a love story should be traced to his desire for a more favourable reception of his work following the public debacle of *Ajace*.[21]

Foscolo's choice of where to set *Ricciarda* can also be seen as an attempt to appeal to contemporary Italian audiences.[22] He had enjoyed an immense amount of success with his 1807 *Dei sepolcri*, which glorified burial sites. By setting *Ricciarda* in the burial room of the palace, the audience would have been instantly reminded of Foscolo's seminal solemn poem. He similarly returned to the language of *Dei sepolcri*. Even though Foscolo composed the overwhelming majority of verses in *Ricciarda* in a simpler, purer Italian style (in contrast to his Homeric efforts with *Ajace*), he did included specific Latinisms that he also memorably used in *Dei sepolcri*. Specifically, those for altars (*are*) and tombs (*avelli*) are found throughout his third tragedy.[23]

Yet, the love story, the familiar setting, and the simpler Italian verse do not stand out in Foscolo's third tragedy. Instead, his near-obsession with the success or failure of *Ricciarda* led him to oversimplify his verse and action to such a degree that the actual tragedy reads as superficial and almost comical, proof of which lies in the final two acts. These acts should contain the most action, teasing out Ricciarda's internal conflict between love for her father and that for her lover, and they should swiftly bring the reader or spectator to the tragic conclusion. Yet, this modern approach to the psychological development of the tragic character is overshadowed by the actual instrument that seals her tragic fate – the dagger.

Acts 4 and 5 are essentially a non-stop discussion of this weapon. Indeed, Foscolo chose to use the term *ferro* twenty-four times, twenty of which occur in the final two acts. He also elected to use the term *daga* five additional times and either *pugnal* or *pugnale* five other times during acts 4 and 5. Foscolo refers to the dagger nine times in act 4, scene 2 alone. It is here that the first instance of Ricciarda pleading Guido for the weapon appears. "Guido, give me that dagger" (*Guido, dammi quel ferro*) appears at verse 117.[24] She then repeats her plea seven verses later with "Give me that dagger, Guido" (*Dammi quel ferro, Guido*).[25] Reluctantly, he finally agrees by verse 139, stating "Have the dagger" (*Abbi il pugnale*).[26] Ricciarda leaves the dagger on the ground, where her father Guelfo discovers it in scene 4. In this scene, Foscolo refers to the dagger in eight more verses. As one reads through, it becomes almost absurd how many times Foscolo refers to the weapon. The frequency is not necessarily surprising. After all, the dagger does serve as the definitive prop that ultimately concludes the tragedy. But the circumstances in which it is mentioned are repetitive, simple, and quasi-comical. These perpetual discussions of the object render *Ricciarda* ultimately lacking in the requisite tragic *gravitas*. If a twenty-first-century reader's attention is easily drawn to and distracted by the object, how would an early-nineteenth-century Italian spectator react to Foscolo's attempt at a simpler Italian verse?

The Performance of *Ricciarda*

Foscolo's concern about *Ricciarda*'s success was not limited to his subject matter or the actual verses he wrote. It actually spread to the performance of the work itself. He wrote to Quirina Mocenni Magiotti on 30 August 1813 and described his waning trust in the actors, explaining that he felt he needed to be in Bologna to oversee the production: "But in any event, by the 12th I must find myself in Bologna where *Ricciarda* will make her first public appearance; and I cannot abandon her to the actors."[27] Foscolo wanted so badly to avoid any acting mishaps that he even wrote a series of detailed stage directions and instructions for the actors entitled *Per gli attori*, which he submitted to the director, Salvatore Fabbrichesi, before the opening night performance.[28]

Ricciarda debuted on 17 September 1813 at the Teatro del Corso in Bologna. It ultimately fared no better than *Ajace*. Foscolo was in attendance at the performance, and he composed a complete account of the opening night in a letter to the Countess of Albany on 19 September 1813. This letter contains both a factual account of the events surrounding *Ricciarda*'s opening night and Foscolo's own opinion of the performance. In his own words, "The tragedy was most poorly performed."[29] For Foscolo, this failure of *Ricciarda* rested solely on the acting company's interpretation and portrayal of his text, and certainly not on the inadequacy of his own verse.

Foscolo's letter focuses on the performance and not the text of *Ricciarda*. He included a comprehensive description of each actor's abysmal performance in his letter to the countess, outlining a laundry list of complaints, ranging from overacting to ridiculous portrayals:

> *Guelfo* would have done excellently if he had not wanted to do too much; *Ricciarda* seemed to be a sentimental girl, rather than a princess completely in love; the audience liked it [her performance] nevertheless; I greatly disliked it. *Averardo* was played reasonably. But *Guido* was performed in such a way that I myself, who had thought about it and wrote it and reread it

never intended what that wretched puppet dressed up like a Hero wanted to say ... Guido, I'm afraid to say, will be a character Quixotically-Petrarchan: in other words, ridiculous.[30]

Foscolo believed that the cause of any deficient performance invariably rested with the inadequate actors. Their misinterpretation of his script was, at its core, the primary reason for the disastrous opening performance.

Following his general scathing critique of *Ricciarda*'s performers, Foscolo's letter continues with an act-by-act account of opening night. His negative focus shifts from the acting company to the Bolognese theatre-going public. As Foscolo recounted, the performance of the first act generated moderate applause. This might seem like a positive and cordial gesture to most, but Foscolo was insulted by it. He remarked, "After the first act, the audience was clapping their hands; and I, in my heart, would have beaten all of those blockheads who did not know that the best gift one can give to an author is silence."[31] Foscolo's emphasis on the audience's applause must be contrasted with his 1797 account of *Tieste*'s opening night, at which the audience honoured Foscolo with their silence.[32] Sixteen years later, Foscolo yearned for this very same silence – and yet, the audience did not oblige him. He explained how "the public benevolence" irritated him even more after the second act, when they "called out to the author with applause," and they "screamed" his name, calling for him to take the stage and accept their accolades.[33] Here, a seemingly modest Foscolo recounted his refusal to take the stage. Yet the reason for this refusal remains murky – was it genuine modesty, or was Foscolo again attempting to adhere to the writings of Cesarotti and not disrupt the verisimilitude of the tragedy?[34] Foscolo not only expressed contempt with the public and their lack of reverence for his effort in this passage, but also alluded to his second tragedy and its misfortune in Milan two years earlier.

The Bolognese reacted negatively to Foscolo's snub. His refusal to take the stage and acknowledge the spectators' praise quashed any hope for a silent and attentive audience. They became extremely restless when the third act began, and as a result, the already feeble performances of the actors only deteriorated. But at least the audience was attentive for the fifth and final act. This courtesy was a stroke of luck that Foscolo attributed to the decidedly negative quality of the performance; the actor playing Guelfo was shouting.[35]

Foscolo was furious with the manner in which the acting company delivered his play, but the worst was yet to come. Foscolo, like the architect of Como's theatre, was a victim of random bad luck. He explained the performance's catastrophic conclusion:

> With regard to the last scene, neither the public nor the comedians themselves could have known how it was to end … It happened that while Averardo and Corrado burst onto the stage with arms and torches – I am laughing at it, and you will certainly laugh while reading this – it happened that one of those torches set fire to the horse-haired beard of an extra … and the fire from one beard set fire to the others; and then laughter gave way to terror, since the essential oil of the large stage lamps, falling on the boards of the stage, burned them; and meanwhile, the spectators' attention was divided between the strikingly ridiculous, but real, incident, and the imaginary catastrophe of the unhappy Ricciarda.[36]

Foscolo watched in utter disbelief as the opening performance of his tragedy ended with the fiery destruction of the whole stage. He explained to the countess how he was "spellbound" in his box, like the "fatalistic Turk who, while his house collapsed on top of him, continued to smoke his pipe and sip his coffee."[37] He concluded his letter by again emphasizing – perhaps justifiably – that the horrible staging of his work should not solely dictate whether the work was judged as a success or a failure. Foscolo pleaded that it would be unfair to form an opinion of *Ricciarda* based on this inaugural performance.[38] This statement implies that he had no intention of accepting any form of criticism of his *Ricciarda* (whether positive or negative) that was based on this bizarre opening night performance. *Ricciarda*'s botched debut may be the only aspect of the work that the public and critics remembered, but Foscolo preferred to act as if it had never taken place.

Italian Reception

A 21 September 1813 anonymous review, "Sulla *Ricciarda*: Cenni sulla tragedia del sig. Ugo Foscolo," recounted *Ricciarda*'s debut. The article was published in the *Giornale del Dipartimento del Reno*, and subsequently reprinted on 1 October 1813 in Milan's *Giornale Italiano*.[39] Many of today's scholars credit the authorship of the article to Francesco Tognetti, the editor of the *Giornale del Dipartimento del Reno*, but the article's striking similarity to Foscolo's letter to the Countess of Albany seems to suggest that it was ghostwritten or at least directly influenced by Foscolo.

The review expresses disappointment with the opening night performance of *Ricciarda*, the abysmal performances of the actors, and the harsh negative reaction expressed by the audience and the critics alike. It begins by describing the perceived hasty and unjust criticism that Foscolo and his tragedy received immediately following its debut. The article emphasizes that neither the literary critic, nor the audience, can or should rely on a single performance as the basis for their judgment of a theatrical work. "Sulla *Ricciarda*" echoes sentiments expressed by Foscolo in his letter to the Countess of Albany by recalling Alfieri's claim that critics must see a tragedy performed on several occasions before rendering final judgment.[40] "Sulla *Ricciarda*" ultimately argues that the failure of a tragedy's performance cannot, and should not, be attributed to the tragedian alone. It provides a rather convincing defence of Foscolo, the victimized tragedian, by placing the blame for the tragedy's failure on extenuating circumstances, or *estranei accidenti*. The article suggests that *Ricciarda* is perhaps much more worthy of praise in its written form than would be suggested by the dismal opening night performance, and that one must read the play in order to appreciate it fully. "Sulla *Ricciarda*" speculates that if the tragedy had been read instead of performed, it likely would have received more praise.[41] The reality of the situation, however, is that even when read and not viewed, *Ricciarda* does not pass muster as a great Italian tragedy of the period. Despite the fact that Foscolo intended to compose in a less-classical Italian, his lines are tedious and fail to drive the action forward.

The article goes on to describe two extenuating circumstances that directly contributed to the disastrous inaugural performance. It portrays these misfortunes as being completely separate and unrelated and bearing no relationship to the text itself. The first was Foscolo's refusal to take the stage to accept the audience's praise following the performance's second act. Much as Foscolo did in his letter to the Countess of Albany, "Sulla *Ricciarda*" emphasizes Foscolo's desire for a silent and attentive audience, the audience's lamentable failure to comply with this wish, and its disappointment at Foscolo's perceived snub when he declined to show himself to the public.[42] The article continues by describing the fire as the second extenuating circumstance.[43]

It is remarkable the extent to which "Sulla *Ricciarda*" echoes Foscolo's attempts in his letter to the Countess of Albany to explain that these two incidents were unrelated to the literary merit of *Ricciarda* and should not impact any review of the work. But this is not the only similarity. The review continues by focusing on the inadequate acting of the production company. It argues that the primary reason for the tragedy's poor reception lay with the actors' terrible performances, and urges that readers reconsider the value of *Ricciarda* and the literary prowess of Foscolo as a tragedian on their own merits and disregard the conspicuous lack of talent on stage. The remainder of the article berates the actors.[44] It ultimately argues that the poor acting actually confused the audience and perhaps even portrayed an action quite different from that which was intended.[45] This scathing critique serves to shift all blame from Foscolo to the production company.

"Sulla *Ricciarda*" concludes with a discussion of the work's playwright. It argues that Foscolo deserved any and every benefit of the doubt, since fire and poor acting have nothing to do with one's prowess as a tragedian. "Sulla *Ricciarda*" even includes laudatory remarks about the way the characters are drawn, highlighting Foscolo's literary innovation on the whole, and giving the author very favourable treatment.[46] And if the modern critic might view these remarks as excessively complimentary to Foscolo, the conclusion of the article is even more ingratiating. "Sulla *Ricciarda*" favourably compares Foscolo to the major European tragedians, including Alfieri, Monti, Voltaire, Corneille, and Crébillon.[47] This sentiment is strikingly similar to that expressed by an anonymous author in the 1797 review of Foscolo's first tragedy *Tieste*, "Notizie storico-critiche sul *Tieste*," which hailed Foscolo as worthy of accompanying many of these literary giants in the annals of literary history.[48] Thus, as was the case with the "Notizie," "Sulla *Ricciarda*" should be seen as a blatant attempt to sway public opinion in favour of Foscolo by prominently placing him in the canon of Italian literature as a tragedian.

Unfortunately for Foscolo, any attempt to manipulate the public via his or anyone else's literary journal contributions ultimately had little effect on *Ricciarda*'s lifespan on the Italian stage. The harsh censorship from the occupying Austrian government resulted in variations of Foscolo's original *Ricciarda* being performed without the playwright's consent in Padova, Venice, Parma, and Brescia, but not Milan, where Foscolo faced significant political opposition. Austrian censors in the city did not approve of the message of the liberator versus the tyrant, which was prevalent throughout the play. The Austrians worried that the protagonist's love for his *patria* and direct defiance of the reign of the ruling monarch (who was also his brother) might inspire Italians to rise up against their foreign occupiers. The Milanese censors thus demanded that Foscolo cut and rework the text before *Ricciarda* could be performed there. *Ricciarda* contained too many patriotic allusions according to these officials, and they decreed that it needed to be substantially revised in order to be suitable for production. Yet Foscolo refused to succumb to the pressures of the occupying government by editing – and inevitably altering – his literary creation. As a result, Foscolo's third tragedy was never performed in Milan. On 6 December 1813 he wrote to Quirina Mocenni Magiotti that he had ceased production of his work, and observed that it was "neither the right country nor the right time for tragedies."[49]

Foscolo's decision to withdraw *Ricciarda* was yet another bitter failure for him as a tragedian. His overarching goal of achieving renown on stage was thwarted for the third and final time. This failure only reinforced his belief that a gauntlet of spiteful literary journal critics, an ignorant public, and the harsh governmental censors awaited each and every one of his compositions with sharpened knives. Foscolo would not attempt to write another tragedy, believing that any future theatrical efforts would be similarly doomed. Yet despite the end of his career as a tragedian, Foscolo was not finished with the genre. Instead, the overwhelming rejection of his tragedies was an important catalyst for Foscolo's critical works in the field during his last eleven years in England.

Foscolo's involvement with the Italian literary journal scene similarly did not end with his decision to withdraw *Ricciarda*. Count Karl Ludwig Ficquelmont (1777–1857), a major-general in the occupying Austrian government who became foreign minister in 1848, approached him in 1815 about founding and directing a new literary journal. Foscolo accepted Ficquelmont's proposal and commenced planning for the new periodical. He composed "Opinion on the institution of a literary journal" (Parere sulla istituzione di un giornale letterario), in February 1815, one month before his final departure from Milan and eventually Italy.[50] In its first section, "Errors to avoid" (Errori da evitarsi), he argued that previous periodicals invariably committed egregious errors that tarnished both the reputations of the authors reviewed and those of the reviewers.[51] Foscolo described these errors as the publication of articles that failed to correspond to the journal's mission statement, typographical errors, and even publication delays. He also cautioned against the manner in which governments, who controlled journals with their censors, gave unjust preferential treatment to charlatans, or unworthy journalists. Foscolo concluded that these potential mistakes must be addressed and avoided at all costs.[52]

Foscolo's negative experiences with *Il Poligrafo* and *Giornale Italiano* provided the underpinnings for his "Parere." He intended to elevate the status of the literary journal to that of "real" literature, arguing that it could assist with documenting the spirit of a nation and that "it could be a mediator between the reason of state and the passion of the people."[53] Foscolo planned that his new journal would successfully avoid the errors of its predecessors. He offered three rules that he believed the journal must follow: it should (1) be published with the welfare of its citizens as its primary goal, and not for financial gain, (2) allow only the most learned intellectuals to contribute, and (3) show an interest in writing not only for contemporaries, but also for posterity.[54] Foscolo's "Parere" was accepted by Vienna without objection.

Unfortunately, he did not remain in Italy long enough to see these ambitious designs realized. Foscolo could not accept the Austrian occupation of northern Italy and the possibility that he would somehow be in their service with the creation of this periodical. As a result, he left Italy for Switzerland (and ultimately England) on 30 March 1815. He would never return. His departure marks the end of one of the most impressive and prolific literary careers in the history of Italian literature. He would make feeble attempts at creative writing while in exile, but his place in the Italian literary canon already had been secured many years earlier with such works as *Ultime lettere di Jacopo Ortis* and *Dei sepolcri*.

Exile and the "Essay"

Foscolo's self-imposed exile fundamentally shaped his future works and his reflections on Italy. This should not be surprising when viewed through a contemporary lens. The topic of an exile's feelings towards his abandoned homeland has been extensively discussed in recent times by literary critics, historians, and sociologists alike. The most prominent example is the late Edward Said's "Reflections on Exile." Said observed that an exiled individual often experiences a heightened sense of self-awareness and national pride while living outside his or her native land.[55] D. Keith Simonton offered a more psychoanalytical viewpoint in his book *Greatness: Who Makes History and Why*. Simonton speculated that an exile's desire for "greatness" may reflect the innate longing for success in a culture from which one is estranged.[56] These sentiments go a long way in explaining Foscolo's efforts after leaving Italy. Indeed, it is easily conceivable that living outside of Italy actually compelled Foscolo to closely focus on his role in the Italian literary tradition in a more intense manner than he ever did while still there.

Foscolo's critical writings during the exile period examine past and contemporary Italian literature. They focus on, among other aims, elevating his own works and status as a prominent author. Instances abound of Foscolo's awareness of his homeland's emerging national identity and his own place in its literary pantheon. One such example is Foscolo's 1816 privately published anthology of Italian sonnets, which he compiled in Switzerland immediately following his departure from Italy. Foscolo's *Vestigi della storia del sonetto italiano* offers a history of the Italian sonnet that was modelled after Ludovico Antonio Muratori's 1706 *Della perfetta poesia italiana*, in both structure and critical style.[57] Foscolo analysed twenty-six sonnets dating back to the 1200s, underscoring his interest in promoting his own notion of a "proper" Italian literary history.[58] He included his own 1802 sonnet "In morte del fratello Giovanni," without critical commentary, as the final selection in the anthology.

Foscolo's remarkable poetic career in Italy warranted his self-inclusion. He also was no stranger to touting his own works. But Foscolo's self-reflection and attempts at self-promotion while in exile were different in both quality and quantity. They were more than mere puffery; they were the efforts of an exile to reclaim a place for himself in his home country's literary tradition. Maria Antonietta Terzoli cites Foscolo's personal struggle to come to terms with his exile as a reason why he chose to include one of his own sonnets.[59] The anthology summarizes Foscolo's thoughts on the evolution of the Italian sonnet over six centuries, and it also allows him to establish himself as the culmination of this Italian tradition, tying him back to his *patria*, Italy. This self-selection easily could be seen as a precursor to the decision to include himself in later critical articles that Foscolo published in England.

Foscolo arrived in England during the second week of September 1816. During his first few years in London, Foscolo occupied himself with several creative projects: he began an epistolary novel, *Lettere scritte in Inghilterra* (which he would never complete), he translated several more chapters of Sterne's *A Sentimental Journey* into Italian, and he published a new edition of *Ultime lettere di Jacopo Ortis* (John Murray, 1817). Greek and Italian studies were fashionable in London at this time, and Foscolo soon became a regular guest both at Holland House and at the home of Sir Roger Wilbraham (1743–1829) – residences frequented by prominent English intellectuals.[60] During his visits to these homes, Foscolo worked with England's most prominent publisher of the time, John Murray (editor of the prestigious London literary journal the *Quarterly Review*), and he established the connections necessary to enable him to create a place for himself in England's literary circles.

Foscolo soon abandoned his creative writing and began publishing numerous critical articles for English literary journals and prominent publishing houses. It was a complete shift from contributing to the Italian literary tradition to writing about it. His works focused on Italy's emerging national identity through her literary history.[61] Joseph Luzzi ponders on Foscolo's production in exile by noting both the positive impact Foscolo had in bringing Italy to the forefront and the negative and glaring void his exile created in the world of Italian literature:

> The essays on Italian history and culture that Foscolo produced during this time helped rally European support for the Risorgimento and eventual unification ... One can only speculate as to the poetry and prose, that without exile, might have followed his rejection of these self-sacrificial bodies in favor of the life-breathing pores of his diaphanous Graces, the subject of his last major poem, *Le Grazie* (The Graces), left unfinished in 1815.[62]

Foscolo's work on Italian history and culture in exile stoked the already piqued English interest in all things Italian. One cannot overlook the fact that he also discussed his tragedies and his theories on tragedy in several of these articles, creating the impression that he was one of Italy's most prominent tragedians.

This manner of self-reflection and self-promotion is particularly evident in Foscolo's 1818 "Essay on the Present Literature of Italy."[63] The "Essay" was widely read when it was first published, and was intended to raise European awareness of Italian literary theory and practice of the late eighteenth century. The widespread distribution of the "Essay" should not be surprising given its backing by several influential English intellectuals. It was published by John Murray, and it appeared in conjunction with the text of Lord Byron's *Childe Harold's Pilgrimage Canto the fourth*. John Cam Hobhouse (1786–1869), a close friend of Byron and one of Foscolo's many patrons, is credited with authorship of the "Essay," but he did not write it. It is widely accepted that Foscolo was in fact its true author.[64] And there is evidence of a connection between the two men. On 23 March 1818, at a dinner gathering at the Wilbraham home, Hobhouse was seated next to Foscolo. He was impressed with the exile on that March evening and considered their meeting to be quite fortuitous. Hobhouse wrote to Foscolo a few days later and invited him to write a piece on the present state of Italian literature.[65] The result was the "Essay."

The "Essay" is a mini-history of late-eighteenth- and early-nineteenth-century Italian literature. It contains a brief introduction and conclusion that bookend portraits of six contemporary Italian authors: Melchiorre Cesarotti, Giuseppe Parini, Vittorio Alfieri, Ippolito Pindemonte, Vincenzo Monti, and, fittingly, Ugo Foscolo himself. Foscolo justified his choice of the six authors by remarking that each of the accomplished men possessed qualities emblematic of the times and of the nation of Italy.[66] Merely by virtue of their inclusion, Foscolo labelled each as representative of Italy. In essence, Foscolo identified the canon as he saw it – or perhaps more precisely, as he wanted it to be. It should go without saying that Foscolo's description of himself is an idealized representation. He unabashedly wrote, "Foscolo is an excellent scholar."[67] This is an accurate assertion, but its accuracy is less interesting than the motivation behind it. The very fact that he would choose to include such commentary indicates that he was not shy about singing his own praises. It is precisely this flawless self-image that makes the work fascinating, especially when evaluating the English perception of Foscolo the tragedian.

Foscolo examined the authors' works in various genres, but his commentary on tragedy is one of the most interesting aspects of the "Essay." To begin with, Foscolo chose to include only those classical, or Alfierian, dramatists with whom he closely identified: Alfieri, Pindemonte, and Monti. Yet Foscolo's discussions of the tragedians included in the "Essay" and their works are not completely favourable. He harshly critiqued the tragedies that strayed from the pure, classical form of the genre, condemning the new and experimental forms of tragedy. Undoubtedly, Foscolo's own formation and implementation of classical ideals in his tragedies coloured his criticisms of others' works. As a result, he indirectly – but unmistakably – justified and exalted the traditional form and subject matter of straightforward neoclassical tragedies. Foscolo harshly criticized mixed genres, Shakespearean influences, and any departure from the traditional Aristotelian "unities." His own tragedies served as the model for what *should* be done, and he consequently labelled works that differed stylistically from his own as examples of what should be avoided.

Foscolo praised the model figure of Alfieri in a unique way. He began the section on the Astian with a generally positive overview of Alfieri's treatises *Della Tirannide* (begun in 1777, published in 1789) and *Il Principe e le lettere* (begun in 1778, published in 1786), noting that "the Italians look upon the prose of Alfieri as a model of style, particularly on political subjects."[68] Foscolo continued Alfieri's portrait by pronouncing his fame as a dramatist. Statements in the "Essay" such as "His [Alfieri's] tragedies have been criticized in every European language"[69] and "Perhaps he was born to shine in tragedy and in tragedy alone,"[70] highlight Alfieri's celebrity.

Foscolo did not dwell extensively on Alfieri's influence as a dramatist, however. He chose not to discuss the numerous tragedies of the emblematic figure in any significant detail.[71] Instead, Foscolo described Alfieri's *Morte di Abele*, an experimental *melo-tragedy*, a "sort of drama," which combined the music of the theatre with the "grandeur and the pathos of tragedy."[72] Foscolo did not approve of the work's hybrid nature and operatic influences, and he characterized the work as "on the whole, devoid of interest."[73]

It is strange that a tragedian so familiar with Alfieri, who closely modelled his tragedies on Alfierian precepts, thought it more prudent to discuss the great tragedian's least "Alfierian" drama. This surprising presentation of Alfieri requires further explanation. Cesare Foligno, in his introduction to the *Edizione nazionale*'s "Essay," speculated that the absence of Foscolo's remarks on Alfieri's tragedies could only be the result of several of Foscolo's original pages being lost while en route to Hobhouse for translation.[74] There is no evidence supporting this theory, however, and I doubt that it is correct. I argue that Foscolo's discussion of Alfieri's experimental *Morte di Abele* was strategic. It is but the first example in the "Essay" of a dramatic work that Foscolo reviewed and rejected in an attempt to demonstrate the shortcomings of new-fangled forms of tragedy.

At the conclusion of his section on Alfieri, Foscolo remarked negatively on Count Alessandro Pepoli. Pepoli was a Venetian dramatist who enjoyed popular success precisely when Foscolo first arrived in Venice at the end of the eighteenth century. Foscolo labelled Pepoli as "the contemporary [and] the rival of Alfieri."[75] He dismissed and even ridiculed Pepoli's unconventional dramatic attempts of the *fisedia*. Foscolo lambasted Pepoli and his innovative ideas, stating that he "wrote tragedies, he wrote comedies: both the one and the other were applauded on the stage; both the one and the other now slumber in the libraries."[76] Foscolo maintained that popularity and literary excellence are two separate and distinct concepts, and he took great pleasure in highlighting the short-lived nature of Pepoli's fame. Conceivably due to the critical and popular failure of his own tragedies, Foscolo elected to attack those who received some semblance of public admiration and sought to discredit their successes.

The section on Ippolito Pindemonte began with an attack on the author's older brother, Giovanni. Foscolo remarked on the popularity of Giovanni and his works, noting how Giovanni Pindemonte, like Pepoli, "kept for some time possession of the stage."[77] Yet still bruised by the lack of popularity of his own tragedies, Foscolo bitterly discussed the fleeting popularity oftentimes associated with experimental mixed-genre compositions, such as those written by Pepoli and Pindemonte. He lamented, "The tragedies of John Pindemonte, which are now almost forgotten, brought crowds to the theatre at the time that Alfieri was listened to with impatience."[78] This allusion to the public's negative reaction to Alfieri must be seen as dripping with sarcasm. Even though Foscolo did not discuss Alfieri's numerous tragedies in the "Essay," he implied that only the great literary works, such as the strictly classical tragedies of Alfieri, can stand the test of time. Foscolo believed that ephemeral literary fads, while perhaps more easily understood by the public, would come and go – but classical tragedies would enjoy a more permanent respect and even a position of superiority in the annals of literary history.

When Foscolo finally came to Ippolito Pindemonte (at least substantively), he cast his subject in the same negative light as Giovanni. Foscolo belittled Ippolito and his literary achievements, observing that the author "has perhaps less imagination than his brother."[79]

Foscolo did not look favourably on Ippolito's tragedies. More than a decade before the "Essay," in an 1806 letter to Isabella Teotochi Albrizzi, Foscolo criticized Ippolito, stating that he lacked the necessary passion and nerve required to write tragedies.[80] The rift between the two men had only grown wider in subsequent years, possibly due to Pindemonte's unfavourable opinions of Foscolo's literary compositions.[81]

Twelve years later in the "Essay," Foscolo described Ippolito's tragedy *Arminio* (1804) to the English as a combination of the Shakespearean, Greek, and Italian dramas.[82] His description of Ippolito's combination of Shakespearean influences and classical rules in the tragedy is positive, yet Foscolo's overall judgment of Ippolito as tragedian ultimately is unenthusiastic. Foscolo fundamentally questioned the praise enjoyed by Ippolito, claiming that his apparent renown was not actual. Rather, only an insignificant number of journal reviewers touted *Arminio*. In reality, according to Foscolo, the public did not receive Pindemonte's works favourably.[83] He concluded, "Whether the *Arminius* has stood the great test, does not appear in the published play. Perhaps it has been never acted, and perhaps it may be as little qualified for any stage."[84] Foscolo evidently believed that Ippolito's innovative tragedy (a combination of the English, Greek, and Italian schools of tragedy) would suffer the same fate of the attempts of Pepoli and Giovanni Pindemonte – ultimately, this work, like the experimental forms before it, was merely a popular fad, and it would not stand the test of time in the judgment of history.

The "Essay" next turns to Vincenzo Monti, with whom Foscolo had a rather complicated relationship.[85] The two authors experienced an earlier falling out over Monti's involvement with Urbano Lampredi and his negative criticisms of Foscolo's tragedies. Furthermore, Monti was considered by many to be a paid servant of the successive occupying French and Austrian governments.[86] Foscolo consequently viewed Monti as willing to modify his politics with each regime change.

Yet Foscolo chose to include Monti in the "Essay." Much as he did with respect to Alfieri, he began his discussion of Monti's dramatic works with high praise. From the outset, Foscolo applauded Monti's 1786 *Aristodemo*, favourably describing the tragedy's dialogue and noting the author's prominence as a tragedian.[87] However, Foscolo quickly departed from this effusive tone, and turned on Monti in his analysis of the author's later tragedies *Galeotto Manfredi* (1788) and *Caio Gracco* (1788–90).[88] He was quick to catalogue many of Monti's perceived weaknesses as a tragedian: "The defects of Monti's tragedies are reducible to the insignificance of his characters, to the irregularity of his plot, and to a style sometimes too lyrical, sometimes too tame."[89]

Foscolo asserted that *Galeotto Manfredi* was strikingly worse than *Aristodemo*.[90] In *Galeotto Manfredi*, Monti drew inspiration from Shakespeare's *Othello*, both in his plot and with his creation of the Iago-like character of Zambino. Furthermore, echoes of Shakespeare's *Julius Caesar* and *Coriolanus* are prominent in Monti's third tragedy, *Caio Gracco*, perhaps causing the unfavourable public reception of the work. Foscolo reported gleefully that "scenes [from *Caio Gracco*] were expressly imitated from Shakespeare, and succeeded at first – nobody, however, dared to applaud them in the subsequent representations."[91]

The section of the "Essay" on Foscolo himself consists primarily of a glowing discussion of the bulk of his literary works. This is not without justification for he had achieved literary renown throughout

Europe with his epistolary novel *Ultime lettere di Jacopo Ortis* and his solemn poem *Dei sepolcri*. He was indeed a prominent Italian author of the period. Writing in the third person, Foscolo reviewed these works, along with his translation *Viaggio Sentimentale* (1813–17), his lectures in Pavia (1809), and the incomplete poem *Le Grazie* (begun in 1812).

This renown did not immunize Foscolo against all criticism. His literary battles with the Milanese establishment remained remarkably fresh in his mind. Foscolo elected to vigorously defend his reputation in the "Essay," where he wove together both fact and fiction in order to present a highly idealized image of himself. For example, he called Lamberti "a declared adversary of this writer [i.e., of himself]," and he recounted a story emphasizing the distinct differences between himself and Monti. Foscolo's narrative highlights his avowed allegiance to Alfieri. He explained:

> They [Foscolo and Monti] were dining at the house of Count Veneri, minister of the public treasury: Monti, as usual, launched out against Alfieri, according to the court tone of the day: "All his works together," said he, "are not worth a song of Metastasio" – "Stop there, Sir," interrupted Foscolo, "or I will twirl round you and your party as well as ever a top was whipped by a schoolboy." As far as respects his [Foscolo's] other great contemporaries, he has never spoken of Pindemonte but with esteem, nor ever named Alfieri without admiration.[92]

Foscolo characterized Monti (justly, perhaps) as a mere puppet, whose literary tastes were unduly influenced and even controlled by whatever government was in power. In contrast, Foscolo depicted himself as an independent author whose literary tastes were not (and could not be) influenced by the opinions of any others, and whose integrity was beyond reproach.

Foscolo also dedicated a portion of his self-portrait to a discussion of his tragedies. In it, he indirectly – but unequivocally – placed himself in a prominent position in the canon of Italian tragedians. Foscolo took full advantage of his opportunity in the "Essay" to present his own tragedies as model compositions of the genre. He contrasted his prior views on what an author should *not* do when composing a tragedy (i.e., in his discussions of Pepoli, Pindemonte, and Monti) with his own examples of what one *should* do, implying that his own tragedies were composed in the "correct way."

The approach employed by Foscolo may have been persuasive, but that does not make it any less brazen and or inaccurate. For example, in his description of *Tieste*, Foscolo proclaimed:

> He [Foscolo] commenced his career a year before the fall of the Venetian republic, with a tragedy called *Thyestes*. Being angry at the little attention paid by the Venetians to the tragedies of Alfieri, and at the corrupted taste which made them prefer and applaud those of the Marquis [Giovanni] Pindemonte and of Count Pepoli, he resolved that his drama should have only four personages; and that the simplicity and severity of his whole composition should rival Alfieri and the Greek tragedians. With this hardy project, he contrived that his play should be acted on the same night when two new pieces from the pen of the above Marquis and Count were to be represented at other theatres of the same town. The courage and the youth of the author enabled him to triumph over his rivals, and his *Thyestes* received more applause than perhaps it deserved. The actors published it in the tenth volume of the *Teatro Italiano Applaudito*, subjoining to it an account of its great success, and a criticism written in favour of the author.[93]

Foscolo's "anonymous" (more accurately, pseudonymous) presentation of the story behind the staging of his tragedy is a first-rate drama in its own right. It resembles a David and Goliath scenario, in which the obscure young playwright conquers the giants of the stage. And yet, as Nicola Mangini explains in the article "La vita teatrale nella Venezia del Foscolo e la rappresentazione del 'Tieste,'" Foscolo's report of the performances of two new pieces from Pindemonte and Pepoli the very same evening as *Tieste*'s opening night is inaccurate. It is true that Pindemonte's *Donna Caritea* was, in fact, performed on the same evening as *Tieste* at San Giovanni Grisostomo. However, the last play of Pepoli's to debut in Venice was *Ladislao*, which premiered almost one year before.[94] Through his hyperbole and inaccurate bragging, Foscolo characterized himself as a brave and bold artist utterly unwilling to compromise his artistic convictions for the sake of public success or acclaim, unlike his "lesser" rivals, Pindemonte and Pepoli. This portrayal serves to elevate Foscolo above his contemporaries, based in large part on his strict adherence to the compositional guidelines set forth by the classical school.

Foscolo's subsequent recounting of the events surrounding the debuts of *Ajace* and *Ricciarda* is also heavily complimentary – and, again, quite inaccurate. He acknowledged the critical and popular failures of these works, but even still he omitted the more embarrassing details explaining their failure. Foscolo only blamed the strict government censors for the failure of these two tragedies. He conspicuously ignored the negative public reception, poor acting, bad luck, and poor artistic choices on the part of the tragedian that were all more responsible culprits. Foscolo wrote:

> Two tragedies, the *Ricciarda* and the *Ajax*, by the same author, were stopped by the government after the first representation. They excited a great curiosity from motives not altogether poetical. It was reported that Moreau was his Ajax, that Napoleon was to figure in his Agamennon [*sic*], and that his holiness the Pope would be easily recognised in Chalcas. The known principles of Foscolo facilitated the recognition of the originals, who, after all, perhaps, never sat to the poet for their likeness.[95] Whatever were his intentions, he received immediate orders to quit the kingdom of Italy, and to reside in some town of the French empire.[96]

According to Foscolo, he and his tragedies were undeserving victims of political persecution. Yet by concentrating on the censorship of his works, Foscolo was promoting them, at least to some degree – he realized that the public is attracted to literary works that are "forbidden," and he took advantage of that sensationalism. Furthermore, Foscolo's emphasis on the unfair censorship of the ruling French government only underscores his intrinsic "Italian-ness." Above all, in the "Essay" Foscolo boldly – though anonymously and largely inaccurately – presented himself as a prolific, innovative, emblematic *Italian* tragedian who was worthy of a place in the canon along with his many brilliant contemporaries.

Foscolo's political persecution complex, as evidenced by his discussion of his latter two tragedies in the "Essay," constitutes only a portion of the larger self-portrait that Foscolo attempts to paint for his readers. He concluded the section on himself by focusing on nationalist passion, which directly tied the "Essay" to a passage in Byron's *Canto the fourth* in which Byron recounted Venice's history of foreign occupation and lamented her subservience to Austria.[97] Here, Foscolo reprinted an excerpt of one of his earliest articles from his self-imposed exile, entitled "Senza querele impotenti, né recriminazioni da servi," which was published in the *Lugano Gazette* on 14 April 1815:

He [Foscolo] became a voluntary exile, and his adieus to his countrymen are couched in the language of proud resignation. "Let not the minister of the Austrian police continue to persecute me in my Swiss asylum; tell him that I am far from wishing to excite the hopeless passions of my fellow citizens. We were in want of arms; they were given to us by France, and Italy had again a name amongst the nations. In the access [sic] of our inflammatory fever, the loss of blood could not harm us, and the death of a single man would have inevitably produced changes favourable to all the nations who should have courage to profit by the happy juncture. But it was ordained otherwise: the affairs of the world have been turned into another and an unexpected channel. The actual disease of Italy is a slow lethargic consumption, she will soon be nothing but a lifeless carcass; and her generous sons should only weep in silence, without the impotent complaints and the mutual recriminations of slaves."[98]

Nationalist passion and heartache clearly reverberate throughout this passage. Foscolo's account echoes his David-and-Goliath sentiment first present in his account of *Tieste*'s opening. Foscolo essentially presents himself as a champion of Italy, who chose to fight so that his adoptive homeland might once again have "a name amongst the nations."

English Reception and Success

The "Essay" reached an extraordinarily wide audience. Foscolo hoped that the article would inspire a renewed European appreciation of Italian literature and its key participants. It almost immediately impacted Italian theatrical trends, and Foscolo's thinly veiled attempt to include only those he preferred in his constructed canon met heavy resistance in Italy immediately following its publication.[99] For example, Ippolito Pindemonte never forgave Byron and Hobhouse for his portrayal. Pindemonte went so far as to refuse Hobhouse's 1826 request for assistance in memorializing Byron with a monument two years after the English poet's untimely death.[100]

The "Essay" spurred a larger and more publicized reaction from those whom Foscolo chose to exclude. Hobhouse discussed the "Essay's" negative reception in Italy in his 1859 book *Italy, Remarks Made in Several Visits from the Year 1816–1854*. He wrote that "the Essay was assailed by the friends of Monti and the partisans of the Romantic school in Italy."[101] Ludovico Di Breme (1780–1820) objected with the loudest voice and Eric Reginald Vincent thoroughly documented in his 1949 book *Byron,*

Hobhouse, and Foscolo Di Breme's displeasure. He wrote scathing letters to both Hobhouse and Byron in June 1818, questioning why no Romantic authors were profiled in the "Essay." Similarly, according to Vincent, Di Breme "suffered the mortification of not finding any mention of his name whatever."[102]

Foscolo was fortunate, then, that the English reception of the "Essay" was largely favourable. According to Marvin Carlson, as the Italian debate surrounding the "Essay" unfolded, "Foscolo had established himself as an authority on Italian letters in the London literary world and in Whig society, and his indifference, if not antagonism, to Romantic experiments colored English views of these works [the texts discussed in the "Essay"] for much of the next decade."[103] The widespread popularity of the "Essay," along with the heightened English interest in the debate between Classicists and Romantics, also increased Foscolo's renown in England. This new-found popularity was exactly what Foscolo needed to establish himself in English society, and for the next nine years he would enjoy his reputation as a prominent Italian tragedian and England's resident Italian literary expert.

Foscolo even was able to forge an indirect relationship with one of England's most prominent authors, Lord Byron, through the "Essay." Since his arrival in Italy in 1816, Italian Romantic intellectuals had hailed Byron as an emblematic Romantic author. In reality, however, Byron wanted nothing to do with Italy's literary wars, and he rejected the Romantic label. His tastes instead echoed Foscolo's literary preferences, and Byron looked to the Alfierian school for inspiration. In a letter to Murray dated 14 July 1821, he even expressed his interest in the Alfierian style of tragedy:

> My object has been to dramatize like the Greeks (a *modest* phrase!) striking passages of history, as they did of history and mythology. – You will find all this very *un*like Shakespeare – and so much the better in one sense – for I look upon him to be the *worst* of models – though the most extraordinary of writers. – It has been my object to be as simple and severe as Alfieri. (Byron's emphasis)[104]

Byron looked to Foscolo as England's resident expert on Italian letters for assistance when composing his Venetian tragedies, *Marino Faliero* (1820–1) and *The Two Foscari* (1821). Foscolo edited Italian passages of the *Marino Faliero*, and Byron asked him (via Hobhouse and Murray) to read and comment on the complete drafts of both works.[105]

Foscolo's opinions in the "Essay" on Italian tragedy also spurred Hobhouse to continue with additional projects. Hobhouse had translated portions of Silvio Pellico's tragedy *Francesca da Rimini*, which he planned to accompany with another essay on Italian theatre soon after the publication of the "Essay." He turned to Foscolo for his opinion on the translation and asked whether Foscolo might be amenable to providing assistance with the new essay. Foscolo agreed to both requests.[106] Hobhouse also expressed interest in translating and publishing Foscolo's *Tieste*. Neither the new essay on Italian tragedy nor the *Tieste* translation ever materialized, but Hobhouse's heightened interest almost certainly can be attributed to Foscolo's positive self-portrayal as an emblematic Italian tragedian in the "Essay."

It is hard to dispute that England was the right place at the right time for Foscolo. He recognized the potential to engineer the positive reception that eluded him in Italy and submitted a proposal to John Murray to publish a London edition of *Ricciarda* in 1820, as explained in a 12 May 1820 letter to his friend Lord John Russell.[107] The tragedy was published shortly thereafter and, in direct contrast to its hostile reception by the Italian public, was well received by the English public. In a letter to Gino Capponi from 23 to 30 May 1820, Foscolo was enthusiastic that his tragedy was an English success and that Murray was selling numerous copies of it.[108] The English scholar and poet John Herman Merivale (1779–1844) also praised *Ricciarda* in a letter to Foscolo on 24 May 1820. Merivale wrote:

> My dear Sir – I cannot refrain from telling you how much I have been delighted by Ricciarda, which I devoured, rather than read, this morning, but must study somewhat more attentively before I can be quite satisfied that I fully appreciate all its excellences. It is indeed a perfect Dramatic Poem, constructed on the severest model of ancient simplicity, progressively and powerfully advancing in interest; – the fable unfolding itself gradually, and apparently by accident, and every successive scene tending to a catastrophe, at once probable and terrible in the extreme.[109]

It is difficult to say whether or not the English really did love *Ricciarda*, or whether they were simply paying lip service to their favourite exile. Italian studies were quite popular during this period, and it is possible that the reason why the English embraced Foscolo's work rests more with the fact that he was a bona fide Italian author rather than with his prowess as a tragedian.

In any event, this turn of fortune soon spread beyond England. A few months after *Ricciarda*'s publication, Italy's *Biblioteca italiana* reviewed this edition of Foscolo's final tragedy.[110] Seven years after the disastrous debut in Bologna, the anonymous author, presumed to be Paride Zajotti (1793–1843), reviewed the drama positively, writing, "in a word the tragedy is precisely that which will bring honor to Italy."[111] According to Zajotti, previous reviewers were influenced by the circumstances of the times and the public's reception of the work, and they simply did not wish to see the merits of the play. Yet despite Zajotti's positive review, Foscolo's vindication in Italy was a fleeting moment, and *Ricciarda* was soon all but forgotten among Italian audiences.

But the popularity of *Ricciarda* among English audiences was not a passing fad. Foscolo received additional letters of praise in the years that followed. The translator James Atkinson (1759–1839) even prepared an English version of the work for him.[112] Atkinson remarked on the classical beauty of *Ricciarda* in a 7 December 1823 letter from Calcutta, India. He explained: "I herewith beg [to] present to you a copy of my translation of your Tragedy of Ricciarda. Poetry and painting form the occupation chiefly of my leisure hours, although there can hardly be a less literary place in the world than Calcutta, but I was so much pleased with the classical manner in which you have embodied the characters in that work."[113] This letter emphasizes the ideal neoclassical nature of *Ricciarda*. And so, while in England, Foscolo seemingly achieved his long-sought-after status of prominent Italian neoclassical tragedian after all.

In addition to these epistolary records of the triumph of the 1820 edition, articles touting Foscolo began to appear in English journals. The writer and translator Thomas Roscoe (1791–1871) published the article "Remarks on the Life and Works of Ugo Foscolo," in which he lauded Foscolo's third tragedy. The article appeared in the first volume of *New Monthly Magazine*, in January 1821. The *New Monthly Magazine* was owned by Henry Colburn from 1821 to 1830 and edited by Cyrus Redding (1785–1870) and the famous Scottish poet-critic, Thomas Campbell (1777–1844). Interestingly, Foscolo was a featured contributor in this very same volume with his article "Learned Ladies," which criticizes as unjust the common English practice of abridging, or simplifying, the translations of great works of foreign literature in order to make it "more appropriate" for English female audiences.[114] Foscolo would publish five more articles in Thomas Campbell's journal during the next year and a half.[115]

Foscolo did not personally compose "Remarks on the Life and Works of Ugo Foscolo," but he very likely was involved in its publication. Thomas Roscoe served as Foscolo's translator for the articles published in Campbell's journal. The two men also collaborated on the creation of a newly planned literary journal, which unfortunately never materialized.[116] It is not hard to imagine that Foscolo assisted with Roscoe's "Remarks," given their close relationship and the article's highly complimentary tone. Roscoe praised Foscolo's *Ultime lettere di Jacopo Ortis* and his poetry, and presented all of his important biographical facts. He also emphasized Foscolo's importance as an Italian tragedian. The effort is an unabashed publicity plug for Foscolo's recently published London edition of *Ricciarda*:

We now come to a more mature and important production from the pen of Ugo Foscolo – a work in which the fair promise of excellence held out in his "Tieste" is amply redeemed, in a harvest of rich poetic fruit, worthy of so fresh and so full a spring. His "Ricciarda" is a perfectly original exhibition of dramatic power and skill. We are at a loss to say, whether the sentiments, or the individual passages and fine bursts of poetry, most richly abound. It bears the same stamp of passionate character as the drama of Alfieri, though it is quite new in its conception, and in the style and execution of the piece. With the same breathless haste, and terrible manifestation of fatality, shown in the progress of the stories of his predecessor, it has a richer poetical diction and an eloquence of passion to which Alfieri never attained. The "Ricciarda" is also entitled to the best praise to which tragedy can aspire – that of nationality and a native growth of thought and feeling, derived from the motives and habits of a people, and without which, the drama can never be a complete representation of human action and character. Foscolo divides the honour with Monti and Manzoni of having achieved a more national and peculiar species of dramatic writing – at once more simple and natural, and more in unison with the mind and genius of modern Italy … The bold and shadowy power – the terrible delineation of passion – and the masterly touches of character, with richness of poetic thought and expression, are above any praise which we can bestow upon them.[117]

Foscolo must have relished Roscoe's glowing remarks. The review not only favourably promoted his newly published *Ricciarda* (thus ensuring its financial success), but also erased to some extent the bitter memory of the tragedy's Italian reception nearly eight years earlier.

 Ricciarda's success and Foscolo's renown as a prominent Italian tragedian endured in England, even after his death on 10 September 1827. A month later, the *New Monthly Magazine* published an anonymous obituary of Foscolo. The author touted *Ricciarda*'s literary excellence and popularity. The obituary states: "'*Ricciarda*,' a tragedy, is one of Foscolo's most celebrated works, built on the simplest and most severe school of the drama."[118] The author failed to note that *Ricciarda* was famous only among English audiences, nor did he mention the tragedy's poor Italian reception. Perhaps he had never heard about *Ricciarda*'s failure in Italy, or perhaps he refrained simply out of respect for the dead. Likewise, in his September 1828 article "The Works of Ugo Foscolo," Thomas Roscoe continued to praise Foscolo's third tragedy, writing that *Ricciarda* "contains many passages of splendid power and beauty; and it is doubtless the most complete and national, if not the most poetical of his [Foscolo's] dramas. The style is bold and impassioned."[119] Whether or not it was their original intention, both of these articles succeed in portraying the tragedy as more popular than it truly was.

Chapter Five

Curtain Call from Exile

The Italian tragedy continued to be a "hot topic" in England following the publication of Foscolo's "Essay" and *Ricciarda*.[1] The Reverend Henry Hart Milman (1791–1868) published a widely read article entitled "Italian Tragedy" in the October 1820 issue of the *Quarterly Review*.[2] The article consists of a general history of the Italian tragedy and a review of three recent tragedies – Alessandro Manzoni's 1820 *Il Conte di Carmagnola*, Foscolo's 1813 *Ricciarda*, and Silvio Pellico's 1815 *Francesca da Rimini*. In general, Milman strongly agreed with Foscolo's previously stated opinions on the genre in the "Essay." This should not be surprising; although Foscolo did not write directly to Milman during this period, the two men surely knew each other. Foscolo had written a letter of presentation for Milman to Isabella Teotochi Albrizzi in 1818.[3] In addition, the *Quarterly Review*'s publisher, John Murray, was also the publisher of the "Essay," and he had recently published the 1820 edition of Foscolo's *Ricciarda*. Yet despite the lack of direct evidence supporting Foscolo's involvement with Milman's article, the presence of Foscolo's interpretation of the history of the Italian tragedy should be seen throughout the work.

Milman aptly outlined a complete history of the Italian tragedy throughout his article. He discussed the highlights of the Renaissance to the present day in the first fifteen pages.[4] Milman concluded that the Italian tragedies generally were low-quality works, stating, "Italy has been singularly barren of excellence in the higher walks of the drama. Indeed, with the exception of Alfieri, she has no one great name in tragedy."[5] The author described how, contrary to the English dramatists, the Italians had not used their own historical tales as their subject matter, instead drawing from the stories of the ancient Greeks.[6] He condemned this practice, suggesting that it had been the downfall of the genre in Italy.[7] Milman went on to discuss Scipione Maffei and his 1713 tragedy *Merope*, as well as the works of Alfieri.[8] Although he credited Alfieri with preserving the tradition of Italian tragedy, Milman ascribed numerous defects to him, observing that his steadfast adherence to the three unities was a highly limiting and negative quality.[9]

Milman then turned to late-eighteenth-century Italian tragedies, including the works of Vincenzo Monti, Giovanni Pindemonte, Alessandro Pepoli, and Ippolito Pindemonte. Milman cited Foscolo's 1818 "Essay" (though he understandably attributes it to Hobhouse) to begin his discussion of Monti.[10] He agreed with Foscolo's negative review of Monti, and he concurred in the criticism that Monti shifted his allegiance to whichever government was in power. He further commented – as Foscolo did – on the lack of plot in Monti's *Aristodemo* and the mediocrity of *Galeotto Manfredi*.[11] Milman despaired at how the modern Italian tragedy might have been lost again with the works of Monti, Giovanni Pindemonte, and Pepoli, but for the efforts of Foscolo and Silvio Pellico.[12]

Milman elaborated on this point by enthusiastically praising these two saviours. He explained, "We now arrive at the most recent, and, we are inclined to say, the most successful attempts to found Italian Tragedy upon Italian subjects, the *Ricciarda* of Foscolo, and the *Francesca da Rimini* of Pellico."[13] Foscolo excluded Pellico from his 1818 "Essay," but they had always remained loyal friends. Milman's decision to include Pellico could be interpreted as yet further proof of his connection with Foscolo. In any event, Pellico's tragedy enjoyed success in English literary circles. John Cam Hobhouse became interested in Italian tragedy immediately following the publication of the "Essay," and he translated portions of Pellico's *Francesca da Rimini*, asking Foscolo to review the effort.[14] Beatrice Corrigan argued in her 1954 article "Pellico's 'Francesca da Rimini': The First English Translation" that Milman actually reprinted parts of Hobhouse's incomplete translation of Pellico's work.[15] And Milman was thoroughly impressed by it.[16] He argued that Pellico's tragedy was the perfect example of how Italians should use their own history as the subject matter of their tragedies. Milman wrote, "What they will lose in that conventional grandeur which our imaginations attach to the heroic and mythological ages of Greece, they may gain in the truth and natural eloquence of their delineations from the human heart."[17]

Milman proceeded with a warm review of Foscolo's *Ricciarda*. I believe that the reason for this praise might lie outside the literary content of *Ricciarda* and might actually have been a result of the recent publicity and success of Foscolo's 1820 edition of the work. Milman summarized each act, faulting Foscolo only for his "pregnant style" of verse and repetitive attempts at frightening the audience with the idea that Guelfo was going to harm his daughter.[18] Milman explained that although Foscolo displayed "indeed great mastery over the language," he missed the mark when addressing the spectator's emotions.[19] Milman more than balanced his criticism of these shortcomings, with effusive praise for Foscolo's original characters and the overall impact of *Ricciarda*. He gushed, "But these defects are nobly counterbalanced by the general impression of poetic power which the whole piece bears; by the conception and execution of the characters which appear to us truly tragic and original."[20] Milman further elaborated on Foscolo's innovative characters:

> There is something tremendous in Guelfo, whose vigilant suspicion finds aliment in the most trivial circumstances; and who is so deep in guilt, as to take pride in hardening himself in his atrocity." ... Ricciarda is uniformly pleasing: willing to be the sacrifice, and only anxious that her father may escape the guilt of her death; for this, foregoing even her love for Guido – for this, offering herself to commit suicide." ... [Guido] is more inactive than we should have wished; but there is something imposing in his calm and uniform generosity.[21]

Milman's positive conclusions are based on reading *Ricciarda*. He did not see it performed. His analysis corresponds to the speculation in "Sulla *Ricciarda*" that if the tragedy had been read instead of performed, it likely would have received more praise.[22]

The similarities between Milman's positive treatment of Foscolo and Foscolo's praise of his own work in his 1818 "Essay" are clearly identifiable. For example, Milman encouraged readers to think beyond Foscolo as the author of the novel *Ultime lettere di Jacopo Ortis* – he had many other talents, including (Milman claimed) his prowess as a prominent Italian tragedian. This assertion closely mirrored Foscolo's own self-criticisms in the "Essay."

Milman's account of each of Foscolo's tragedies also echoed Foscolo's own interpretation of those works. He focused on Foscolo's young age when writing *Tieste* and perpetuated the myth that "Alfieri is reputed to have said, 'if the author be only nineteen he will surpass me.'"[23] This angle seems obviously designed to impress readers with the ambitions of a young poet, and it is markedly similar to Foscolo's own commentary in the "Essay" and the 1797 "Notizie storico-critiche sul 'Tieste.'" Like Milman's article, these earlier works focus on Foscolo's youth when discussing his first tragedy.[24] (See chapter 2.)

Milman concluded his lengthy review of the Italian tragedy tradition by commenting on Foscolo's general character. He effusively praised Foscolo's abilities as an intellectual, proclaiming that he was "a scholar in the highest sense of the word."[25] This also invokes Foscolo's self-description in the "Essay": "Foscolo is an excellent scholar."[26] Milman also alluded to Italy's present political predicament – Austrian occupation – while promoting Foscolo's literary fame, again echoing Foscolo's sentiments expressed in the "Essay."[27]

Milman's article has enjoyed notoriety throughout the centuries for one major reason: his negative remarks about Alessandro Manzoni's first tragedy, *Il Conte di Carmagnola* (1820).[28] This book's main subject is Foscolo, and not Manzoni. Yet a brief digression here is warranted. By 1820, Foscolo had sparsely mentioned the young Milanese author. Manzoni had not yet published his tragedy by the time the "Essay" was in print, so it is understandable why Foscolo did not include him. But Foscolo did praise the young Manzoni for his patriotic poetry years earlier, in his 1807 *Dei sepolcri*.[29] In order to understand the context in which Foscolo would write his final theoretical works on Italian tragedy, however, a succinct retelling of Manzoni's first tragedy's reception in Europe merits our attention.

Milman similarly touted the poetic genius of Manzoni in his 1820 article. He concluded, however, that the author was a better poet than tragedian. Milman was decidedly unimpressed with *Il Conte*, and he dedicated only one paragraph of the lengthy thirty-one-page article to Manzoni. He described how Manzoni boldly cut against the Italian neoclassicist tradition and defied the unities of time and place.[30] But Manzoni's innovation was not praiseworthy. Milman ultimately concluded, "We confess our hopes that the author will prefer, in future, gratifying us with splendid odes, rather than offending us by feeble tragedy."[31] The only aspect of Manzoni's "feeble" tragedy praised by Milman is the chorus at the end of act 2, and indeed he followed his sparse commentary with a complete translation of this passage.[32]

Although Milman only dedicated one paragraph to Manzoni, a brief examination of Manzoni's new approach to the tragedy was the subject of Foscolo's response in his final articles on tragedy. In the "Prefazione" to *Il Conte di Carmagnola*, Manzoni explained his shift away from the neoclassical form of tragedy and his rejection of the unities of time and place. He implored that each and every new composition be critiqued not on the basis of rigid or formalistic rules, but instead, on whether or not the author achieved his goals. Nonetheless, despite this neoclassical break, Manzoni insisted on upholding the unity of action and maintaining the separation of the tragic and comic genres. Federica Brunori Deigan remarked in her introduction to her 2004 translation of Manzoni's tragedies that "Manzoni's reason for eliminating the unities [of time and place] was strictly connected with shifting the focus of tragedy away from an abstract and absolute treatment of human passions and toward historical truth."[33] Manzoni proceeded to warn against relying on the unities to create verisimilitude in a tragedy; instead, he argued, the author should create verisimilitude through the imitation of human passions and portrayal of believable sensations.

Manzoni further advocated grounding the action in human rationality. He specifically referred to the Romantic theories of the German intellectual August Wilhelm von Schlegel when explaining his inclusion of the chorus following act 2. Manzoni cited Schlegel's description of the Greek choruses found in Lesson 3 of *Über dramatische Kunst und Literatur* (*Course of Lectures on Dramatic Art and Literature*). He remarked that "the Chorus is to concern itself with the personification of the moral thoughts inspired by the action, like the organ of the feelings of the poet who speaks on behalf of all of humanity."[34]

Manzoni firmly took the helm of the new Romantic school of tragedy. He entered into the Italian Classicists-Romantics debate on the genre by repudiating the neoclassical form. Many European literary journals reviewed Manzoni and his tragedy, including J.J. Victor Chauvet's notoriously harsh review of *Il Conte* in the Parisian journal *Lycée français, Mélanges de littérature et de critique* in the spring of 1820.[35] Chauvet believed that the story of *Il Conte* was utterly ruined by Manzoni's blatant disregard for the unities of time and place. This letter spurred Manzoni to further develop his own tragic theories, and in the following summer of 1820 he responded in a long letter, *Lettre à M. C*** sur l'unité de temps et de lieu dans la tragédie.*[36] Manzoni provided an elaborate historical commentary and proceeded to divide his characters into the categories of "historical" and "invented."[37] This division was Manzoni's significant contribution to the genre and would become the very subject of Foscolo's criticisms in later years.[38]

But before Foscolo would respond, the German literary giant Johann Wolfgang Goethe (1749–1832) entered into the discussion, defending

Manzoni from both Milman's and Chauvet's criticisms. Goethe was no stranger to publically presenting his opinions of the Milanese author. He expressed his admiration for Manzoni's published hymns, the *Inni sacri*, in his 1820 essay "Classicists and Romantics Engaged in Fierce Struggle in Italy" (published in the literary journal *Über Kunst und Althertum*).[39] Goethe returned to the subject of Manzoni and the ongoing Italian Classicists-Romantics literary debate in 1821, in the first issue of the journal *Über Kunst und Altertum*. In his article, "On Criticism," the German intellectual boldly defended Manzoni.[40] He began by citing Milman's paragraph that criticized the Milanese's talents as a tragedian. Goethe proceeded to contradict Milman's analysis and praised every aspect of Manzoni's first tragedy.[41]

Goethe famously distinguished between the destructive and the productive critic in his article. The former blindly applies present rules and expectations to new works, while the latter approaches the work with an open mind and attempts to judge it in the light of its own goals and assumptions.[42] Goethe pointedly used the destructive-critic label when describing Milman. He also presented the famous "three questions" of constructive criticism in his article – "What did the author set out to do? Was his plan reasonable and sensible, and how far did he succeed in carrying it out?"[43] With these questions, Goethe actually quoted (without attribution) the opening paragraph of Manzoni's "Prefazione," in which Manzoni espoused the requirements for good criticism: "quale sia l'intento dell'autore; se questo intento sia ragionevole; se l'autore l'abbia conseguito."[44] Goethe's article brought Manzoni recognition in Europe as one of Italy's foremost tragedians.

Foscolo and the Imitation of Nature

So how did Foscolo react to the new character of Manzoni on the Italian tragic stage? To begin with, the Italian Classicists-Romantics debate presented a bit of a problem for Foscolo. He found it difficult to contribute to the discussion, since he had left Italy in March of 1815, a year before the debate had officially begun in earnest with Madame De Staël (1766–1817) and her illustrious letter published in the *Biblioteca italiana*.[45] It is perfectly understandable that in 1818 Foscolo neglected to include the followers of the Italian Romantic movement in his "Essay on the Present Literature of Italy," instead calling the whole debate an "idle inquiry" – he did not have any memory of the controversy, and therefore, it did not exist for him.[46]

Real-world events also significantly influenced Foscolo's plans to contribute to this literary discourse. Foscolo's lifestyle was extravagant at first upon his arrival in England, but by the early 1820s he could no longer pretend to be wealthy. He was forced to assume numerous aliases and frequently changed residences to avoid creditors. Foscolo gave several paid lectures in 1823 on Italian literature, and in a letter to Silvio Pellico from 30 September 1818, he referred to his lectures *Epoche della lingua Italiana* or *Epochs of the Italian Language*. One of his primary objectives was to ameliorate his deteriorating finances through the lecture series. Foscolo desperately needed the money, but he was concerned with what the members of the elite English literary circles might think of such an endeavour. He expressed this fear about his reputation to his friend Lord John Russell (1792–1887), asking if his new profession as lecturer was undignified. Russell reassured Foscolo in early 1824, advising: "Dear Foscolo, – I think you are quite right to adopt the plan of your friends of giving lectures – it is not in this country any way degrading. Campbell and Sydney Smith have done so very lately."[47] Foscolo was encouraged by this advice. He lectured the English on Italian literature and seized the opportunity to address the unfolding Italian literary debate.

Foscolo divided his lectures into epochs or periods, each representing a specific era in Italian literary history.[48] He came close to providing a single, complete history of Italian literature through these orations, despite the fact that the complete work was never finished, and for several of the later periods, the text consists merely of sketchy notes. Foscolo initially planned to publish each lecture, though only the first nine (spanning the years 1180 to 1600) appeared in print.

Foscolo published the first article of the series, "Principles of poetical criticism, as applicable, more especially, to Italian literature," in the *European Review* of July 1824. "Principles" corresponds to the first lecture of the series, "On the origin and object of poetry." Foscolo built upon the theories that he had previously expressed in his earlier literary-critical works, presenting his general opinions on the form and function of poetry to English literary audiences. He began "Principles" by acknowledging the then-current Classicists-Romantics debate taking place in Italy. Foscolo summarized the two schools of thought as they were represented by their constituent Italian authors. For the most part, he fairly and objectively described the two camps, explaining how each side faulted the other's representation of nature.[49]

Foscolo certainly aligned himself more closely with the neoclassical school. Yet it was not in his best interests to attack the *Romantici* lest he risk the accusation of being out of touch with the contemporary Italian literary movement. This fear was well founded. Foscolo previously had been the target of Ludovico Di Breme's complaints and criticisms about his omission of Romantic authors in his summary of current Italian literary trends in the "Essay."[50] Perhaps as a result, he did not openly endorse his preference for either position in the debate. Instead, Foscolo used the collective "we" to explain that the *European Review*'s opinions did not identify with either group without significant reservation. He specified: "We must either preserve a silent neutrality, or speak at the risk of provoking the two armies to combat against us, who stand alone."[51] Thus, Foscolo avoided the fray, at least on his article's face, preferring to concentrate on the one area of common ground between the two camps – the imitation of nature.[52]

Foscolo asserted that a poet should combine factual and fantastical elements in a seamless fashion so that a reader is unable to distinguish between the two. He argued in favour of balancing poetical fact and fantasy in order to perfect nature.[53] Foscolo observed that if the ideal imagined scene was not grounded in some aspect of the truth, it would be rooted in fantasy and simply not credible. But if the scene was based solely on truth, it would seem like a weak imitation of reality – and not poetry.[54] Foscolo continued by observing that poetry should not be an absolute representation of reality. He believed that it is meant, above all, to be a pleasurable escape from reality for the reader. The reader is therefore denied that pleasing diversion if the poet's imitation of nature is too realistic.[55] Foscolo offered a suggestion for combining truth and imagination to imitate nature, proposing a manner in which a poet could successfully elicit terror in his readers while still imitating nature. He cited Dante's story of Count Ugolino in canto 33 of the *Inferno* as an excellent example of how a poet can blend imagination and truth.[56] Foscolo greatly admired Dante's ability to elicit the sentiment of terror in the reader.

Foscolo's detailed discussion of terror in "Principles" might lend one to believe that he also discussed the genre of tragedy in his article. Yet Foscolo avoided any mention of it. He did, however, return to the notion of *discordia armonica*, which he had described in the 23 February 1813 letter to Silvio Pellico, when defending *Ajace* (see chapter 3). In "Principles," Foscolo discussed the notion of harmonious discord in more general terms, pointing out its role in nature.[57] According to Foscolo, because this sort of harmonious discord exists in nature, a poet had the duty to imitate it. He also warned that poetry would be boring if it only represented facts of real life.[58] Foscolo concluded "Principles" by re-emphasizing a poet's important responsibility to combine truth and imagination in his imitation of nature. He reiterated that it is this refined imitation of nature, not one's affiliation with one school or another, that should govern one's artistic choices.

Public Perception and the Imitation of Nature

Foscolo's desire to please his audience and to avoid confrontation should not be surprising. He famously explained his views on public opinion in 1826, writing, "*Public* opinion is the most powerful instrument in every country for influencing the actions of the great" (his emphasis).[59] Foscolo wanted to appeal to English audiences as an Italian literary authority and, more specifically, an Italian authority on tragedy, immediately following the publication of *Ricciarda*. The poet Thomas Campbell and Foscolo's translator Robert Campbell suggested that if the Italian wanted to further his popularity in England, he should reach out to his English audience and submit an article on English literature in early 1821. Foscolo agreed and published the article "On Hamlet" in Campell's *New Monthly Magazine* in April 1821.[60]

Foscolo focused his analysis of the famous Shakespearean tragedy on the central issue of the Classicists-Romantics literary debate – the imitation of nature. Shakespeare, of course, was one of the most beloved figures during the Romantic period, and in 1818, Samuel Taylor Coleridge (1772–1834) re-stoked English interest with lectures on the legendary playwright. Throughout early-nineteenth-century Europe, Shakespeare symbolized the voice of the popular writer for the Romantics, unbound by the confining rules upheld by the followers of the neoclassical school.

Foscolo's appreciation of Shakespeare differed from that of the new Romantic poets. Foscolo respected Shakespeare's contributions to poetry and literary history, but he was unsympathetic to Shakespeare's disregard for the Aristotelian unities. Nevertheless, Foscolo viewed the English icon from a historical, or Vichian, point of view: Shakespeare was a primitive poet who, like Homer and Dante, can be seen a significant cornerstone of his nation's literary history, regardless of his adherence to any classical rules.[61]

Foscolo's "On Hamlet" relies heavily on other European discussions of the tragedy. He began the article with an English translation of a passage from Goethe's *Wilhelm Meisters Wandeljahre*.[62] The passage from Goethe's novel that opens Foscolo's article involves the protagonist, the actor Wilhelm, preparing for the role of Hamlet. Wilhelm summarizes the tragedy and offers his own opinions on the character. He muses on the delicate, yet consistent, psychological nature of Hamlet.[63] For Wilhelm, Hamlet is "an oak tree planted in a china vase" – too fragile to take on such weighty action and he is more or less the same character throughout the tragedy.[64]

Foscolo expressed his own opinions on Hamlet's complexities after this translation. He centred his article on the imitation of nature, especially focusing on a discussion of the opinion of the inestimable poet-critic Samuel Johnson (1709–84). Johnson had argued that Hamlet's actions were consistent with those of a person dealing with grave circumstances (i.e., the murder of his father) in his famous 1765 note on *Hamlet*. There is no reason to suspect that Shakespeare portrayed the Danish prince as mad – rather, Johnson believed that he was faithfully mirroring the human nature of a person living through such trying times. He also touched upon Shakespeare's skill at mirroring life and the common nature of his characters in his 1765 preface to his edition of the Bard of Avon's works.[65] Foscolo clearly relied on this assessment of Shakespeare's accurate portrayal of human nature in "On Hamlet." Hamlet's actions may *seem* sporadic and *appear* to be the workings of a madman, but on closer examination they are easily explained as the direct result of the circumstances affecting him. Foscolo agreed with Johnson in his analysis – Shakespeare is the master at imitating human nature, especially the most difficult, seemingly "inconsistent," aspects of humanity. Foscolo concluded "On Hamlet" by acknowledging Shakespeare's unparalleled poetic prowess, observing that "the character of Hamlet, though perfectly true to nature throughout, is one to which Shakespeare alone perhaps could have done justice."[66]

The actual content of "On Hamlet" is worthy of note – about half of the text is the translation from Goethe. Foscolo's critical opinions (even those agreeing with Johnson) were few and far between. Regardless of his rationale for including the character Wilhelm's analysis, it is also interesting that Foscolo does not comment extensively on Goethe's opinions. In his article, Foscolo makes a simple and vague statement that "the main idea on which the foregoing estimate of Hamlet's character is supported, appears to me to be very accurately conceived."[67] But he does not specify what this "main idea" is, and does not elaborate on Wilhelm's musings. The absence of substantive commentary suggests that perhaps Foscolo did not completely understand Goethe's text and merely was agreeing with the reputed critic in an effort to be seen as sufficiently erudite.

This theory is consistent with much of the available evidence. In his 1928 article "Un articolo shakespeareano di Ugo Foscolo," Vittorio Cian claims that Foscolo was not able to read or speak German, and therefore he questions Foscolo's understanding of Goethe's work.[68] As for the English translation of that passage of Goethe's text, Cian does not attribute it to Foscolo or his translator, Robert Talbot; instead, he credits the Scottish essayist Thomas Carlyle (1795–1881), who published a translation of *Wilhelm Meisters Wandeljahre* in 1824. Like Foscolo, Carlyle was a frequent guest at Holland House, and several years before the publication of his translation, he circulated drafts to various members of the group, eliciting suggestions. It is at least plausible that the opening English translation of Goethe's work was based, to some extent, on Carlyle's work in progress.

These language difficulties might easily have led Foscolo to include the Goethean passage without fully comprehending the text. After all, at the time of publication of "On Hamlet," both Goethe's and Johnson's opinions on Shakespeare were generally accepted by the English literary circles. "On Hamlet" essentially reinforces most of the specifics of Goethe's and Johnson's previously stated literary opinions. Foscolo agreed without reservation with Goethe's analogy of Hamlet as a fragile china vase containing an oak tree. Likewise, he agreed with Johnson about Shakespeare's accurate portrayal of nature. It is a simple and safe analysis that would not upset or offend the English reader – perhaps not a surprising result, given that one of Foscolo's goals was to endear himself as a serious critic to the same English public. This article therefore might best be seen as Foscolo's attempt to convey to the public that he was knowledgeable of the critical history of Hamlet and of the works of Goethe and Johnson, and most importantly, of England's great sixteenth-century playwright.

Foscolo, Goethe, and Manzoni

Foscolo's reverence for Goethe was short lived. He made it a priority to respond to the German literary giant after Florence's Giuseppe Molini published his 1825 edition of Manzoni's tragedies *Il Conte di Carmagnola* and *Adelchi* (1822), along with Goethe's defence of Manzoni.[69] Foscolo weighed in on the debate more than a year later in what many critics believe to be his most original and forward-thinking literary-critical work, "Della nuova scuola drammatica italiana" (begun in 1826).[70] Foscolo began the ultimately unfinished essay for John Bowring, editor of the *Westminster Review*, who had requested a piece on Manzoni. As it grew, Foscolo began to think of turning "Della nuova scuola" into a "little book" (*libretto*) entitled *On Literary Criticism*. He never completed the article (much less this entire planned book), but in this final work he nonetheless managed to hone and present his opinions on (1) tragedy, (2) the imitation of nature, and (3) the role of the critic. The result was far from inconsequential. René Wellek, in his *History of Modern Criticism: 1750–1950*, hailed "Della nuova scuola" as "the most brilliant flash of Foscolo's critical activity."[71] Indeed, Foscolo's "Della nuova scuola" was more than a mere response to Goethe and critique of Manzoni – it was the critical culmination of the author's lifelong preoccupation with tragedy and literary criticism.

In "Della nuova scuola," Foscolo acknowledged the two competing schools and summed up their conflict by noting its focus on the imitation of nature.[72] Foscolo returned to his 1824 "Principles," discussing the poetic concept of the imitation of nature. But this time, he directly addressed the tension between the Classicists and Romantics. He pondered whether the term "imitation" had ever been well defined, and if the word "nature" could ever even be defined.[73] Foscolo answered this rhetorical question by again arguing that imitation was accomplished through an equal and seamless combination of realistic and fantastic elements.[74] Foscolo described the cold and ordinary – and certainly uninteresting – nature of a wholly truthful and accurate representation of nature. He advocated the inclusion of the fantastical with the truthful in order to create a sense of *meraviglia*, or wonder.[75] Foscolo insisted that a poet could not solely rely on historical facts, but instead must also include creative components in order to imitate nature poetically.

Foscolo went one step further in "Della nuova scuola" than he previously had by fundamentally defending Italian literature against foreign commentary. Contrary to the suggestions offered by Madame de Staël in her 1816 article "Sulla maniera e l'utilità delle traduzioni," Foscolo urged his countrymen *not* to rely on foreigners for guidance in matters of literature. He argued that Italians should not look to the French or German or even English models of the modern tragedian when composing their own *Italian* tragedies.[76] Foscolo did not approve of foreigners, and especially Germans, defining "good" Italian literature. Accordingly, in his "Della nuova scuola" he attempted to bring his Italian colleagues together against one common enemy: the foreign critic. In his mind, Goethe had no business commenting on a literary debate between Italians concerning Italian literature.[77] Foscolo implored Italians to ignore Goethe's evaluation of Manzoni and the Italian Classicists-Romantics debate altogether because Goethe was a foreigner and not Italian, and he could not truly understand literature written in another language.

Foscolo instead proposed that Italians should imitate the tragedies of Alfieri – the quintessential neoclassical *Italian* tragedian. He further observed the existing similarities between then-contemporary Italian tragedies and Alfieri's.[78] Foscolo went on, in what would prove to be the remainder of "Della nuova scuola" to dismissing the literary distinctions of the two competing schools. He even went so far as to imply that Alfieri might even be deemed to be a Romantic tragedian. But Foscolo's final assessment is that Alfieri should not be labelled either Classicist or Romantic. Indeed, he blurs the lines between the two schools in order to make his final reflections on literary history.

This re-evaluation of Alfieri is surprising but understandable given Foscolo's overwhelming preoccupation with his own popularity. He was an Alfierian by training, and therefore he inevitably was seen as a member of the "old school" of tragedy by most critics. Yet if Foscolo could succeed in refashioning Alfieri as the first *Romantic* tragedian, he would necessarily become part of this new and more popular group. So by arguing that Alfieri's works were a perfect example of the modern Italian tragedy, Foscolo was also, at the same time, attempting to legitimize his own efforts.

Foscolo concluded in "Della nuova scuola" that Italian literary movements are primarily based on what is fashionable at any given period in history, and these trends rise and fall in popularity to reflect the changed attitudes of the public. He speculated that even though it was fashionable at the time for his colleague poets to deify Dante, future generations might laugh at this idolatry, just as Foscolo's contemporaries mocked the *petrarchisti* of an earlier era. He explained:

Style in Italy is an object of fashion; changing once from century to century, or maybe from month to month ... Now the idol is Dante, they justly say, and I believe it; but when one thinks about the devotions that Petrarch

> won in another time, it would not seem odd to predict that the decedents
> looking back to the present mania of *dantifying* will mock us, like we mock
> the Petrarchists of another century. (Foscolo's emphasis)[79]

For Foscolo, there was no potential benefit in supporting either side of the tragedy debate; both schools would – or at least could – become unfashionable in the years to come. Foscolo instead concluded that the universality of the effective imitation of nature (i.e., the "heart" of a tragedian's purpose) would remain fashionable forever.

Foscolo not only provided a possible new interpretation of the Italian tragedy canon, but also anticipated a new, modern approach to literary criticism with his rereading of Alfieri's seminal tragedy. It is a critical approach that De Sanctis later employed in his 1870–1 *Storia della letteratura italiana* – one primarily centred on capturing the spirit of an author and his times, and not an adherence to any formal set of rules. Foscolo's critical writing here signals an important turning point in the history of Italian literary criticism from the encyclopaedic to the passionate. He illustrated, in a very clear fashion, the complexity and intensity of what it meant to define Italian identity in the period leading up to the Risorgimento.

Yet Foscolo was writing from outside Italy and for a non-Italian audience. His physical marginalization did not, however, dissuade him from actively participating in the cultural debates of his time. On the contrary, he was perhaps better equipped to address these debates precisely because of his unique perspective from outside of Italy. Foscolo was actively working to shape English opinions of Italian literature. He was able to defend his own artistic choices and simultaneously bolster Italian cultural identity with his critical writings.

And there at the centre of it all remained tragedy. Foscolo concluded his thirty-year preoccupation with tragedy with his final critical reflections in England. Each of his writings on tragedy on its own is not especially prominent. In the aggregate, however, they paint a more cohesive portrait of the figure of Ugo Foscolo.

Epilogue

The final years of Ugo Foscolo's life were marked by dramatic emotional highs and lows. He experienced immense joy with his estranged daughter, Floriana, who entered into his life in 1821, following the death of her maternal grandmother, with whom she lived. The father and daughter lived together in Foscolo's custom-designed home, "Digamma Cottage," in Regent's Park. His lavish tastes and expenditures provided brief moments of pleasure. But this new-found happiness was short lived, when in 1824 Foscolo and Floriana were forced to leave the villa due to his outrageous debts. Foscolo lived beyond his means and was forced to don various masks and assume numerous aliases.[1] He ran from creditors for much of the rest of his life.

Foscolo continued to write and to teach in an effort to ameliorate his dire financial situation. He even gave Italian lessons at the Quaker school for girls.[2] Foscolo published his last two articles in 1827: "Memoirs of Casanova" (*Westminster Review*) and "History of the Democratical [*sic*] Constitution of Venice" (*Edinburgh Review*). The city in which he first entered into the world of the Italian theatre apparently was on his mind while he was working on "Della nuova scuola drammatica italiana."

This "return to Venice" was bittersweet, however, and Foscolo's financial woes were not the worst of his troubles. For most of his life, he was plagued with poor health, which only worsened in the English climate. By 1827 he had moved to the London suburb of Turnham Green, where he would spend the final days of his life. Foscolo's health was at its worst in June, when he was so physically depleted and exhausted that he spent countless hours in bed, drifting in and out of troubled sleep. Foscolo's doctors, Gaetano Negri and George Frederick Collier, informed the exile that he was suffering from dropsy in the first days of August. He endured many excruciatingly painful treatments over the next month. Foscolo ultimately succumbed to the dropsy following an operation to treat it on 10 September 1827. He was buried in the Chiswick churchyard. Following the unification of Italy, Foscolo's remains were reinterred alongside those of other famous Italians in the church of Santa Croce in Florence on 24 June 1871.

Foscolo's literary renown fundamentally rests with his *Ultime lettere di Jacopo Ortis* and his *Dei sepolcri* for their patriotic sentiments and intense desire to foster a collective Italian identity. Perhaps mostly due to these works, he was elevated to the standing of national hero during the Risorgimento and has since enjoyed an almost mythical status as one of Italy's most celebrated literary figures. Yet his work in the tragic genre should not be overlooked.

It is true that Foscolo's recognition in this field remained elusive in Italy. The Italian literary elite and the public insisted on relying on more persuasive evidence than his own preoccupation with tragedy to evaluate Foscolo's prowess – his mediocre and relatively unsuccessful tragedies themselves. Italian audiences' and the critics' tastes of the period turned away from Foscolo's tragedies. They no longer revered the Alfierian form of tragedy on which Foscolo predominantly relied when composing all three of his tragedies. They certainly were not receptive to Foscolo's homage to Homer, both in robust verse and in excessive length, in *Ajace*. And they were unforgiving to poor *Ricciarda*, whose abysmal acting and actual catastrophic conclusion trumped Foscolo's attempt at contributing a tragedy all about love to the Italian tragedy tradition. He clearly did not become the canonical figure that he strove to be in this genre.

But whether or not he achieved recognition as a tragedian is irrelevant and inconsequential when the reader looks beyond Foscolo's actual tragedies. His later writings on tragedy and on Italian literary history actually allowed Foscolo to reinsert himself into the Italian canon as a tragedian. For this reason alone, he was not a complete failure in the genre. To the contrary, Foscolo managed to achieve a surprising level of success as a literary critic working on, among other topics, the tragedy during the years he was self-exiled in England.

Alas, even this foreign success did not long outlive Foscolo. Evidence appeared in London's *Foreign Quarterly Review* by 1832 that Foscolo's legacy as a prominent Italian authority on tragedy did not stand the test of time. In his article "Foscolo and His Times," the soldier-turned-writer

André Vieusseux accurately portrayed Foscolo's third tragedy as mediocre, and decisively put an end to *Ricciarda*'s successful run in England. Vieusseux wrote: "Foscolo, persisting in his dramatic attempts, in spite of former failures, wrote a third tragedy, *Ricciarda*, a subject from middle age history. It has the same faults as the other two, poverty of invention, monotony of tone, and want of dramatic interest. The language is fine, and the verse harmonious. But his literary fame will not rest on his dramas."[3] Likewise, Mary Shelley echoed this ultimate judgment in her 1835 biography of Foscolo in the widely read *Lives of the Most Eminent Literary and Scientific Men of Italy, Spain and Portugal* (volume 2). She concluded, "As an author, he may be said to be a bad tragedian, and not a good novelist; but he was an elegant writer, conversant with the depths and the refinements of the human heart."[4]

Shelley's nuanced and forthright assessment is particularly notable. Lia Guerra convincingly demonstrated in 2005 how Foscolo's self-representation in the "Essay" served as the primary source for Shelley's biography.[5] But the biographer did not merely regurgitate Foscolo's words. She decisively rejected the exile's positively spun portrayal of his tragedies. Shelley departed from Foscolo's self-design and affirmed his failed status as a tragedian. She was cognizant of his efforts at self-promotion, and she took a more clear-headed view of his prowess as a tragedian and the characterization of our subject as a self-absorbed figure. This was an honest, albeit complex, critical assessment of Foscolo's tragedies.

Scholarly recognition of Foscolo's self-promotion must not be seen as a condemnation of the author. On the contrary, if anything, it assists with illustrating the interesting and important times in which he lived. Shelley clearly and unapologetically supported this interpretation of Foscolo, characterizing him, along with Alfieri and Monti, as one of the three greatest modern Italian authors. Yet, her praise was tempered with the equally strong assertion that Foscolo was vain and "impelled to produce and reproduce himself."[6] She continued:

> And yet to this assertion we must put some limit, for Foscolo was a man of learning and taste, and he was capable of giving light to compositions formed by the rules of art, and adorned by the graces culled from an intimate knowledge of the finest of human works. But vanity was still the mainspring, – a vanity accompanied by honesty of principle and independence of soul, and yet which was vanity – the worship of the self – the making his own individuality the mirror in which the world was reflected.[7]

But what do we do with this seemingly contradictory evaluation? One approach is to return to the historical context in which Foscolo lived. A perfect storm of sorts emerged, capable of sparking an author's simultaneous positive and negative reception. The viral impact of contemporary mass media (journalism), the emergence of literary histories and the surge in self-representation all converged throughout late-nineteenth- and early-nineteenth-century Europe. Scholars must equally weigh these factors, combined with a conventional reading of a particular literary work's compositional merits. Evaluation of a particular work alone only scratches at the historical reality in which it was produced. This type of reading also limits our understanding of a particular work's influence on an author and his or her future writings. But fortunately in the case of Foscolo the tragedian, he left many articles and commentaries that when examined in conjunction with his tragedies, his epistolary accounts, and contemporary reviews of his work provide a more complete portrait of the canonical author.

This book aimed to address Foscolo's multifarious nature with an analysis of Foscolo the tragedian. Employing a critically sensitive and nuanced literary-historical and biographical analysis, I have illustrated Foscolo's complex, yet undeniably vain, personality, literary prowess, and preoccupation with tragedy for the majority of his life. The book opens the door to interpreting Foscolo by examining the intersection of both his writings on tragedy and this vanity, but it by no means completes the study. It has been my intention to spark future inquiry to urge scholars to continue to unpack the complex figure of Foscolo from new perspectives. Foscolo's own prolific and diverse corpus of work requires such continued devotion. He should be remembered (though not necessarily revered) as more than just the author of *Ultime lettere di Jacopo Ortis* and *Dei sepolcri*. Only then will Foscolo find some sense of redemption from the suffering he endured while pursuing his tragic vision.

Original Reviews of *Ajace*

1. Francesco Pezzi, *Corriere Milanese*, 10 December 1811, 1179–1180.

NOTIZIE INTERNE
Regno d'Italia
Milano 10 dicembre

Jeri a sera i commedianti italiani hanno rappresentato l'AJACE, nuova tragedia del sig. *Ugo Foscolo*. La folla degli spettatori era straordinaria: l'ampio ricinto del nostro grande teatro non bastò a contenerla tutta; molte persone furono obbligate di ritornarsene indietro per mancanza di posto. Il pubblico ascoltò in silenzio tutta la recita, talchè quelli ch'erano collocati il più da lungi, hanno potuto comprendere facilmente dalla prima all'ultima parola. S'udì talvolta batter le mani ad alcune sentenze, a qualche immagine ben colorita, e a certi squarci di poesia che il meritavano. Moderati furono gli applausi fra un atto e l'altro. Appena terminate la tragedia, il pubblico stanco dall'eccessiva prolissità del componimento, soprattuto dell'atto 5, ed impaziente d'uscir del teatro, dopo avervi fatto una sì lunga ed incomoda stazione, non manifestò il suo giudizio con verun' segno d'aggradimento; ma due minuti dopo, parecchi di quegli spettatori ch'erano rimasti, si mossero a batter le mani, e fu allora che s' intese qualche indiscreto ed anco ingiusto fischio mescolarsi coi plausi. Ma quest'ultimi furono vittoriosi; la procella parve dissiparsi, e tre degli attori hanno creduto bene di comparire sul palco scenico per ringraziare i plaudenti. La tragedia di replica questa sera.

2. Lattanzi, *Corriere delle Dame*, 14 December 1811, 425–6.

R. Teatro Della Scala

Quanto sia difficil cosa l'ottenere il voto comune del pubblico, e quanto più difficile sia il tessere una perfetta tragedia, lo hanno sperimentato molti scrittori, e fra questi recentemente il Sig. Ugo Foscolo, cui niuno contrasta feracità d'ingegno, e dignità di stile. È difficile l'immaginarsi l'affollamento degli spettatori, che attirati dalla meritata riputazione del Sig. Foscolo, accorsero ad udire lunedì scorso la sua nuova Tragedia l'*Ajace*; come pure a quelli che non vi assistettero riescirà difficile il credere che il Sig. Foscolo non ottenesse pieni, e generali applausi. Prescindendo dalle varie osservazioni che varj han fatte, esternerò francamente, e brevemente la mia opinione. Il Sig. Foscolo ha scelto un soggetto più favoloso che storico. Essendo sterile l'argomento in cui aggirasi la condotta de' primi personaggi, e particolarmente di Ajace ambizioso di ottenere le armi del morto Achille, era quasi impossibile al Sig. Foscolo di trar partito dal movimento delle passioni che più valgono ad interessare gli spettatori. Per quanto egli abbia ben sostenuta la dignità di carattere in Agamennone, ed in Ajace, altrettanto l'ha avvilita in Ulisse, ed in Calcante: il primo lo fa comparire un basso intricante da commedia, ed il secondo, nell'atto quinto principalmente, lo trasforma da Sacerdote in Telegrafo, facendogli narrare dall'alto di una collina alla moglie di Ajace, che trovasi nella pianura, gli accidenti li più minuti d'una lontana battaglia fra i greci, ed i trojani. Il Sig. Foscolo sentiva bene che doveva per necessità scolarsi dalla storia e dalla favola, che dimonstrano essersi Ajace crudele, bestiale, ed impetuoso, ucciso come un pazzo, e non come un Eroe; ma a parer mio avrebbe con miglior effetto condotta la sua tragedia se si fosse attenuto all'opinione di molti, che dicono aver Ulisse di concerto con Agamennone fatto uccidere Ajace. Qual vasta risorsa non avrebbe allora trovata egli nel giro dell'andamento, e nelle passioni del despota Agamennone, e dell'astuto Ulisse? Queste mie ingenue avvertenze nulla tolgono al merito poetico del Sig. Foscolo, sia per la elocuzione, che per le sentenze ed immagini di che ha dato nuovo e luminoso saggio in questa tragedia.

3. *Giornale Italiano*, 15 December 1811, 1395–6.

Milano, Domenica, 15 Dicembre 1811
VARIETÀ

L'*Ajace*, tragedia del sig. Ugo Foscolo già da lungo tempo annunziata fu finalmente esposta nella sera del giorno nove sulle scene di questo R. Teatro della Scala, e fu pure riprodotta nella susseguente. Forse non mai fu questo Teatro si ridondante di spettatori, nè mai sì grande fu la pubblica aspettazione. Noto già l'autore di essa pel suo igengno, per la fervida sua immaginazione e pel *Tieste*, altra tragedia da lui composta negli anni giovanili, ci avea destato la curiosità di vedere ciò ch'egli fatto avrebbe in età più matura, e dopo un lungo studio su gli umani affetti, e sui più famosi tragici specialmente della Grecia. La sua tragedia però non riscosse quella corona, a cui sembrava di dover aspirare, e malgrado alcuni pregi che in essa risplendono, lasciò o freddo, o indifferente il cuore degli affollati spettatori. Noi ben lungi dall'alzarci in censori, ci faremo anzi a brevemente rintracciare d'onde mai avvento sia, che questa tragedia ottenuto non abbia l'effetto che ne attendevamo; e ciò faremo noi tanto più volontieri, quanto che le nostre osservazioni servire potranno di avvertimento all'autore nella tragica carriera, per la quale sembra che voglia incamminarsi.

L'*Ajace furioso* è uno di que' difficili argomenti, che mentre dimostrano il lodevole ardire di chi ha il coraggio di trattarli, ne rendono ad un tempo assai periglioso il cimento. Sofocle il più grande de' tragici della Grecia non potè in esso riescire che coll'introdurvi il personaggio di Minerva, e col dividere la favola quasi in due azioni, nella prima delle quali si espone il contrasto per le armi di Achille, nella seconda la disputa pel cadavere di Ajace, al quale gli Atridi accordare non volevano l'onoro del sepolcro. La *macchina* di una divinità, e questa quasi doppia azione, artifici ch'essere poteano accetti ai Greci, non lo sono egualmente per noi, nè perciò la tragedia di Sofocle fu esente da qualche censura anche presso gli antichi. Forse il desiderio di fare meglio eccitò l'ingengno di altri scrittori a maneggiare lo stesso argomento, e fra essi vuoli essere nominato Cesare Augusto. Ma questi dopo d'avere incominciato il suo *Ajace*, abbandonò l'impresa forse convinto delle difficoltà ch'essa presentava. Più ardito e più felice di Augusto il sig. Foscolo condusse a fine la sua tragedia, schivò la macchina del personaggio di una deità, non meno che il difetto di una seconda azione, e tutta aggirò la sua favola sulle furiose smanie di Ajace. Ma esso con questo artifizio resi i primi tre atti presso che totalmente privi di azione, a cui fu costretto di supplire con una certa oratoria o lirica declamazione, che alletare può bensì gli orecchi coll'armonia de' numeri e de' versi, ma non mai scuotere e commovere altamente il cuore, unico scopo della tragica poesia. Ecco il primo difetto della tragedia del nostro poeta. Noi dunque spargeremo di giuste lodi lo stile e i versi di questi tre primi atti; e lode ancor maggiore accorderemo alla bella scena fra Agammenone, Ajace, ed Ulisse nel terzo atto, scena che per la forza delle sentenze riscosse i più grandi applausi anche dal pubblico spettatore. Eguali lodi meriterebbe pure la scena fra Agammenone e Calcante nell'atto secondo, se non lasciasse travedere una troppo servile imitazione di una simile scena nel Saulle di Alfieri.

Negli altri due atti il poeta tenta di rendere più viva e commovente la sua tragedia coll'artificio di Ulisse che allontanò del campo Teucro il fratello, ed il più caro amico di Ajace spargendo contro di lui neri sospetti di fellonìa; e coll'introdurre ad imitazione di Sofocle il personaggio di Tecmessa già schiava e poi sposa di Ajace. Noi non negheremo che questi due artifici non siano atti e destare gradi affetti, e che la civile discordia e pugna che nasce dal primo, e la conseguente strage delle greche schiere non debba forse anche anterporsi al macello, che presso di Sofocle viene dal furibondo Ajace fatto del gregge e degli armenti. Ma in questi due atti più non si parla delle armi di Achille, che sono pure la base della favola, e, nel quinto, Ajace s'immerge nel seno il brando per tutt'altro motivo, che per la disperazione che le armi fatali state siano aggiudicate ad Ulisse; nè di esse più si parla se non nelle ultime parole di Teucro ritornato dalla battaglia, e quando Ajace di già ferito trovasi agli ultimi aneliti della vita. Pare che quivi il nostro poeta dimenticato siasi di quel precetto del Venosino

Aut famam sequere, aut sibi convenientia finge.

Un argomento mitologico e già consecrato dall'autorità de' più insigni poeti, o non debb'essere trattato, ed espor si debbe scrupolosamente secondo l'opinione, che domina da lungo tempo inalterabile nelle genti. Tale è il secondo difetto dell'Ajace del sig. Foscolo. Al precetto di Orazio pare che si oppongano pure i caratteri di Ulisse e di Agammenone. Il primo è rappresentato e da Omero, e dagli altri scrittori come un uomo astuto bensì, ma però grande e sempre eroe. Presso di Sofocle, Ulisse sostiene sempre la nobilità del suo carattere, ed egli medesimo con quella saggia facondia, ch'era propria di lui, estingue lo sdegno del maggiore Atride, e lo dissuade dall'inveire contro l'estinto Ajace. Nella tragedia del sig. Foscolo, Ulisse non è più il saggio figlio di Laerte, ma un vile adulatore del Re dei Regi, un ambizioso che si fa reo de' più bassi stratagemmi, uno scellerato che nulla tralascia per ottenere il suo intento. D'Agammenone poi ha voluto il nostro autore un ambizioso politico modellato più sui precetti di Machiavello e di Hobbes, che sull'archetipo che viene da Omero presentato. Presso Sofocle, Tecmessa per distorre Ajace dal disperato divisamento fa uso de'più teneri affetti, nè si dimentica di richiamargli l'imagine del pargoletto Eurisaceo: Ajace ne è sì commosso, che pur chiede d'abbracciare l'innocente figlio, e finalmente ritirarsi fingendo di voler purificarsi in un fonte lustrale, e seppellire il brando di Ettore, e quindi si uccide. Il sig. Foscolo fa che l'Eroe fugga dall vista della sposa per non funestarla colla sua morte. Quale di questi due artifici è più degno del nipote di Alcide?

Come difettoso venne pure censurato il lungo e freddo soliloquio di Ajace allorchè sta per uccidersi, ed il prolisso dialogo in cui egli ha parte dopo d'essersi ferito. Pare che la disperazione non debba dar luogo a tanti riflessi, nè a tante apostrofi quante sono quivi in bocca di Ajace furioso. Ben più saggiamente Ovidio non fa dire al suo Eroe che le seguenti terribili parole:

......, arripit ensem
Et meus hic certe est: an et hunc sibi poscet Ulysses?
Iloc, ait, uteudum est in me mihi; quique cruore
Saepe Phrygum maduit, domini nunc caede madebit,
Ne quisquam Ajacem possit superare, nisi Ajax.

Tali sono, se noi non andiamo errati, le ragioni per cui questa tragedia non fu accolta con quegli applausi che sembrava doversi aspettare. Maggior campo di gloria si aprirà forse il nostro autore, se abbandonando i mitologici argomenti rivolgerà il suo ingegno a quelli che trarre si possono dalla storia. Allorchè dal pubblico di Parigi fu freddamente accolto il quinto atto dell'Oreste di Voltaire, troppo fedele imitazione del greco, *c'est pourtant Sophocle*, diceva l'autore a madame de Graffigny, e questa gli rispose colla piacevole parodìa di un verso delle *Femmes savantes*:
Excusez nous, monsieur, nous ne sommes pas Grecs.

A.C.

4. Urbano Lampredi, *Il Poligrafo*, 15 December 1811, 589–92.

IL TEATRO ALLA SCALA
AJACE, Tragedia nuovissima del sig. Ugo Foscolo

Esciva io la sera del 9 dal Teatro della Scala, premuto d'ogni parte dalla grandissima folla di persone accorse ad udire la novissima Tragedia di Ugo Foscolo, intitolata l'Ajace, quando fra le varie osservazioni, che l'uno a l'altro faceva,[1] due ne udii, che si attirarono la mia attenzione. Voltosi un uomo di bella presenza al suo vicino – *Io per me*, diss'egli in buon Milanese, *non ho potuto capire perchè Ajace siasi data la morte … Ciò per me a nulla monta*, rispose l'altro, con un tal poco di cattiva cera; *Io mi sono annojato moltissimo, e la Tragedia mi è sembrata troppo lunga.* Dopo questo discorso gli perdei ambedue di vista, e distrigatomi dalla calca, e postomi a considerare sopra questi due diversi giudizj, mi parve di intravedere che, quantunque a prima vista sembrassero disparati, pure esser potevano due conseguenze diverse d'un medesimo principio. Allettato da questo barlume, mi sforzai di richiamare al pensiero i fondamenti dell'Arte, ed a farne l'applicazione al Dramma rappresentato. Il discorso che intendo fare al pubblico in questo Articolo, ed in altri ancora, se troppo lungo mi venisse, non è che la semplice esposizione di quanto mi venne in mente per conciliare questi due giudizj, che ho poi trovato conformi a quelli della maggior parte degli Spettatori.

E siccome quando vuolsi ragionare sopra un suggetto qualunque, bisogna fondare il discorso sopra la definizione delle idee principali, così, io domandai a me stesso. Che cosa è un Dramma Tragico? Egli è un Dialogo grave e sostenuto fra diverse persone di alto affare sopra un fatto importante, i cui accidenti o narrati o rappresentati, destano negl'interlocutori diverse forti passioni, le quali passano nell'animo degli Ascoltanti, che a quell'azione vivamente s'interessano. Perchè dunque appena viene annunziata la rappresentazione d'un Dramma, particolarmente se sia nuovo, tutti accorrono il folla a goderne? Perchè, come dice Schlegel, l'*attività è il vero godimento della vita, anzi è la vita stessa.*[2] Ma siccome non possiamo continuamente operare, perchè tanto il corpo quanto lo spirito nostro hanno bisogno d'un tempo di riposo per riprendere nuove forze, così per supplire alla mancanza attuale di azione, nella quale azione consiste il godimento della vita, e la qual mancanza di godimento chiamasi *noja*, così ci affrettiamo ad assistere ad uno spettacolo, affinché non potendo operare, e cangiare il nostro stato d'animo per noi stessi, altri con la loro azione suppliscano alla mancanza della nostra, cioè in una parola, vogliamo vivere per due o tre ore a spese del Poeta, e degli Attori. Tanto più grande dunque sarà il piacer nostro, e però tanto minore la noja, quanto più viva, e ben condotta sarà l'azione; cioè quanto più saranno i cambiamenti di stato negli attori per i quali l'azione si affretta progressivamente all'evento, ed allora essendo noi passati per questi diversi stati e generi di passione, possiamo dire d'aver vissuto, perchè da questi cambiamenti appunto è stata sbandita la noja, che minacciava d'invaderci. Pertanto se il Poeta non disegna e non conduce bene la sua azione, talchè sia verosimile nella sua totalità, e ben connessa nelle sue parti, se ne' suoi personaggi non si vedono quei caratteri, e nelle loro parlate quella scelta di pensieri, che convengono all'azione stessa, e che la fanno procedere al suo fine per passioni successivamente destate, se in una parola parla il Poeta, e non l'Attore, allora non vi ha più illusione, l'azione illanguidisce, e l'anima dello Spettatore non si occupa più, e si annoja; allora finalmente non si sa perchè Ajace sia morto.

Posti tali principi inconcussi, diamo un'occhiata al disegno e economia della Tragedia del sig. U. F. ed ai caratteri de' suoi personaggi. Si trattava d'imitare l'azione, cioè la serie de' fatti che condussero Ajace ad ammazzarsi. S'introduce dunque nel primo Atto, Ulisse, che astutamente procura d'indisporre Agamennone contro Ajace, già indisposto, nè si sa perchè, e disporlo in suo favore, onde a lui sien date le armi d'Achille. Poscia Ulisse stesso (nè s'intese bene con quali arti)[3] inganna Teucro fratello d'Ajace, e lo induce a partire del campo coi suoi Saettieri. Fin quì nessun interesse nè per le armi, nè per Ajace. Nell'Atto secondo, Agamennone alterca con Calcante per sue private passioni, e si parla d'Ajace, e dell'armi, ma in maniera che gli Uditori non possono molto interessarvisi, perchè si riferisce a fatti accaduti durante la spedizione, e non relativi all'azione presente. Sopragiunge Ajace, che vede in Agamennone un Carlo V che aspira alla monarchia universale, e si mostra tutt'altro, che il propugnacolo degli Achei. E neppur fin quì nessun o poco interesse nè per Ajace, nè per l'armi. Nel terzo Atto, Ulisse fa un freddo, ed artificioso racconto di quanto è accaduto nel parlamento, e narra che il parlamento[4] stesso ha statuito, che le armi sarebbero aggiudicate dai Re prigionieri (eranvi prigionieri, ma non Regi) conformemente al volere d'Agamennone, il quale dimostra con ciò la sua imparzialità, mentre il Poeta ha insinuato fin quì tutto il contrario. Si noti poi che i Greci, allorché introducono alcuno a fare un racconto, non usano d'introdurre mai un personaggio interessato al fatto, ma un messaggero, che non abbia una parte essenziale nel fatto, perchè non si sospetti che possa alterarlo. Quindi comparisce Ajace infuriato non già per le armi d'Achille, ma perché non trova il fratello Teucro nel campo; ed ecco un nuovo interesse nel Protagonista. Nel IV Atto lunghe declamazioni fra Calcante, Agamennone ed Ajace, ne mai o poco si parla delle armi, e di Teucro, finchè comparisce Tecmessa, con la quale Agamennone fa una scena indipendente affatto dall'azione principale, e poi parte per assalire le rocche di Troja.[5] In quest'atto vi aveva una ridicola declamazione di Ulisse verso Ajace, che l'Autore ha tagliato prudentissimamente nella seconda rappresentazione. Nel quinto Atto finalmente, Calcante sopra una collina serve di Telegrafo a Tecmessa nel piano, per indicarle con la voce, e coi gesti gli accidenti dell'attacco; Ajace poi entra furibondo in iscena perchè crede e non crede, che il fratello sia un traditore, perchè i prigionieri durante la battaglia hanno dato l'arme d'Achille ad Ulisse, perchè teme che Teucro ammazzi il suo figlio, perchè teme ancora di passare egli stesso per un traditore, perchè[6] ... insomma si ammazza per molti motivi passati, presenti e futuri; ma prima d'ammazzarsi, Ajace stesso (chi lo crederebbe!) parla filosoficamente sul Suicidio, come l'Amleto di Shakespeare, o come Jacopo Ortis, (cioè Werther) si prepara a morire, filosofando, dopo aver costretto Calcante ad andarsene. Sta poi una mezz'oretta prima di morire affinchè Teucro possa con lui discolparsi, (e Dio sa come e perchè!) e finalmente muore vedendo giungere Agamennone, il quale dice che per la morte d'Ajace diviene più potente, e più infelice. Ora io domando, con questo disegno di scene bizzarre, slegate, si può egli fare una vera e buona Tragedia? Egli è chiaro, che si è perduto di vista l'oggetto principale, con avvenimenti mal a proposito immaginati, e l'attenzione, che fissa sopra un solo oggetto si sarebbe a quello interessata, è andata errando sopra circostanze estranee al punto principale,[7] e lo ha perduto di vista? Non era egli dunque permesso di domandare, perchè Ajace si fosse data la morte? Non era egli permesso di dire: io mi sono annojato, e la Tragedia è stata lunghissima?

Gl'inconvenienti, e gli sbagli di questa Tragedia compariranno in più chiara luce, quando esamineremo i caratteri o falsi o grotteschi che U.F. ha dati agli Eroi d'Omero. Anzi siccome è stato detto, che questo soggetto non è suscettivo d'esser posto in azione Tragica, noi speriamo di potere dimostrare il contrario, delineando un disegno, sopra il quale si può fare, a parer nostro, una buona Tragedia d'Ajace. Noi lo metteremo nel venturo Poligrafo sotto gli occhj de' nostri Leggitori, e del Pubblico. Ci sembra, che dopo aver veduto come questa Tragedia non deve farsi, abbiamo potuto immaginare come debba farsi.[8]

Parleremo infine anche dello stile e modi di dire usati dall'Autore, ed in ciò avremo qualche cosa da dire in favore della sua Tragedia.

Del resto, che il disegno di questa Tragedia sia stato mal concepito, si deduce ancora da ciò, che non ha potuto schivare una fredda accoglienza per parte del Pubblico neppure per l'impegno col quale fu recitata dagli Attori; essi potevano esser accusati d'una certa uniformità di tuono, e d'inflessione, la quale ha quasi sempre luogo, quando uno solo ha il diritto di fargli declamare secondo il suo gusto, le sue maniere, e la sua fantasia, ma non già di non aver fatto uso di tutte le loro forze, ed abilità. Prepiani rappresentò l'Agamennone con la dignità conveniente, e con la conveniente gravità Bettini rappresentato la parte di Calcante. Blanes, la seconda sera, declamò con gran vigore, e se egli ed anche Tessari, non riscossero corti applausi, ciò deve attribuirsi in qualche parte all'Autore della Tragedia, il quale, come abbiam promesso di dimostrare, si è ingannato moltissimo nel determinare i caratteri d'Ulisse, e di Ajace. Il primo doveva essere ammirato, come il *prudentissimo* Ulisse d'Omero, e fu aborrito come il perfidissimo Abner d'Alfieri; il secondo doveva esser compianto come vittima d'altissimo senso d'onore, e fu deriso come vittima di calamità immaginarie.

Nulla possiamo dire di Teucro, e quel che più ci rincresce di Tecmessa, perchè come i primi quattro parlarono troppo, e ciascuno pareva farla da Protagonista, così questi due parlarono pochissimo quanto all'intrigo, ed erano personaggi piuttosto di terzo che di secondo ordine.

A.

5. Urbano Lampredi, *Il Poligrafo*, 22 December 1811, 594–8.

LETTERATURA

Nel numero antecedente abbiamo già dimostrato che la Tragedia dell'*Ajace* è un vero mostro per rispetto al disegno, simile in tutto al libro descritto da quel povero uomo di Orazio

> ... ceius velut aegri somnia, vanae
> Reddentur species;[9] ut nec pes nec caput uni
> Reddatur formae ...

il quale difetto si deve attribuire all'ignoranza o al disprezzo dei buoni precetti dell'arte; precetti che si derivano, non già dal capriccio di coloro che li dettarono, ma dalla esperienza, universale maestra, e dalle giuste e ben fondate considerazioni sull'indole e sullo scopo dei componimenti drammatici, e sulla natura dell'intelletto umano e del cuore.

Ed ecco un nuovo argomento per dimostrare, che il *Genio*, ossia Demone inspiratore, celebrato cotanto, ma non ancora ben deffinito [*sic*] dai supremi moderatori ed arbitri dell'odierna letteratura, ha pure non picciolo bisogno di qualche norma che dirigga [*sic*] gli alti ed impetuosi suoi voli, sicch'egli nell'elevarsi, e nel battere le ali, non dia del capo nelle volte o nel muro, e non istramazzi stroppiato ed esanime sul pavimento. Con un tantino di arte, studiata per esempio sulla poetica del re dei pedanti, Aristotele, o del suo seguace Orazio, l'illustre Autore avrebbe potuto preparare assennatamente e rendere ragionevole e necessaria la miserabile fine di Ajace, in guisa che lo spettatore ne rimanesse vivamente commosso, non già la odiasse, come incredibile.

Ma per difetto di arte è stato bisogno che la morte venga a togliere sagacemente di mezzo ogni difficoltà, e così si è sempre più confermata quella sentenza del celebre Lessing, cioè che il quinto atto delle Tragedie suol essere una scortesissima epidemia, la quale viene a levare subitaneamente dal mondo alcuni personaggi, che nei quattro primi atti ci avevano dato speranza di una vita più lunga. Si schiamazzi pur dunque, e si gridi e si tuoni, quanto più puossi, che noi torneremo sempre a ripetere, che senza le saggie norme dell'arte i veri, *Genj*, non produrranno mai cosa perfettamente buona, e i falsi ne produrranno sempre di pessime. E qualunque volta con gli abbaglianti sofismi ci si vorrà mostrare il contrario, noi appelleremo pur sempre a quelle opere che furono scritte senza la guida dei sani precetti, e la noja e il fastidio, e l'invincibile sonnolenza, che da quelle si diffonderà su i pazientissimi ascoltatori, sarà ottimo argomento per porre in chiaro, chi s'abbia la ragione od il torto, se quelli che raccomandano lo studio delle regole, o quelli che lo proscrivono.[10] Nè quì possiamo astenerci dall'esclamare. Oh! Pedanti, Pedanti, ai quali finora fu esclusivamente accordato il gran privilegio di seccare le persone dabbene con le insipide inezie, ecco i vostri pacifici possedimenti già minacciati di tremenda invasione, e da pericolo tanto maggiore, quanto chi aspira ad occupare i vostri diritti si fa innanzi circondato di splendide pompe, e si trae dietro gran popolo con la seduzione dei fastosi spettacoli.[11]

Ma se l'Ajace è un vero mostro, quanto al disegno, esso non lo è punto meno per rispetto ai caratteri dei principali personaggi. E da questo lato ancora qualche studio sull'arte avrebbe giovato al poeta per insegnargli, che i caratteri degli Eroi famosi si debbono rappresentare, quali le storie, o le tradizioni degli Autori più riputati, ce [*sic*] gli hanno costantemente dipinti. "L'Istoria, dice un famoso Tedesco, non è per la Tragedia, che un repertorio di nomi, ai quali noi siamo soliti di attaccare l'idea di certi determinati caratteri." Dunque il Poeta o debbe, nelle qualità essenziali dei caratteri stessi, seguire fedelmente la storica narrazione, o volendone formare di nuovi, debbe applicarli a personaggi ugualmente nuovi, ed inventare totalmente il suggetto del suo dramma, siccome fece il Voltaire nell'Alzira e nulla Zaira, il Belloi[12] nella Zelmira, ed altri ben molti in altre Tragedie. Adunque e perchè applicare le qualità, ora di un ambizioso Carlo Quinto, ora di un ostuto Filippo, ora di un sospettoso Saule, a quell'Agamemnone [*sic*], che da Omero, primo pittore delle antiche memorie, e da Eschilio e da Euripide ci fu con ben altri colori rappresentato? E quel pensiero di figurarlo, com'uomo, che presumesse e studiasse di rendersi tirannicamente padrone di tutta Grecia, è ella cosa che possa conciliarsi, non dirò già con le istoriche tradizioni, ma col senso comune?[13] E chi era, e dove stava, e con chi si univa egli Agamemnone [*sic*], mentre avvenivano i fatti che sono l'argomento della Tragedia? Agamemnone [*sic*] non era Signore che di una piccola parte di Grecia,[14] si ritrovava in una terra straniera, separato per molto mare dalla propria patria, circondato da guerra pericolosa, in mezzo ad un esercito confederato, e ad un'armata di mille e dugento navi, delle quali solamente censessanta, o al più al più dugento venti gli appartenevano, se a quelle ch'erano condotte da lui e da Menelao, si volgiano aggiungere le sessanta degli Arcadi, ai quali, come al popolo mediterraneo, le aveva somministrate egli stesso. Ma un tal uomo, e in tali condizioni constituito, poteva egli entrare nella stolta intenzione di spegnere tutti i capitani alleati, molti de' quali erano più arditi e più valorosi di lui, com'egli stesso ben conosceva, od aver la speranza d'indurli, non già con le dolci maniere e con le insidiose lusinghe, ma con le ingiurie e col superbo parlare, a lasciarsi trarre di mano l'imperio de' loro regni? E quand' anche gli avesse spenti, o domati tutti, è egli credibile che i soldati, che a quelli obbedivano, si sarebbono sottommessi ugualmente, e l'avrebbero ciecamente seguito in Grecia per soggiogare le provincie, che a loro medesimi erano patria, e dove si tenevano fermi e ben muniti i padri di alcuni dei capitani che avevano navigato a Troja, come fra gli altri erano Peleo e Telamone? Per porsi dinanzi alla mente queste naturalissime osservazioni non è bisogno di studiare nè Aristotele, nè Orazio; una scintilla sola di buon criterio è sufficiente per suggerirle. E Ulisse? quell'Ulisse che gli antichi rappresentarono ispirato e diretto da Minerva, come l'autore stesso della Tragedia ha pure ripetuto in qualche suo verso, contraffacendo così coi detti al fatto, quell'Ulisse in somma, che ne fu dato per simbolo della prudenza congiunta al valore, e per dimostrarne, *quid virtus et quid sapientia possit*; che cosa è egli divenuto nello scritto del nostro Autore? non altro certamente, se non un perfido e fraudolento Abner, di cui diffida quello stesso Agamennone, che pur vuole giovarsi della perfidia di lui, od un vile e sciocco ingannatore, le cui astuzie direttamente conducono a distruggere i buoni successi di quella rilevantissima impresa, per la quale egli stesso sosteneva da molti e molti anni e fatiche e pericoli, e mancanza di tutte le cose più care. Ma già mi pare di udire Ajace, il Protagonista della Tragedia

> Il qual mi grida, e di lontano accenna,
> E prega ch'io no 'l lasci nella penna.[15]

Or bene, dimmi, formidabile Ajace, tu, dopo il tuo cugino Achille, valorosissimo degli Achei, tu che vedendo il campo involto da folta nebbia, ti volgevi al Tonante, dicendo

> Giove Padre, deh! togli a questo bujo
> I figli degli Achei, spandi il sereno,
> Rendi agli occhi il vedere, e poiché spenti
> *Ne vuoi, ci spegni nella luce almeno.*

Omer. Trad. Monti.

tu finalmente, che in mezzo alla pugna, rispondesti ai consigli di Pallade con queste parole: *assisti Diva agli altri guerrieri, poichè dove io combatto, i nemici non prevarranno*; dimmi ripeto, avresti tu riconosciuto te stesso, se fossi venuto a vedere la nuova Tragedia, che s'intitola del tuo gran nome? Ohimè! ohimè! tu avresti sicuramente rinnovato la strage delle pecore, e la flagellazione dell'irco, e ti sarestj ammazzato la seconda volta, vedendoti effigiato in sì strana caricatura, e rappresentato ora come un furioso, che imbestialische senza motivo, ed ora come un timido novizietto, che consapevole di sue mancanze palpita e trema al cospetto del P. Abate. E del P. Abate Calcante, nel quale a moltissimi già apparve raffigurato l'Achimelecco di Saule, non diremo noi qualche parola? Ma e che dirne! di un personaggio sì stravagante, sì contradditorio in se stesso, investito, quando di una paurosa virtù, e quando di un eccessivo ardimento, ora strapazzato, ed ora strapazzante, non si può dar ragione, nè conto. Con tutto ciò diremo, che se l'Autore avesse ben letto od inteso i Greci maestri, avrebbe potuto discernere, con qual fino accorgimento essi furono soliti d'introdurre ne' poemi i ministri de' loro Dei. Quindi avrebbe veduto, che i saggi re, lasciando ai sacerdoti l'esercizio del loro ministero, e secondandoli in ciò che strettamente apparteneva agli ufficj sacerdotali, in tutte le altre cose poi, senza maltrattarli fuor di ragione, li tenevano per sudditi non diversi dagli altri tutti, e li volevano interamente subordinati alla politica autorità.

Noi avevamo scritto sin quì, e volevamo procedere innanzi, quando un amico de' nostri ci s'accostò, volle udire ciò che avevamo posto in sulla carta. Finita la lettura, l'amico si alzò come sdegnato, e sclamò: che Achimelecchi, che Abner, che Filippi, che Saulli! Tutti questi confronti sono fuori di luogo, nè paragoni sì alti possono applicarsi alla nuova Tragedia. Cotesta non è Tragedia affatto, ma una miserabile parodia di un pezzo di Storia Eroica, nella quale Agamemnone [*sic*] è trasformato nel Capitan Covriello, Ulisse in Brighella, Teucro in Arlecchino, Calcante in Pantalone, Tecmessa in Rosaura, ad Ajace in Meneghino Pecenna. Questo inaspettato discorso, che in parte ci mosse a riso, in parte a dispetto, sconvolse per modo tutte le nostre idee, che non potemmo più ritornare posatamente in sulla traccia dei primi pensieri. E però risolvemmo di lasciare pel numero venturo alcune altre considerazioni su' varii punti della Tragedia, non meno che sulla scena su' vestimenti, e sulle decorazioni, nelle quali cose tutte dimostreremo, grandissimo essere stato il dominio di quello spirito di stravaganza, e d'incongruenza, che si è mescolato all'azione del dramma, e al carattere dei personaggi in quello introdotti.

A.

6. Urbano Lampredi, *Il Poligrafo*, 29 December 1811, 610–13.

LETTERATURA
Continuazione delle Osservazioni sopra l'Ajace

L'Autore della Tragedia, non contento di trasformare il prudentissimo Ulisse in uno scellerato, si è pure dato la nobile cura di farne un traditore ed un pazzo. Quell'Ulisse adunque, che già tanto si celebrò, come un prodigio di accorgimento e di senno, quell'Ulisse, che così ben conosceva, quanto pel buon esito delle grandi imprese sia necessario l'affidarne il governo all'autorità di un solo, e che, per indurre a obbedienza la tumultuante moltitudine dei Greci, andava un giorno gridando:

> Un sol comandi, e quello
> Cui scettro e leggi affida il Dio, quei solo[16]
> Ne sia di tutti correttor supremo.

Iliad. I. 2. Trad. Monti.

Quell'Ulisse d'altronde, che per le scarse forze da lui somministrate alla confederazione Greca, era de' meno potenti, quello nella nuova Tragedia si arroga il diritto di comandare movimenti a un corpo dell'esercito, e di sospingere ad imprese arbitrarie uno de' capitani. Noi appelliamo a tutti quelli, che sano alcun poco delle discipline guerresche, e lasciamo a loro il decidere, se una si ridicola[17] invenzione abbia punto del verisimile. Ma e con chi si avvisa egli Ulisse di comunicare il suo sciocco e temerario pensiero? Con Teucro ch'era perfettamente ligio in tutte le cose alla volontà del suo famoso fratello, con Teucro che certamente non fu uomo nè insensato, nè timido, ma saggio ed ardito, come Omero se lo dipinse. Con tutto ciò quando ancora si supponesse che Ulisse potesse essere abbastanza stolido per dare il fraudolento consiglio, e Teucro mal'accorto abbastanza per aderirvi, si dovrà di necessità domandare, quali erano le soldatesche, a cui Teucro potea comandare di seguire i suoi passi. E noi risponderemo: nessune affatto. Teucro non aveva milizie sue proprie, e perciò nella rassegna de' capitani arrecataci nel secondo libro dell'Iliade, non si fa alcuna menzione di lui. In fatti i Salaminj venuti a Troja erano così pochi, che loro non poteva essere assegnato che un solo condottiero, e questi era Ajace, senza l'espresso comando del quale essi non si sarebbono mai arditi di porsi ad alcuna impresa. Ma noi vogliamo usare di straoridinaria generosità con l'illustre Autore, e concedere che Ulisse, e Teucro, e tutti i soldati del Telamonio possano rappresentarsi come una coorte d'uomini sconsigliati: saremmo per altro assai vaghi di sapere, come in un giorno di tanto pericolo, e già presso all'estremo termine della tregua, un certo numero di truppe potesse muovere fuori dalle trinciere,[18] e dalle fosse che assicuravano il navile Greco, senza che dalle sue tende, ch'erano erette nel dritto mezzo della linea anteriore dell'armata, dovesse avvedersene quell'Agamemnone, che dall'Autore ci viene descritto così geloso del suo supremo potere, e così attento nel conservarlo; e come tutta quella schiera potesse uscire non osservata da un campo, che con tanta cura si custodiva, e dove noi sentimmo dalle frequenti sentinelle, annunziare l'arrivo anche di un uomo solo, nello stesso modo, che si suol praticare nelle anticamere dei grandi.[19] Noi abbiamo voluto fermarci con tante parole su questa grottesca parte dell'invenzione, acciocchè si veggia, da quale e nobile, e giusta e probabile origine, il giudiziosissimo Autore abbia fatto quasi interamente dipendere tutta la catastrofe del suo dramma.

> Caetera de genere hoc, adeo sunt multa, loquacem
> Delassare valent Fabium ...

Onde ci faremo a dire dell'altre cose, che abbiamo osservate nello spettacolo.

Scena. Alto colle con Tempio di Giove. – La quistione per le armi di Achile [*sic*] si fece presso alle navi, e lungo la riva del mare, come racconta lo stesso Ulisse nel nono libro dell'Odissea. Ma nelle pianure di Troja, e in quella parte, dove stava ordinato il navile de' Greci, non erano nè monti nè colli. Quanto al Tempio posto all sommo della collina, noi ameremmo di sapere chi potesse averlo edificato, e come a' tempi della guerra Iliaca si conoscesse già l'architettura dell'età di Pericle.

Abiti, armi ec. – A chi volesse ragionare minutamente di questa parte della rappresentazione, troppo lunga ora bisognerebbe. Pertanto in quattro parole ce ne varcheremo, dicendo, che i vestimenti inargentati, indorati, ingemmati, e la forma dell'armi tanto da offesa quanto da difesa, e tutto ciò in somma, onde si formavano l'esterne decorazioni della Tragedia, tutto corrispondeva assai male ai semplici costumi, e alle usanze de' secoli Eroici, tramandateci dai libri e dai monumenti antichi.

Gli è vero, che siffatte colpe si dovrebbero attribuire al pittore, ai sartori ed al *berettonaro* del Teatro, ma siccome sappiamo che l'illustre autore ha voluto dirigere in tutto e per tutto gli accessorj dello spettacolo, fino alla declamazione degli attori, così ci teniamo in buona coscienza obbligati di aggiugnere alla sua partita anche la somma di questi errori.

Una sentenza fra le altre molte ci ferì particolarmente gli orecchi, là dove uno de' personaggi disse che *Achille era tornato al cielo, dond'era disceso*. Achille non venne al mondo dall'alto sereno, ma dalla profondità dei mari. Da un altro canto la Religione Pagana non mandava gli uomini virtuosi o gli Eroi all'olimpo, a meno ch'essi non ottenessero l'apoteosi, del qual privilegio non godè il filgio di Peleo, ma agl'Inferi, e quivi appunto lo ritrovò Ulisse, come si narra nel citato libro dell'Odissea. Alcuni bensì credettero, che il Pelide, uscendo dalla vita mortale si fosse ricondotto all'elemento natio, e ciò sta scritto in un Inno a Tetide, che i Tessali navigatori solevano cantare, quando di nottetempo si approssimavano co' loro legni alla terra; ma niun autore approvato trasportò mai Achille alla abitazione dei Celesti.

Alcuni, ponendo da un lato i vizj dell'Ajace per rispetto al disegno, all'azione, alla peripezia, ai caratteri, alla mancanza di esposizione nel principio, e di ogni buon fine morale nella conclusione, mettono poi dall'altro alcuni bei concetti, e alcuni bei versi che vi sono sparsi per entro, e si ostinano a pretendere, che il buono e il cattivo si equilibrino per questo modo insieme. Noi concederemo che nell'Ajace si trovi qualche giusto pensiere, e parecchie undicine di sillabe bene accozzate. Ma che perciò? Anche in quel *Diluvio Universale* del P. Ringhieri, dove sono miseramente affogate tutte le buone regole della Drammatica, e del *Buonsenso*, nuotano qua e là di belle sentenze e di be' versi. Con tutto ciò il *Diluvio Universale* non cessa dall'essere una Tragedia assolutamente ridicola. Pochi e radi difetti non distruggeranno mai il valore di un componimento, che sia veramente buono nelle parti essenziali; ma un componimento cattivo nella sua totalità, rimarrà pur sempre cattivo, a malgrado di qualche bellezza che vi risplenda, come un abito di rozzo panno, mal tagliato, peggio cucito, e non punto adattato al dosso di una persona non farà meno brutta comparsa, perchè vi si attacchino alcuni pezzi di broccato o di porpora, e come sotto un cielo povero di luce propria, alcuni moccolini disposti in un vastissimo campo, non renderanno mai luminosa una buja notte.

Molti cenni d'imitazione di antichi scrittori abbiamo riscontrato nella Tragedia: e per questa parte sarebbe assai da lodarsi l'illustre Autore, s'egli avesse saputo copiare i famosi esemplari con quel fino giudizio, con cui Orazio *rubò tutte le sentenze e le immagini delle sue Odi a' Lirici, ed a'cori de' Tragici Greci*, come, facendone rimprovero al Romano poeta, altamente pronunzia un venerabile Maestro moderno nell'ultimo volume degli Annali di Scienze e Lettere. Ma tutto ciò che l'Autore dell'Ajace ha voluto derivare dagli antichi, è stato da lui, per istrana maniera diformato o nella sustanza, o nell'ordine, o nella collocazione; e però teniamo per fermo, che l'antica Sapienza, potendo vedere quella

Tragedia, direbbe all'autore di essa con assai più di ragione, che non diceva Eschilo al suo rivale: *considera quali primamente da me ricevesti gli Eroi; se forti ed altissimi, non ricusanti i pubblici ufficj, nè vagabondi, nè furbi, nè ciurmadori, ma spiranti l'amore dell'armi, e forniti di animo pari a quello di Ajace dal settemplice scudo; e se tu non facesti ciò, ma di buoni e di generosi in scelleratissimi li cambiasti, di quale supplizio sarai tu degno?*

A.

7. Urbano Lampredi, *Il Poligrafo*, 5 January 1812, 3–7.

Letteratura

Al n.36 del Poligrafo promettemmo di dare un disegno secondo il quale, al parer nostro, si potrebbe, tessere una Tragedia sulla morte di Ajace, conforme ai buoni precetti dell'arte, ed atta a muovere potentemente gli affetti. E ciò intendevamo di fare, poichè molti hanno asserito che quel soggetto non è *Tragediabile*. Noi avremmo in questo numero osservato la nostra promessa, ma ci è paruto convenevole di cedere alla preghiera fattaci con la seguente,[20]

Lettera ai Poligrafici,
Appena ebbi osservato l'esito infelicissimo della tragedia, l'*Ajace* di U. Foscolo, ch'io al primo tratto giudicai con molti altri, che il fatto non fosse assolutamente tale da far colpo ai moderni italiani. Ma poco dopo ragionai fra me stesso, e dissi: È vero che l'armi di Achille erano pei Greci una cosa di altissimo pregio, e dovevano conseguentemente presentarsi alla loro immaginazione in un aspetto ben più importante, che adesso, e a noi non farebbero.[21] Egli è vero altresi che Sofocle stimò di dovere in certa maniera dividere l'azione tragica dell'Ajace in due parti, nella prima delle quali si rappresentano i momenti che precedettero la morte di quell'Eroe, e nella seconda i sasseguenti, cioè quelli in cui si tratta della sepoltura di lui. E in questo maniera pare che il sommo Tragico credesse di poter rendere il suo Eroe sempre più degno di compassione facendo che i Greci dopo di avergli negato le armi da lui tanto disiderate, volessero ancora privarlo dell'onor del sepolcro; la qual cosa,[22] giusta le opinioni religiose di quei tempi, si reputava disaventura[23] o punizione maggiore di ogn'altra. E su questo proposito permettemi di osservare che nella Tragedia di Sofocle, mentre Agamemnone e Menelao resistono a Teucro, volendo pure che il cadavere di Ajace rimanga insepolto, colui che giugne a rendere inefficace questo

obbrobrioso e terribile decreto, è appunto Ulisse: e basterà leggere il dialogo tra lui[24] ed Agamemnone per conchiudere che U.F.[25] non poteva immaginare una più bassa, e più ridicola parodia del nobile e generoso carattere di quell'Eroe, trasformandolo com'egli ha fatto, e come voi già avete saggiamente notato,[26] in un personaggio da farsa. (*)

Ma per tornare al primiero argomento, io sostengo che al malgrado di quanto ho poco sopra osservato, la sola quistione dell'armi può destare nello spettatore una viva attenzione, e tutti quei movimenti di affetti che più si richiedono, ond'egli resti vivacemente toccato all'azione, lo voglio bensì concedere, che la qualità di quelle armi, fabbricate dallo stesso Vulcano alle preghiere di Tetide, e la predizione che senza di esse Troja non sarebbe mai espugnata, non sieno cose le quali possano colpire l'animo nostro, con tanto vigore, con quanto scuotevano quello dei Greci. Con tutto ciò a quelle armi un'altra particolarità si conguingne, atta, siccome io credo, a destare una gagliarda emozione inqualsivoglia cuore che sia capace di generoso e nobile orgoglio; e questa è, che quegli a cui esse si sarebbero aggiudicate, veniva ad essere proclamato come il più valoroso e il più accorto fra un grandissimo numero di suoi eguali. Imperocchè la madre di Achille aveva deliberato e prescritto che le armi del proprio figlio si dessero per ricompensa al guerriero che più di tutti aveva contribuito a sottrarne il cadavere alle mani e alla vandetta degl'inimici. Ora, domanderò io, può ella reputarsi cosa poco lusinghevole, o indifferente l'essere dichiarato primo per gagliardia e per senno in mezzo a molti valorissimi capitani![27] La maggiore difficoltà adunque sta nel porre opportunamente in usole regole dell'arte, (e quando parlo di arte, non parlo coi moderni Genj delle nostre lettere) per isvillupare l'accennata passione in sul bel principio della Tragedia, e farla, per così dire, varcare nell'anime degli spettatori; e poscia con soccorso dell'arte medesima, accrescerne il movimento mercè di ostacoli imprevisti sì, ma naturali e probabili e non punto contrarii alle idee che universalmente si hanno intorno al carattere degli Eroi, che s'introducono sulla scena.[28] Con questi fondamenti presi io a delineare un *piano* d'azione, distribuita in cinque atti, indi mi occupai a distinguere le scene che dovevano comporre gli atti medesimi e a determinare il numero dei personaggi, e la qualità delle materie, che trattar si dovevano acciocchè l'azione e l'importanza di essa andasse successivamente crescendo in maniera, che finalmente si pervenisse ad

---

* Crediamo opportuna cosa di qui appore il dialogo fra Agamemnone ed Ulisse, da noi letteralmente tradotto dal testo di Sofocle.

eccitare quelle passioni generali, ch'io mi era prefisso di risvegliare nell'animo degli spettatori. Per questo lavoro, non è necessario l'avere cognizione dei principj essenziali dell'arte, e l'essersi con discernimento, e con buon gusto, trattendo nello studio dei grandi esemplari antichi, e nella ricerca delle naturali disposizioni dell'uman cuore. Io non tralascerò di sottoporre l'opera mia all'esame di tali che sappiano più di me, e quando ne ottenga il suffragio, mi accingerò a colorire la mia tela, come meglio per me si potrà.

U. E che t'ha egli (Teucro) fatto che si t'offenda?

A. Egli protesta di non volere permettere che si lascri senza sepoltura questo cadavere (d'Ajace); ma vuol seppellirlo a mio dispetto.

U. Un amico che ti dica la verità può egli sperare di non divenirti men caro di prima?

A. Parla: altrimenti io non sarei savio; poichè ti ho pel mio megliore amico fra gli Argivi tutti.

U. Odimi dunque: non ti soffra il cuore di abbandonare così spietatamente insepolto cotesto Eroe; ne te vinca in alcun modo la violenza fino ad odiarlo cotanto, ed a calpestare così la giustizia. Che a me ancora costui già si fece inimicissimo, più che altri mai, dal momento in ch'io ottenni le armi d'Achille ma lui, comunque tale per me, non io disprezzerei al segno di non confessare d'averlo riconosciuto come il più valoroso degli Argivi, fra quanti venimmo a Troja, eccetto Achille. Per lo che non giustamente egli sarebbe da te privato dei debiti onori. Poichè in ciò non tanto faresti oltraggio a lui, quanto alle leggi degli Dei. E non è lecito di offendere un uom valoroso, poich'egli è morto, neppur quando tu l'avessi in odio.

A. E così, o Ulisse, ingrazia di costui a me contrasti?

U. Si: io l'odiava quando stava bene l'odiarlo.

A. E non ti conviene l'odiarlo ancorchè morto?

U. Non t'allegrare, o Atricle, di non onesti vantaggi.

A. Non è facil cosa ad un Re il mostrarsi sempre pietoso.

U. Ma gli è facile per altro l'avere in onore gli amici che ben consigliano.

A. Conviene che l'uomo onesto obbedisca ai superiori.

U. Cessa: tu non ti mostri men forte, lasciandoti vincere dagli amici.

A. Considera a qual'uomo tu dia il tuo favore.

U. Cotes'uomo m'era inimico, ma un dì fu valoroso.

A. E a qualcosa varrai tu, se rispetti cotanto il cadavere d'un inimico?

U. Me vince assai più l'altrui valore, che l'odio.

A. Gli uomini di tale animo sono riputati codardi.

U. Pur troppo molto ora sono amici, e poco dopo inimici.

A. Credi tu bello l'acquistare siffatti amici?

U. Io non suglio chiamar bello un animo inesorabile.

A. Tu giugnerai oggi a farci apparire deboli.

U. No; anzi giusti in Facca a tutti i Greci.

A. Mi consigli dunque di lasciar seppellire il cadavere?

U. Si, perchè anch'io un giorno ad uguale necessità mi ritroverò.

A. Oh! Come ogni uomo si affatica per amore di se.

U. E per chi digg'io più travagliarmi che per me stesso?

A. A te dunque quest'opera, non a me sarà imputata.

U. Com l'avrai prestata, giusta e buono ne sarai chiamato per tutto.

A. Or sappi, Ulisse che io intendo di concederti una grazia anche maggiore. E vivo ed estinto costui mi sarà del pari odiosissimo: pure sia in te l'arbitrio di fare tutto ciò che conviene.

CORO

Chiunque, o Ulisse, non istima te d'animo sapientissimo, quale pur sei, quegli a un uomo veramente insensato.

Notes

The following notes include the textual variations between the original 1811–12 reviews and the published reviews in *Lettera apologetica di* Urbano Lampredi *seguita da alcuni articoli e dialoghi letterarii Estratti dal «Poligrafo» Milanese in risposta ad un'articolo oltraggioso intitolato Ugo Foscolo Pubblicato nel Giornale Inglese «Foreign Quarterly Review» e riportato tradotto in Francese nella «Revue Britanique» che si pubblica a Parigi n. 2 Août 1830* (Naples: dai torchi di Porcelli, 1831), 25–55. Giuseppe Nicoletti reprinted these 1831 reviews in 2011 in the second volume of the Edizione Nazionale's Appendice. The variations included below are followed by the page number on which they appear in the Appendice. Minor variations, including capitalizations and subtle changes to punctuation are not included.

1 "che gli uni ed altri facevano," 20.

2 "Perché, risponde Schlegel, l'attività è il vero godimento della vita, anzi è la vita stessa." 20.

3 "(nè s'intese bene con quali arti di lui degne)" 21.

4 "è accaduto nel Congresso, e narra che il Congresso stesso ha statuito" 21.

5 "alle rocche di Troja, e si propone al tempo stesso di bruciar le tende de' prigionieri; ma tal feroce proponimento eccita la resistenza di Ajace, e s'impegna fra entrambi una guerra civile. In quest'atto," 22.

6 "gli accedenti del combattimento; Ajace poi entra in iscena risoluto di uccidersi, perché crede e non crede che il fratello sia un traditore, perché dispera di avere le armi di Achille ed è persuaso che di diano ad Ulisse, perché teme ancora di passare egli stesso per un traditore, perche …" 22.

7 "è andata errando sopra incidenti estranei al punto principale," 22.

8 "Anzi, siccome è stato detto che questo soggetto non è suscettivo d'esser posto in azione tragica, un amico nostro carissimo spera di poter dimostrare il contrario, delineando un disegno, sopra il quale si può fare, a parer suo, una buona tragedia d'Ajace. Noi lo comunicheremo a suo tempo col pubblico nei seguenti Quaderni del Poligrafo. Imperocché ei

sembra, che dopo aver veduto come questa tragedia non deve farsi, possa uno immaginare come debba o possa farsi." 22.

9 *"Fingentur species;"* 23.

10 "prescrivono." 24.

11 *"chi aspira ad occupare i vostri diritti si fa innanzi circondato di splendide pompe, e si trae dietro gran popolo con la seduzione dei fastosi spettacoli."* Lampredi's emphasis, 24.

12 "Belloni," 24.

13 "ma col senno comune?" 25.

14 "parte della Grecia," 25.

15 "nol lasci" 25

16 "quel solo" 27.

17 "sì ridicola," 27.

18 "trincee," 27.

19 "e dove si dovea sentire annunziare dalle frequenti sentinelle l'uscita anche di un uomo solo, nello stesso modo, che si suol annunziare l'entrata di qualsivoglia persona nelle anticamere dei grandi." 28.

20 Lampredi erroneously wrote that the first article appeared in number 36 of *Il Poligrafo* in the 1812 original. It actually appeared in number 37. The opening paragraph is completely different from the original in the 1828/1831 version. Lampredi clearly admitted to not fulfilling his intended goal of offering a workable design for a tragedy based on the story of Ajace in this later version of the review.

"Nell'articolo 1.° abbiamo promesso di comunicare col pubblico un disegno, secondo il quale un valente letterato sperava che si potrebbe tessere una tragedia sulla morte di Ajace, conforme ai buoni precetti dell'arte ed atta a muovere potentemente gli affetti. Ed a questo lavoro egli attualmente intende, benché, come abbiamo sopra notato, molti abbiano asserito che quel soggetto non è *tragediabile*. Noi non possiamo in questo numero osservare la nostra promessa, ma ci è paruto convenevole di cedere alla preghiera fattaci con la seguente" 30.

21 "che adesso a noi non farebbero." 30

22 "la quale cosa," 30.

23 "disavventura," 30.

24 "dialogo fra lui," 30.

25 "U. Foscolo," 30.

26 "voi avete saggiamente notato," 30.

27 "capitani?" 32.

28 "s'introducano nella scena." 32

Notes

Introduction

1 Ugo Foscolo, *Edizione nazionale delle opere di Ugo Foscolo*, ed. Plinio Carli (Florence: Felice Le Monnier, 1954), 17: 333. Hereafter, all citations from the 22 volume *Edizione nazionale delle opere di Ugo Foscolo* will be cited as *E.N.*

2 *E.N.*, 8: 367–71.

3 "Si può veramente dire che una Tragedia è la più bell'opera dell'umano ingegno," *E.N.*, 17: 217. Unless otherwise indicated, all translations from the Italian are mine.

4 The one notable exception is Ettore Catalano and his studies on the three tragedies in three books: *La spada e le opinioni: Il teatro di Foscolo* (Foggia: Bastogi, 1983); *Foscolo "tragico": Dal Tieste alle ultime lettere di Jacopo Ortis* (Bari: Laterza, 2001); and *Le trame occulte: L'Ajace e la Ricciarda nel percorso teatrale di Ugo Foscolo* (Bari: Laterza, 2002).

5 Sandra Parmegiani discusses Foscolo's tragic vein in chapter 1 of her book *Ugo Foscolo and English Culture* (London: Legenda, 2011), 7–60. See also Ettore Catalano's thorough examination of tragic elements in Foscolo's early years. Catalano, *Foscolo "tragico."*

6 *E.N.*, Appendix 2, 20–32.

7 Frederick May, "Calliroe e Ifianeo: Work in Progress on the 'English' Period of Ugo Foscolo," *Italica* 41, no. 1 (March 1964): 68.

Chapter One

1 See Boileau-Despréaux's 1674 *L'art poétique*; Rapin's 1674 *Réflexions sur la poétique*; and Bouhours's 1671 *Entretiens d'Ariste et d'Eugène* and his 1687 *La manière de bien penser dans les ouvrages d'esprit*. For a general overview

of French criticisms of Italian literature, see J.G. Robertson, *Studies in the Genesis of Romantic Theory of the 18th Century* (New York: Russell & Russell, 1962), 1–23. For a comprehensive and intricate analysis of the perceptions of France and Italy during the late seventeenth and early eighteenth centuries, see Françoise Waquet, *Le modèle français et l'Italie savante: Conscience de soi et perception de l'autre dans la République des Lettres (1660–1750)* (Rome: École française de Rome, 1989). For more on the Italian response to French criticisms, see Francesco Bruni's chapter 12, "Rinuncia alla cultura barocca, tradizione, tempi nuovi," in *Italia, vita e avventure di un'idea* (Bologna: Mulino, 2010), 419–82.

2 *Considerazioni sopra un famoso Libro Franzese intitolato La Manière de bien penser Dans les Ouvrages d'esprit, cioè La Maniera di ben pensare ne' componimenti, divise in sette dialoghi, Ne' quali s'agitano alcune Quistioni Rettoriche, e Poetiche, e si difendono molti Passi di Poeti e di Prosatori Italiani condannati dall'Autor Franzese* (Bologna: Costantino Pisarri, 1703). The work was first published anonymously after Bouhours's death and Orsi's name did not appear until the 1735 edition. Giuseppe Toffanin emphatically affirmed that Orsi's *Considerazioni* was an "integral and philosophical defence of the Italian Aristotelian-tradition," in *L'eredità del Rinascimento in Arcadia* (Bologna: Zanichelli, 1923), 89. Toffanin continued, asserting that Orsi's *Considerazioni* demonstrated that "the French were neither Aristotelian nor classical" (89).

3 For a comprehensive discussion of Orsi's *Considerazioni*, see Bruni, *Italia, vita e avventure di un'idea*, 427–34.

4 Rome's Biblioteca Angelica holds the manuscript for this essay: *Osservazioni generali su la francese letteratura*, in *Arcadia manoscritti* 29, 97r-109r.

5 See Crescimbeni's account in *Storia dell'Accademia degli Arcadi* (London: T. Becket, 1804).

6 For more on *katharsis* in Aristotle's *Poetics*, see chapter 6, "Tragedy Defined and Analyzed into Parts," where Aristotle remarks, "Thus, Tragedy is an imitation of an action that is serious, complete, and possessing magnitude; in embellished language, each kind of which is used separately in the different parts; in the mode of action and not narrated; and effecting through pity and fear [what we call] the *catharsis* of such emotions." Aristotle, *Aristotle's Poetics*, trans. James Hutton (New York: W.W. Norton & Co., 1982), 50–2.

7 Enrico Mattioda, *Tragedie del Settecento*, vol. 1 (Modena: Mucchi Editore, 1999), 44–6.

8 See, for example, Alfredo Galletti's oft-cited description of the Italian frenzy surrounding the creation of the Italian tragedy: "Several writers, more

erudite than brilliant, noticed that Italy was lacking a tragic theatre, and this absence seemed to them more humiliating compared to the dramatic richness of other countries; they called Italians' attention to this defect and proposed several solutions. And then all throughout the peninsula, with a fervour and commendable enthusiasm, the tragic attempts multiplying themselves, poets, theorists, critics rising up, from every part dissertations, projects, treatises were raining down, in all the most educated parts of the nation, attempting to contribute to that desire and to that aspiration. The need, as a Darwinian would say, must have created the organ, and after eighty years of sterile discussions and mediocre attempts, we had Alfieri." Alfredo Galetti, *Le teorie drammatiche e la tragedia in Italia nel secolo XVIII (1700–1750)* (Cremona: Fezzi, 1901), 5.

9 See Gian Vincenzo Gravina's seminal treatises *Della ragion poetica* (Rome, 1708) and *Della tragedia* (Naples, 1715); Peitro Calepio's *Paragone della poesia tragica d'Italia con quella di Francia* (Zurich, 1732); Antonio Conti's *Prefazione alla tragedia Druso* (Venice, 1748); and Giuseppe Giorini Corio's *Trattato della perfetta tragedia* (Milan, 1729). For more on these works and numerous others on tragedy produced during the first half of the eighteenth century, see Enrico Mattioda, *Teoria della tragedia nel Settecento I* (Modena: Mucchi Editore, 1994). Mattioda's insightful analysis, meticulous interpretation and presentations of the previously neglected writings on tragedy of the period are paramount in Italian eighteenth-century drama studies.

10 Mattioda, *Tragedie*, 1: 7.

11 Ibid., 9–23.

12 Ibid., 23–48.

13 Ibid., 48–71.

14 Ludovico Antonio Muratori, *Della perfetta poesia italiana*, ed. Ada Ruschioni, 2 vols. (Milan: Marzorati Editore, 1971).

15 See Ruschioni's introductory commentary on Muratori's treatise, Muratori, 1: 13–24.

16 Ibid., 112.

17 Ibid., 114–15.

18 Ibid., 115. Muratori explained that a poet must base his literary creation on some form of the truth. Two fundamental truths exist in nature according to Muratori: "One is that Truth that in fact is, or ever has been," while "the other is that [which] seemingly has been, or even was able to be or should have been according to the forces of Nature." Ibid., 120.

19 Ibid., 125.

20 Ibid., 129.

21 For more on the Foscolo-Muratori connection, see my article "Making Histories and Defending Reputations: Ludovico Antonio Muratori and Ugo Foscolo," *Rassegna Europea di letteratura italiana* 36 (December 2010): 111–28.

22 "Poets aim at giving either profit or delight, or at combining the giving of pleasure with some useful precepts for life … The man who has managed to blend profit with delight wins everyone's approbation, for he gives his reader pleasure at the same time as he instructs him" [aut prodesse volunt aut delectare poetae, aut simul et iucunda et idonea dicere vitae … omne tulit punctum qui miscuit utile dulci, lectorem delectando pariterque monendo]. Horace, *Epistles Book II and Epistle to the Pisones*, ed. Niall Rudd (Cambridge: Cambridge University Press, 1989), 69–70.

23 Marshall, "Rousseau and the State of Theater," *Representation* 13 (1986): 84–114. See also Timothy M. Costelloe, "The Theater of Morals: Culture and Community in Rousseau's *Lettre à M. d'Alembert*," *Eighteenth-Century Life* 27, no. 1 (Winter 2003): 52–71.

24 Marshall, 86.

25 A third edition of Cesarotti's *Poesie di Ossian* was published in 1801. See Cesarotti, *Poesie di Ossian*, in *Dal Muratori al Cesarotti*, ed. Emilio Bigi (Milan: Riccardo Ricciardi Editore, 1960), 4: 87–269.

26 See Cesarotti, "Ragionamento sopra il diletto della tragedia," in *Dal Muratori al Cesarotti*, ed. Emilio Bigi (Milan: Ricciardi, 1960), 4: 27–53.

27 Ibid., 27–9.

28 Ibid., 35.

29 Ibid., 46–7.

30 Ibid., 38–9. For more on the concepts of pity and fear in Aristotle's *Poetics*, see chapter 14, "How to Arouse Pity and Fear," 58–60.

31 Cesarotti, "Ragionamento," 39.

32 Marvin Carlson asserts that Arcadian beliefs were "reinforced at the close of the century by the appearance at last of a tradition of significant modern neoclassic Italian tragedy, beginning with the works of Alfieri." Carlson, "The Italian Romantic Drama in Its European Context," in *Romantic Drama*, ed. Gerald Gillespie (Amsterdam, Philadelphia: John Benjamins Publishing Co., 1994), 238.

33 Alfieri's wrote his twenty tragedies between 1775 and 1795: *Cleopatra, Antigone, Polinice, Virginia, Agamennone, Oreste, La congiura de' Pazzi, Don Garzia, Maria Stuarda, Rosmunda, Ottavia, Timoleone, Merope, Agide, Sofonisba, Bruto I, Bruto II, Alceste seconda, Saul,* and *Mirra.*

34 Vittorio Alfieri, "Parere sulle tragedie," in *Opere di Vittorio Alfieri da Asti*, ed. Morena Pagliai (Asti: Casa d'Alfieri, 1978), 35: 81–167. First published in Paris, 1789.

35 Ibid., 81.

36 Ibid., 83.

37 Ibid., 144–5.

38 Ibid., 145.

39 Ibid., 157.

40 Ibid., 145.

41 Ibid., 146.

42 Ibid.

43 See ibid., 147–9.

44 Ibid., 149.

45 Ibid., 156–7.

46 Foscolo provided his own presentation of both Monti and Pindemonte to the English in his 1818 "Essay on the Present Literature of Italy"; see *E.N.*, 11.2: 442–66.

47 For Foscolo's early poetry, see *E.N.*, 2: 239–84. See also Christian Del Vento's impeccable discussion of Foscolo's early compositions in *Un allievo della rivoluzione: Ugo Foscolo dal "noviziato letterario" al "nuovo classicismo" (1795–1806)* (Bologna: CLUEB, 2003).

48 See Isabella Teotochi Marin Albrizzi's *Ritratti* (1807), in which the author depicted the famous participants of her salon in prose, especially Foscolo, Alfieri, and Byron. Isabella Teotochi Albrizzi, *Ritratti*, ed. Gino Tellini (Palermo: Sellerio, 1992). For more on Teotochi Albrizzi, see Cinzia Giorgetti, *Ritratto di Isabella: Studi e documenti su Isabella Teotochi Albrizzi* (Florence: Le Lettere, 1992) and Adriano Favaro, *Isabella Teotochi Albrizzi: La sua vita, i suoi amori e i suoi viaggi* (Udine: P. Gaspari, 2003). For more on Foscolo's relationship with Teotochi Albrizzi, see Bruno Rosada, *Foscolo a Venezia negli ultimi anni della Serenissima* (Treviso: Grafiche San Vito, 2006). Rosada succinctly described Teotochi Albrizzi's relationship with Foscolo as "lover for five days, but friend for a lifetime." Rosada, *Foscolo a Venezia*, 7.

49 See Foscolo's April 1796 letter to Paolo Costa for evidence of their amicable relationship. *E.N.*, 14: 29–31. See Foscolo's letter to Gaetano Fornasini, May 1795, and his letter to Cesarotti, October 1796, for evidence of Saverio Bettinelli's influence and interactions with the young Foscolo. *E.N.*, 14: 10–13 and 38–9. See Foscolo's letter to Aurelio de' Giorgi Bertola, 28 May 1795, in which the author professed his admiration for the poet. *E.N.*, 14: 15.

50 *E.N.*, 14: 17–18. Guido Bézzola noted in his introduction to volume 2 of the *Edizione nazionale delle opere di Ugo Foscolo* that there is no existing copy of the poem "Il Genio." Although Foscolo mentioned the work both in this letter to Cesarotti and a subsequent letter to his mentor from 30 October 1795 (*E.N.*, 14: 19), it appears that the ambitious poet never completed the

poem (see his *Piano di studi*). The ode "La Verità," however, was completed by Foscolo between 1795 and 1796. See, *E.N.*, 2: 290–3.

51 Foscolo detailed his admiration of Cesarotti in the April 1796 letter to Costa. See *E.N.*, 14: 31.

52 *E.N.*, 6: 1–10.

53 For more on the relationship between Foscolo's *Piano di studi* and Rubbi's *Parnaso*, see Carlo Dionisotti, "Venezia e il noviziato di Foscolo," in *Appunti sui moderni: Foscolo, Leopardi, Manzoni e altri* (Bologna: Il Mulino, 1998), 51.

54 Foscolo, *E.N.*, 14: 6–7.

55 Foscolo's *Piano di studi* includes the following Italian authors: under the heading of epic poets – Dante Alighieri and Torquato Tasso; for lyric poets – Alessandro Guidi; melodious lyric poets – Lodovico Vittore Savioli and Paolo Rolli; love poets – Francesco Petrarca and Antonio Conti; dramatists – Pietro Metastasio; pastoral poets – Jacopo Sannazzaro; rustic poets – Aurelio de' Giorgi Bertola; satirical poets – Giuseppe Parini; tragic poets – Vittorio Alfieri; narrative poets, Lodovico Ariosto and Lorenzo Pignotti; and under the heading of miscellaneous – Vincenzo Monti.

56 In the *Piano di studi*, Foscolo apparently did not regard Monti as a specialist of any particular genre or style of poetry.

57 Foscolo openly expressed his dislike for Pepoli's and Pindemonte's theatrical works in his 1818 "Essay on the Present Literature of Italy," *E.N.*, 11.2: 441–3.

58 For more on the theatres of eighteenth-century Venice, see Nicola Mangini's "Venezia il Foscolo e la rappresentazione del 'Tieste,'" *Rivista italiana di drammaturgia* 14 (1979): 37–55.

59 Franca R. Barricelli, "'Making a People What It Once Was': Regenerating Civic Identity in the Revolutionary Theatre of Venice," *Eighteenth-Century Life* 23, no. 3 (1999): 38–9. See also Mangini, "Venezia."

60 Shelley, "Ugo Foscolo," in *Lives of the Most Eminent Literary and Scientific Men of Italy, Spain, and Portugal*, vol. 2 (London: Longman, Rees, et al., 1835), 356.

Chapter Two

1 "Ardii scrivere una tragedia sopra un soggetto che fu già toccato da Crébillon e dal gran Voltaire. Sì; scrissi il *Tieste*." *E.N.*, 14: 19.

2 *E.N.*, 6: 8.

3 "Ma il tempo in cui scriveva un atto al giorno (come quando composi il Tieste) è passato con la foga e l'ardire della mia gioventù." *E.N.*, 16: 497.

4 See Alfieri, "Parere," 146.

5 Prosper Jolyot de Crébillon, *Atrée et Thyeste*, in *Oeuvres de Crébillon* (Paris: P. Didot, 1802), 1: 89–155.

6 F.M. Arouet (Voltaire), *Les Pélopides*, in *Oeuvres complètes de Voltaire* (Paris: Chez Furne, 1835), 2: 176–191.

7 P.J. Davis, *Seneca: Thyestes*, Duckworth Companions to Greek and Roman Tragedy (London: Duckworth, 2003), 128.

8 "Yes; I wrote *Tieste*, and with only four characters … If they [the audience] will not accept it among their favourites, the tears and the terror of the ignorant will satisfy me, since they are the main objectives of all of my verses. Of course, I never would have ventured my hard work and my name if Crébillon was less intricate and the great author of *Maometto* more terrible and more decisive." [Sì; scrissi il *Tieste*, e con quattro attori soltanto … S'essi [spettatori] non l'accetteranno fra le lor favorite, basteranmi le lagrime ed il terror degli ignari, che sono i principali oggetti di tutti i miei versi. Certo ch'io non avrei avventurato la mia fatica e il mio nome, se il Crébillon fosse meno intricato, e il grand'Autore del *Maometto* più terribile, e più deciso.] *E.N.*, 14: 19–20.

9 Cesarotti, "Ragionamento," 38–9.

10 Carlo Dionisotti discussed Foscolo's notable decision to adopt the Alfierian structure for *Tieste* when, at the same moment in Venice and Padoa, there was a distinct departure from the Astian model. See Dionisotti, "Venezia e il noviziato di Foscolo," in *Appunti sui moderni: Foscolo, Leopardi, Manzoni e altri* (Bologna: Il Mulino, 1988), 43.

11 Maria Maddalena Lombardi used the term lyrical to define Foscolo's characters of Erope and Tieste. For her, the term "lyrical" is equated with "Metastasian." In her 1994 "Scheda introduttiva" to *Tieste*, Lombardi succinctly examined the difference between Foscolo's use of the prototypical Alfierian tyrant character, Atreo, and the indecisive characters of Tieste and Erope. See Lombardi's "Scheda introduttiva" and "Note" to *Tieste* in Foscolo, *Opere* (Turin: Einaudi-Gallimard, 1994), 1: 722–7, 727–88. Of course, what Lombardi fails to mention is the decidedly different meanings of Alfieri's tyranny vs liberty theme (developed pre-1789) and the weighted meaning of Foscolo's use of the tyrant figure, Atreo, in the aftermath of the French Revolution. For more on the Alfierian nature of Foscolo's *Tieste*, see Christian del Vento's meticulous and subtle analysis in *Un allievo della rivoluzione: Ugo Foscolo dal noviziato letterario al nuovo classicismo (1795–1806)* (Bologna: CLUEB, 2003), 39–47.

12 *E.N.*, 14: 18–20.

13 See chapter 1.

14 See act 5, scene 4. Voltaire, *Les Pélopides*, 2: 190–1.

15 *E.N.*, 2: 55.

16 Ibid., 56.

17 Ibid.

18 "Spiacemi che il Foscolo azardi la sua Tragedia senza domandarne consiglio da chi pò. Questo è un passo che può decidere della sua fortuna. Io non l'ho veduta dopo l'ultima mano. Come stava prima avea varie scene interessanti, ma nel totale v'era molto da correggere." *E.N.*, 14: 41, n. 1.

19 Ibid.

20 Ibid.

21 Luigi Carrer, *Vita di Ugo Foscolo*, ed. Carlo Mariani (Bergamo: Moretti & Vitali, 1995), 69.

22 Nicola Mangini, "La vita teatrale nella Venezia del Foscolo," in *Atti dei convegni Foscoliani* (Rome: Istituto Poligrafico e Zecca dello Stato, 1988), 3: 251. For more on Pellandi and Foscolo see also Rosada, *Foscolo a Venezia*, 23–7. Other members of the original cast included the playwright Giulio Domenico Camagna as Tieste, and Gaetano Businelli as Atreo.

23 "Si temeva molto del *Tieste* a S. Angiolo, tragedia ristretta a quattro personaggi d'argomento terribile. Non vi fu azione quella sera che più di quello piacesse: il suo giovine autore fu sollevato dagli applausi alle stelle; il suo genio promette al tragico italiano teatro de' nuovo onori, e il nome suo si ripete ovunque con ammirazione ed elogi." *Gazzetta Urbana Veneta*, 7 January 1797.

24 The second positive review includes the following succinct description of the tragedy: "Una tragedia di quattro attori, di scena stabile, d'argomento terribile, in cinque atti, sena' alcun esterno soccorso per il materiale dell'occhio e dell'udito, ha da essere molto ben ideata, e condotta e scritta, e molto bene rappresentata, per avere tanta fortuna. Ecco l'elogio del suo giovin Autore e de' personaggi che la eseguiscono." *Gazzetta Urbana Veneta*, 14 January 1797.

25 "Mio padre – Si vide il *Tieste*; si tacque, si pianse. Ecco l'elogio ch'io faccio al Foscolo di diciott'anni." The date of Foscolo's letter to Cesarotti is unknown. However, as Plinio Carli remarks in his annotation of the letter, "It must be from the final days of January or the first days of February 1797." *E.N.*, 14: 39. Foscolo's use of "Ecco l'elogio" is conspicuously similar to the review from 14 January in the *Gazzetta Urbana Veneta*.

26 "fortunata tragedia." Printed in *Giornale dei Teatri*, vol. 7 of the *Teatro moderno applaudito* (Venice, January 1797). As quoted in Foscolo, *Opere*, ed. Franco Gavazzeni, Maria Maddalena Lombard, and Franco Longoni (Turin: Einaudi-Gallimard, 1994), 1: 723.

27 This evaluation of the historical significance of Foscolo's ten performances of *Tieste* has been thoroughly discussed by Nicola Mangini.

28 "Il *Tieste* fu giudicato da un populo non filosofo in cosa alcuna, e meno in questa: felice dunque l'autore di diciott'anni che seppe capire la fama dalla bocca di una capitale mal prevenuta per lo stile, per la semplicità, e quel ch'è piú per le passioni grandi ed energiche. Ma nel *Tieste,* benché di stile istudiato, di purissima semplicità, e di sommo calore, non avvi né lo stile vero, né il semplice nobile, né la passione ben maneggiata e dipinta." *E.N.,* 14: 39.

29 Ibid.

30 "giudicatela dunque severamente," *E.N.,* 14: 40.

31 "My dear Foscolo – I have already heard with utmost satisfaction, the applause made at your tragedy; but I was also surprised, mortified, and almost irritated to not hear them from you … But I am very glad that you have not let yourself be inebriated from the applause, since your work needs revising." [Mio caro Foscolo – Avea già sentito con somma compiacenza gli applausi fatti alla tua Tragedia; ma fui anche sorpreso, mortificato, e quasi quasi irritato di non sentirlj da te … Godo assai però che non ti lasci inebbriar dall'applauso, e che vada tuttavia ritoccando il tuo lavoro.] *E.N.,* 14: 40–1.

32 "saranno stampabili." *E.N.,* 14: 41.

33 "coll'interesse del padre e colla severità del critico." *E.N.,* 14: 42.

34 See Guido Bézzola's analysis of the question of authorship, *E.N.,* 2: xvi.

35 *E.N.,* 2: 203.

36 As was customary during the period, Stella, as editor of the collection, was morally (if not legally) obligated to show his edition to the author of the piece before publication.

37 See, for example, Foscolo's letters to Cesarotti from 30 October 1795 (*E.N.,* 14: 18–20) and late January and early February 1797 (*E.N.,* 14: 39–40), as well as his letters to Vittorio Alfieri and Diodata Roero on 22 April 1797 (*E.N.,* 14: 42–4).

38 "È fuor di dubbio che quella del signor di Voltaire ha servito più d'ogni altra al piano del nostro autore." *E.N.,* 2: 206. This observation is conspicuously similar to what Foscolo wrote in his 30 October 1795 letter to Cesarotti, when, before composing *Tieste,* he remarked on how he intended to improve upon Voltaire's tragedy. See *E.N.,* 14: 19.

39 Foscolo acknowledged that a teenager such as himself might be too inexperienced to compose the highest quality of tragedy, conceding that his young age might hinder the success of his theatrical debut. Foscolo concluded his letter by expressing his hope that Cesarotti would not think less

of the tragedy simply because of his youth. He wrote, "In the meantime, I hope that you will not all of a sudden think, as many others do, that he who is young and who sings odes cannot be ready to write philosophical poems and tragedies." [Frattanto io spero che voi non crederete ad un tratto, come tant'altri, che chi è giovane e che canta dell'odi non possa accingersi a scrivere de' poemi filosofici e delle tragedie.] *E.N.*, 14: 20.

40 "Foscolo di diciott'anni," *E.N.*, 14: 39.

41 "un giovane che dee prepararsi con questa sua prima fatica la stima, e la disistima degli uomini." *E.N.*, 14: 40. Similarly, Foscolo sent copies of his first tragedy to both the inestimable Vittorio Alfieri and to the only woman thus far to be invited into the *Accademia privata piemontese*, followed by the *Accademia delle scienze di Torino*, Diodata Roero (1774–1840). Foscolo began the accompanying introductory letters by stating that *Tieste* was only "the first tragedy of a young, Grecian-born man, who was educated in the Dalmatian islands"; "la prima tragedia di un giovane nato in Grecia ed educato fra Dalmati." See Foscolo's letters to Alfieri ("Il Tragico dell'Italia") *E.N.*, 14: 42 and Roero ("La Saffo italiana"), *E.N.*, 14: 43.

42 This effort appears to have been successful; even contemporary critics emphasize the influence of Foscolo's youth on his public's perception of *Tieste*. For example, as recently as 2000, Maria Antonietta Terzoli's book stresses Foscolo's youth when discussing the work: "Who reads *Tieste* today … cannot but ask if the reason for the extraordinary success that smiled on the young author was not perhaps his own impressive youth." See Maria Antonietta Terzoli, *Foscolo* (Rome: Laterza, 2000), 19.

43 "il primo saggio d'un giovanetto che non ha ancora compiuto il diciannovesim'anno dell'età sua," *E.N.*, 2: 203. The author further scattered comments on Foscolo's age throughout the piece, such as "Alfieri's pupil," "our young author," "the age of Mr Foscolo," "other young writers," "if the author was of a more mature age," and even a remark on his "studious youth." The original phrases read, "alunno dell'Alfieri" (ibid., 206), "il nostro giovine autore" (twice on 207), "L'età del signor Foscolo" (208), "altri giovani scrittori" (208), "se l'autore avesse un'età più matura" (208), and "studiosa gioventù" (note 1, 206)

44 See ibid., 206–7, n. 3.

45 See ibid., 206, n. 2.

46 "Sono così mal collocate le massime di politica in questo componimento, che giungono perfino a raffreddare una delle più calde situazioni tragiche, quale si è quella della scena terza dell'atto IV." Ibid., 208, n. 1.

47 "In Atene, a' tempi d'Aristofane, eranvi de' giudici, o commissarj, destinati dal governo per decidere del merito delle composizioni teatrali: … Era

inoltre vietato a' poeti di produrre cosa alcuna sulle scene prima dell'età di trenta, o, secondo altri, di quarant'anni." Ibid., 208, n. 3.

48 For more on Alfieri's "Parere," see chapter 1. See Marvin Carlson's account of Alfieri's rejection of *Cleopatra* in *The Italian Stage from Goldoni to D'Annunzio* (London: McFarland & Co., 1981), 20–1. See also Vittorio Alfieri's version of the story of *Cleopatra* in the "Epoca terza," of his *Vita*.

49 Foscolo, *Opere*, ed. Gavazzeni, Lombardi, and Longoni, 1: 724.

50 The performance was short-lived. *Atreo e Tieste* debuted on 5 August 1808 and ran for three nights. See the *Giornale Italiano* 217–20, from 4–7 August 1808, for the announcements of the performances.

51 "Dimani si rappresenterà la tragedia del sig. Ugo Foscolo intitolata *Atreo e Tieste*. La sera sarà a beneficio della prima attrice sig.a Anna Pellandi." *Giornale Italiano* 217, Milan, Thursday, 4 August 1808.

52 *Corriere Milanese*, 4 August, 1808: "La prima [Pellandi] non è altro, che la scelta e la bella Natura posta sulla scena; sì bene sa essa trasformarsi in tutti i caratteri, e sì bene penetrare ne' cuori o appaja di regal manto decorata, o d'umile od elegante donna adorna" (748).

53 "Essa perciò ottiene omai la primazia fra le attrici d'Italia." *Corriere Milanese*, 748.

54 See G.A. Martinetti, "Sul testo delle tragedie di Ugo Foscolo," *Giornale storico della letteratura italiana* 23 (1894), 215.

55 See ibid.

56 Gianfranco Acchiappati, *Raccolta foscoliana Acchiappati: Edizioni originali e ristampe scritti su riviste letterarie e giornali*, vol. 1 (Milan: Distribuzione Edizione il polifilo, 1988), 150–1.

57 Foscolo had a tendency of not mentioning events in his letters when they occurred and of reflecting on them at a later date. See Sandra Parmegiani's astute commentary on Foscolo's *Epistolario* in *Ugo Foscolo and English Culture* (London: Legenda, 2011), 33.

58 "Se i Veneziani avessero fischiato il mio *Tieste*, com'ei meritava, quand'io avea diciott'anni, non avrei forse più né scritto né letto." From Foscolo's December 1808 letter to Vincenzo Monti, *E.N.*, 15: 542. This letter was subsequently published in the journal *Biblioteca italiana* (n. 180, December 1830).

59 *E.N.*, 11.2: 468.

60 For "Per la istituzione di un teatro civico," see *E.N.*, 6: 723.

61 See *E.N.*, 14: 46–9.

62 Foscolo was so overjoyed with the arrival of Napoleon's troops that he immediately composed the ode *Bonaparte liberatore* while in Bologna.

63 For more on Italian Jacobinism, see Paolo Bosisio, *Tra ribellione e utopia: L'esperienza teatrale nell'Italia delle repubbliche napoleoniche (1796–1805)*

(Rome: Bulzoni, 1990). Bosisio explains that Jacobinism was "passively accepted by the Italians, without originality" (103).

64 *Raccolta di tutte le carte pubbliche stampate ad esposte ne' luoghi piu frequentati della citta di Venezia.* (Venezia, 1797), 1: 161.

65 For more on the society, see Giovanni Gambarin's notes in his introduction to volume 6 of *Edizione nazionale*, E.N., 6: xx.

66 *Raccolta di tutte le carte pubbliche stampate*, 1: 224. See also the report in the public session of 27 May 1797 in *Raccolta di carte pubbliche, istruzioni, legislazioni, ecc. Del nuovo veneta governo democratico* (Venice: Gatti, 1797), 1: 17–18.

67 In Italian, the societies making up the committee were "di censura, d'istruzione, di corrispondenza, di beneficenza, di economia, e d'ispezione della sala." E.N., 6: xxi.

68 The public documents can be found in two different ten-volume collections: *Raccolta di tutte le carte pubbliche* and *Raccolta di carte pubbliche*. The society's minutes of the verbal sessions were published in a single volume. See *Prospetto delle sessioni della Società di pubblica istruzioni* (Venice: Giovanni Zatta, 1797). Venice's Museo Correr library holds the only accessible copy remaining. As Michieli noted in his 1904 study *Ugo Foscolo a Venezia*, this volume does not include every session. Adriano Augusto Michieli, *Ugo Foscolo a Venezia*, in *Nuovo archivio veneto*, 5–7 (Venice: Visentini, 1904).

69 *Raccolta di tutte le carte pubbliche stampate*, 1: 226–7.

70 See Giovanni Gambarin's thorough discussion of the society in his introduction, E.N., 6: xix–xxvi.

71 "Io volo! Io vado a spargere le prime lagrime libere, ed a parlare a' miei concittadini che per tanto tempo soffersero le loro catene."E.N., 14: 50.

72 E.N., 14: 53.

73 See *Prospetto*, 22.

74 Foscolo began his service as recording secretary on 23 July. See Giovanni Gambarin's introduction, E.N., 6: cxlix–cl, for the details surrounding Foscolo's position.

75 See Michieli for a comprehensive examination of Foscolo's participation in the society.

76 For a general overview of the role of the theatre in nation building and that of the citizen/spectator, see Loren Kruger's chapter 1, "Theatrical Nationhood and Popular Legitimation," in *The National Stage: Theatre and Cultural Legitimation in England, France, and America* (Chicago: University of Chicago Press, 1992), 3–39. Kruger also aptly discusses the role of the national theatre in France in the late eighteenth and early nineteenth centuries in chapter 2, "Theatre to Contain a People," 31–82, esp. 31–8.

77 Horace, *Epistles Book II and Epistle to the Pisones*, ed. Niall Rudd (Cambridge: Cambridge University Press, 1989), 69–70.

78 Mario Marcazzan, "La letteratura e il teatro," in *La civiltà veneziana del Settecento*, ed. Diego Valeri (Florence: Sansoni 1960), 201. See Franca R. Barricelli's article "'Making a People What It Once Was.'" See also Martha Feldman, "Opera, Festivity and Spectacle in 'Revolutionary' Venice," in *Venice Reconsidered: The History and Civilization of a City State 1297–1797*, ed. John Jeffries Martin and Dennis Romano (Baltimore, MD: Johns Hopkins University Press, 2000), 217–62.

79 See *Raccolta di tutte le carte pubbliche stampate*, 1: 162.

80 The manifesto was signed by Nicoló Ugo Foscolo, Pietro Buratti, Giacomo Colombina, Antonio Psalidi, Giovanni Comarolo, Francesco Psalidi, Giovanni Bianchi, and Pietro Comarolo. *E.N.*, 6: 717; originally published in *Raccolta di carte pubbliche*, 1, ccxxxix–ccxl. For more on the manifesto, see Giovanni Gambarin, "Note foscoliane," in *Saggi foscoliani e altri studi* (Rome: Bonacci Editore, 1978), 165–78.

81 *Raccolta di carte pubbliche*, 1: ccxxxix–ccxl.

82 See Gambarin's introduction, *E.N.*, 6: cxlix–cl.

83 Franca R. Barricelli erroneously dated the manifesto as being from 13 May 1797. She also inexplicably wrote that the manifesto was reprinted in volume 13 of the *Teatro moderno applaudito* in July 1797; see Baricelli, n. 19. It was not. The introductory remarks comment on the value of a civic theatre. Yet there is no evidence of the society's manifesto in this volume. See *Teatro moderno applaudito* (Venice, 1797), 13: 3–4.

84 Manilo Pastore Stocchi, "1792–1797: Ugo Foscolo a Venezia," in *Storia della cultura veneta* (Vicenza: Neri Pozza, 1986), 6: 21–58.

85 The letter is addressed to both the male and female citizens of Venice ("Cittadini e cittadine"), *E.N.*, 6: 717.

86 "Ora riacquistando novella vita, liberi, sciolti dalle barbare catene del pregiudizio, e solamente soggetti a quelle, ben più soavi, dell'onore, della umanità, del dovere e della Legge possiamo liberamente dar campo ai nostri pensieri, cribrare le nostre idee, render utili i nostri studi." *E.N.*, 6: 717.

87 "Si propone un Teatro Civico. Ci dedicaremo alla declamazione, alla musica ed a comporre per istruire il Popolo, lasciando al nostro genio la scelta se avremo aggravio alcuno; occorrendo qualche momentanea sovvenzione, essa sarà tenue assai, ed a titolo di semplice imprestanza. Tutto ciò che si ritrarrebbe oltre le spese, verrà distribuito ai poveri." Ibid.

88 Ibid.

89 Rebecca Messbarger, *The Century of Women: Representations of Women in Eighteenth-Century Italian Public Discourse* (Toronto: University of Toronto Press, 2002), 6, citing Pierdomenico Soresi, *Saggio sopra la necessità e la facilità di ammaestrare le fanciulle* (Milan: Federico Agnelli, 1774), 32, 38.

90 Messbarger, 6, citing Melchiorre Delfico, *Saggio filosofico sul matrimonio* (Teramo, 1774).

91 Messbarger, 6, citing Saverio Bettinelli, "Lettere sui pregi delle donne," in *Opere edite e inedited in prosa ed in versi* (Venice: Adolfo Cesare, 1799–1801), 13: 261–2. Messbarger also cites from Elisabetta Graziosi's 1992 article "Arcadia Femminile: Presenze e Modelli," explaining the importance of women in the Italian Arcadian Academy: "The Arcadia did something more than propose and change feminine and linguistic paradigms in the course of its century-long existence, gathering together the aristocratic woman in combat with her destiny, the wife and the platonic lover, the cultured actress, the female adventurer, the professional woman poet and playwright. After the conclusion of its first moment under the star of female patronage [Queen Cristina of Sweden] the Arcadia opted for a commingling of the sexes that had as its model the *salon* and that relegated to the past the misogynistic closure of the seventeenth-century Italian intellectual class." Elisabetta Graziosi, "Arcadia Femminile: Presenze e Modelli," *Filologia e critica* 17 (1992): 321–58, trans. Messbarger, 8–9.

92 The important role of women as educators was overshadowed by the very real inequality between the education of men and women during the period. A "free citizen" published an opinion piece, entitled "Sulla nuova istituzione d'un Teatro Civico" in the second volume of the *Raccolta di carte pubbliche*, 2: 37–45. The anonymous author noted that women were at a distinct disadvantage and were not in fact treated equally with regard to the civic theatre. This was the direct consequence of the fact that women did not have the same education. The article proceeds with a presentation of the then-current treatment of women in Venetian society and their morals. This opinion piece is interesting when set against Foscolo's 1826 article "The Women of Italy" in the *London Magazine*. Foscolo attempted to correct the Grand Tour representations of Italian female depravity. He discussed in detail the social condition of women in Italy and focused on their education and morality. See *E.N.*, 12: 418–69.

93 See Barricelli, 46.

94 See Foscolo's letter of 16 May 1797, to the Municipality of Reggio Emilia. *E.N.*, 14: 49–50. He mentions the tragedy more than a year later in another letter to Milan's Society of Patriotic Theatre. Ibid., 70.

95 "Grand'uomo è Alfieri, e grande Scrittore Repubblicano, e degno d'imitazione e di laude. Felice l'Italia, se tutti i tragici lo eguagliassero!" *E.N.*, 6: 27.

96 "Alfieri quindi sdegnossi, e confinò la sua vita in Firenze all'ombra della neutralità del Granduca." Ibid., 27.

97 "Io non sarò forse ascoltato; ma io avrò promulgata la verità. Alfieri tace! Alfieri non parla che per lanciare delle rampogne all'Italia. Alfieri dunque non ha diritto alla stima de' patrioti." Ibid., 29.

98 *Raccolta di tutte le carte pubbliche stampate*, 7: 278–280.

99 "Ancor fanciulli nella carriera della libertà … come nel regno della libertà i progressi dello spirito umano sono più rapidi e sublimi, così dobbiamo lusingarci che presto arriverà il teatro alla più alta perfezione e diverrà scuola di morale costume." *Raccolte di tutte le carte pubbliche stampate*, 7: 279.

100 Foscolo wrote a letter to the provisionary Municipality of Venice asking to be relieved of his position and was excused the following day. See *E.N.*, 14: 56.

101 For more on *Dei sepolcri* see Joseph Luzzi's impeccable analysis in *Romantic Europe and the Ghost of Italy* (New Haven: Yale University Press, 2008), specifically the introduction (1–21), "Did Italian Romanticism Exist?" (25–52), and chapter 8, "The Body of Parini" (195–212).

102 *E.N.*, 7: 3–37. See Emilio Santini's introduction to volume 7 of the *Edizione nazionale* for more information on Foscolo's appointment at the University of Pavia and the five additional lectures he presented, ibid., xiii–xxiv.

103 Ibid., 17.

104 In *Dell'origine*, Foscolo was referring to Gerolamo Tiraboschi, *Storia della letteratura italiana* (Modena, 1772–82); Francesco Saverio Quadrio, *Della storia e della ragione di ogni poesia* (Venice, 1739–52); Giovan Mario Crescimbeni, *La bellezza della volgar poesia* (Rome, 1700; Venice, 1712, 1731); and Muratori, *Della perfetta poesia italiana* (1706).

105 "La letteratura deve, se non altro, nutrire le meno nocive, dipingere le opinioni, gli usi e le sembianze de' giorni presenti, ed ammaestrare con la storia delle famiglie." *E.N.*, 7: 35.

106 Ibid., 37.

Chapter Three

1 See Guido Bézzola's introduction to *Ajace* in *E.N.*, 2: xviii.

2 For more on Foscolo's incomplete tragedy, see also Maria Antonietta Terzoli's brief discussion of *Edippo* in *Foscolo* (Rome: Laterza, 2000), 21–2; Maria Maddalena Lombardi, "Sull'attribuzione al Foscolo dell'«Edippo» tragedia di Wigberto Rivalta," *Studi di filologia italiana* 54 (1996): 291–309; and the introduction to Mario Scotti's edition of the play, *Edippo tragedia inedita* (Milan: Rizzoli, 1983), 7–80.

3 *E.N.*, 2: 226–35. In his outline, Foscolo wrote notes indicating several scenes from Shakespeare's *Richard II* and quoted from *Richard III* in French. He began his notes to *Edippo* by writing "Ricard. II, Sc.6. att. 3 – vol. 8 pag. 104 e seg." *E.N.*, 2: 226. Foscolo erroneously cited this scene – Shakespeare only wrote four scenes in act 3 of *Richard II*. Presumably, Foscolo was citing from Pierre LeTourneur's (1736–88) famous translations of Shakespeare's works, *Shakespeare traduit de l'Anglois*, 20 vols. (Paris, 1776–83).

4 The story of Ajax is also found in Ovid's *Metamorphoses*, book 8.

5 See lines 215–25 of Foscolo's poem *Dei sepolcri*, *E.N.*, 1: 131.

6 See his 23 March 1811 letter to Ugo Brunetti: "On February 2, I finally started, and it was about time, to write *Ajace*; and now I am spending day and night with those heroes and demigods from the *Iliad*." [A' 2 di febbraio incominciai finalmente, ed era ormai tempo, a verseggiare l'Aiace; ed ora mi sto giorno e notte con quegli eroi e semidei dell'Iliade] *E.N.*, 16: 501.

7 See his letter of 6 February 1811: "And now finally I am working on the Heroes of the tragedy that I promised to the director. But the time in which I was writing one act per day (like when I wrote *Tieste*) has passed along with the fire and daring of my youth. Now perhaps I will write better; but in an entire day I cannot extract the meaning that ten years ago I would extract in only one hour. By the end of spring I will certainly have finished." [Ed ora appunto sto addosso agli Eroi della tragedia che ho promessa all'impresario. Ma il tempo in cui scriveva un atto al giorno (come quando composi il Tieste) è passato con la foga e l'ardire della mia gioventù. Ora forse scriverò meglio; ma ora in un giorno intero non cavo il costrutto che dieci anni addietro io cavava in un'ora sola. Per la fine di primavera avrò certamente finito.] *E.N.*, 16: 497.

8 Foscolo mentioned the difficult time he had when composing *Ajace* in his numerous letters to family and friends. See his 11 April 1811 letter to Giambattista Giovio: "Now I have, after three weeks of boredom, given myself again to other prophets, and before reverting to *Ajace*, I would like to piously spend Holy Week rereading Isaiah." [Or io mi sono, dopo tre settimane di noia, ridato ad altri profeti, e prima di ripigliare l'*Aiace* voglio piamente spendere la settimana santa a rileggere Isaia.] *E.N.*, 16: 506; n.b., 11 April 1811 was indeed Holy Thursday. See also Isabella Teotochi Albrizzi's 13 May 1811 inquiry about *Ajace* and Foscolo's 14 May 1811 response: *E.N.*, 16: 512–16; a 28 September 1811 letter from the actor Paolo Belli Blanes, who after hearing that Foscolo had completed *Ajace*, offered to recite a role: *E.N.*, 16: 522–3; and Foscolo's 5 October 1811 letter to Giuseppe Grassi, where he mentioned he had just finished the last verses:

E.N., 16: 525. See Guido Bézzola's introduction to *Ajace*, for the chronology of Foscolo's composition of his second tragedy: *E.N.*, 2: xviii–xxxviii.

9 Alfieri, "Parere," 157.

10 The one hundred lines for Calcante are represented by eleven short lines and three soliloquies (33 lines, 23 lines, and 33 lines, respectively). Yet again, Foscolo strayed from the teachings in Alfieri's "Parere sulle trage- die," which stipulated that secondary characters should not have solilo- quies. See Alfieri, "Parere," 152.

11 Mario Fubini, *Ugo Foscolo* (Florence: Nuova Italia, 1962), 220.

12 Eugenio Donadoni, *Ugo Foscolo: Pensatore, critico, poeta*, 3rd ed. (Florence: Edizioni Remo Sandron, 1964), 409.

13 Giorgio Pullini, *Teatro italiano dell'Ottocento* (Milan: Vallardi, 1981), 45.

14 Roberto Alonge, *Struttura e ideologia nel teatro italiano fra '500 e '900* (Turin: Stampatori Università, 1978), 193.

15 Ciccarelli, "L'*Ajace* di Foscolo fra azione e inazione: Ovvero il rifiuto della storia." *Quarterly Journal in Modern Foreign Languages* 49, no. 3 (Fall 1995): 203–13.

16 See both Maria Maddalena Lombardi's "Scheda introduttiva" and her ex- tensive annotations ("Note") of *Ajace* in Foscolo, *Opere*, 1 (Turin: Einaudi- Gallimard, 1994), 788–96, 796–876.

17 *E.N.*, 3, pt. 1, 13–58. See Gennaro Barbarisi's introduction to the *Esperimento* for more on Foscolo's attempts at replicating the Homeric verse in Italian, *E.N.*, 3.1, xix–xxiv. See also Arnaldo Bruni's *Foscolo tradut- tore e poeta: Da Omero ai "Sepolcri"* (Bologna: CLUEB, 2007) for a thorough examination of Foscolo's translation practices.

18 Lombardi, "Note," 793.

19 *E.N.*, 2, 62 and 3.1, 16.

20 *E.N.*, 2, 65 and 3.1, 31.

21 *E.N.*, 2, 67 and 3.1, 26.

22 *Annali* 2 (1810): 25–78. Emilio Santini aptly describes the content of the ar- ticle in his introduction to the seventh volume of the national edition of Foscolo's works as a biting outburst against his enemies; *E.N.*, 7: xxviii. Two prominent figures in Italian medicine directed the *Annali*, Pietro Moscati and Giovanni Rasori. The *Annali di scienze e lettere* ran from 1810– 13 in Milan. Foscolo published "Sulla traduzione dell'Odissea del Pindemonte" (April–May 1810) in the *Annali*. For more on Foscolo's in- volvement with the *Annali*, see Santini's introduction, *E.N.*, 7: xxxvi–liii.

23 *E.N.*, 7: 231–81.

24 Giuseppe Chiarini recounted Lampredi's reaction in his biography of Foscolo, remarking how Lampredi responded with an extremely biting

article – "un articolo molto frizzante." Chiarini, *La vita di Ugo Foscolo*, ed. Guido Mazzoni (Florence: G. Barbèra, 1927), 217.

25 "Re della lega de'ciarlatani letterari," *E.N.*, 7: 296. Foscolo's "Ultimato di Ugo Foscolo nella guerra contro i ciarlatani, gl'impostori letterari ed i pedanti" remains incomplete. See *E.N.*, 7: 296–316 and Emilio Santini's introduction, *E.N.*, 7: xxxii.

26 Lampredi directed *Il Poligrafo* from 1811 through the beginning of 1812 (when he left for Naples), at which point Luigi Lamberti assumed control until his death in 1813. From its founding in 1811 until early 1812, *Il Poligrafo* printed numerous articles under the direction of Lampredi, criticizing Foscolo's literary and literary-critical works.

27 The feud between the men has been well documented since at least the late nineteenth century. For more on the Foscolo-Lampredi conflict, see G.A. Martinetti, *Delle guerre letterarie contro Ugo Foscolo* (Turin: Paravia, 1881); Aldo Vallone, *La polemica Foscolo-Lampredi* (Galatina, 1946); and Rita Chini, "Il 'Poligrafo' e l''Antipoligrafo': Polemiche letterarie nella Milano napoleonica," *Giornale storico della letteratura italiana* 149 (1972): 87–105.

28 Thomas E. Peterson, "Justice, Modesty, and Compassion in Ugo Foscolo's *Ajace*," in *The Revolt of the Scribe in Modern Italian Literature* (Toronto: University of Toronto Press, 2010), 38. Peterson brought *Ajace* completely out of the shadows and thoroughly introduces today's reader to the tragedy.

29 Giuseppe Chiarini described an audience consisting of both allies and enemies of the tragedian in his 1910 biography of Foscolo. Chiarini, 224. See also Luigi Carrer's similar account: Carrer, *Vita di Ugo Foscolo*, ed. Carlo Mariani (Bergamo: Moretti & Vitali, 1995), 215.

30 See chapter 2 for more on Anna Fiorilli Pellandi. Paolo Belli Blanes played Ajace, Giovanbattista Prepiani was Agamennone, Alberto Tessari was Ulisse, and Giovanni Bettini was Calcante. According to Ettore Catalano, *Ajace*'s actors constituted "a cast of most notable, artistic prominence." Ettore Catalano, *Le trame occulte: L'Ajace e la Ricciarda nel percorso teatrale di Ugo Foscolo* (Bari: Laterza, 2002), 55.

31 Chiarini, 224.

32 Giuseppe Chiarini noted in his biography that Foscolo hid under his cloak and snuck out of the theatre. Chiarini, 224–5.

33 Cesarotti, "Ragionamento sopra il diletto della tragedia," in *Dal Muratori al Cesarotti*, ed. Emilio Bigi (Milan: Ricciardi, 1960), 4: 35.

34 Act 5, ll. 392–4. *E.N.*, 2: 137.

35 Giuseppe Pecchio, *Vita di Ugo Foscolo*, ed. G. Nicoletti (Milan: Longanesi, 1974), 176.

36 As Chiarini described, the actor's pronunciation of the verses sparked an unfortunate reaction from the spectators – that of laughter. Chiarini, 225.

37 Pecchio, 286.

38 See Chiarini, 226–7. Eugenio Donadoni counters the claim that Foscolo based the character Ajace on General Jean-Victor Moreau, stating that Ajace is actually Foscolo himself. Donadoni, *Ugo Foscolo: Pensatore, critico, poeta*, 3rd ed. (Florence: Remo Sandron, 1964), 401. On 13 December 1811 the Viceroy Eugène de Beauharnais posted an announcement banning *Ajace*: *E.N.*, 16: 547, note.

39 "If Your Authority will deign to believe the protests of a man who has never degraded himself to lying, then she will be able to persuade you that while I sought to represent in Ajax the imprudence and accidents of a badly employed heroism, I could not have the foolish intention of agitating a public that venerates the founder of the Kingdom of Italy, that blesses the government of Your Authority." [Se V. A. si degnerà di credere alle proteste d'un uomo che non s'è mai avvilito a mentire, Ella si persuaderà che mentr'io mirava a rappresentare in Ajace le imprudenze e gl'infortuni d'un eroismo mal impiegato, io non poteva avere la stolta intenzione di turbare un popolo che venera il fondatore del regno d'Italia, e che benedice il governo di V. A.] *E.N.*, 16: 547–8.

40 Foscolo's letter to Grassi reads: "Last night I read to a few young men the 1750 verses of *Ajace*. They liked it, or so they made me believe: but I, from their facial expressions, realized that those who had heard it recited in passages other times, liked it much more. In any case, they all judged that the first act was worse than the others, and they recommended that I trim it. How does one do that? You cannot take out even half of one verse without unravelling the entire tragedy; and I am so deadened by that work that I would rather choose to write an entirely new tragedy from scratch than have to rake over the scenes of this one. Plus, it takes time; and the manuscript is already in the hands of the actors, to whom I sent it because so they will learn their lines … *The die is cast*, and God be with me! The fourth and fifth acts come across generally pitiable and quick, and they will balance out the bad of the first three, even though to me the second seems like the best of them all. Tecmessa turned out to be a great character; so it seems to everyone, since everyone cried. To me, the character of Ulysses seems the least imperfect in its genre, perhaps because it cost me so much energy. – In the first few days of December, or soon after, I will see the effect of the scene, and I will be able to make a less inexact judgment, and more duly make corrections." [Ier sera ho letto ad alcuni giovani i mille settecento cinquanta versi dell'*Ajace*. Piacque, o così almeno mi fecero credere: ma io da' muscoli del viso m'accorsi, che a chi l'aveva udito recitare a squarci altre volte, piaceva più assai. Ad ogni modo tutti giudicarono, che il primo atto fosse peggiore degli altri, e mi raccomandarono

d'accorciarlo. Come si fa? Non si può togliere mezzo verso senza sconnett-
ere tutta la tragedia; ed io sono sì esanimato da quel lavoro, che sceglierei
di scrivere una nuova tragedia di pianta, anzichè rimestare le scene di
questa. E poi ci vuol tempo; e il manoscritto è già nelle mani degli attori, a
quali l'ho inviato perchè imparino le parole delle lor parti ... *Jacta est alea,*
e Dio me la mandi buona! Il quarto e quinto atti riescono sommamente pa-
tetici e rapidi, e compenseranno il cattivo dei primi tre, benchè il secondo
a me paja il migliore di tutti. Tecmessa è riuscita bellissimo carattere; così
parve a tutti, perchè tutti piansero. A me pare men imperfetto nel suo genere il carattere d'Ulisse, forse perchè mi è costato sudori sudori sudori. –
A' primi di dicembre o poco dopo, vedrò l'effetto della scena, e potrò farne
giudicio meno inesatto, e correggere più utilmente.] *E.N.*, 16: 531–2.

41 The other journals were the *Giornale di giurisprudenza*, the *Giornale d'indizio*,
 Annali di agricoltura, and *Annali di scienze e lettere*, the journal to which
 Foscolo contributed.

42 For more on the circulation of periodicals during the early nineteenth century, see Carlo Capra, "Il giornalismo nell'età rivoluzionaria e napoleonica," in *La stampa italiana dal Cinquecento all'Ottocento*, vol. 1, ed. Valerio
 Castronovo, Giuseppe Ricuperati, and Carlo Capra (Bari: Laterza, 1976),
 371–537. Capra remarks on the relatively passive nature of most periodicals of the period: "From a table compiled based on the information of the
 chief officers, we learn that the leading journal was the *Corriere Milanese*
 with 3000 subscribers, which was a little more than that of the *Giornale
 Italiano*; further behind was the *Corriere delle Dame*, with 700 subscribers,
 then *Notizie politiche* of Milan, *Il Quotidiano Veneto*, and *Notizie del Mondo*
 (both from Venice), with 500 subscriptions each. All the other papers sold
 at the most 200 or 300 copies, and there were a few that did not even reach
 100. It is important, therefore, to keep in mind that the majority of the journals were passive" (495).

43 Francesco Pezzi, "Notizie interne," *Corriere Milanese*, 10 December 1811,
 1179–80. See Gavazzeni, Lombardi, and Logoni's *scheda introduttiva* of
 Foscolo's *Ajace* in Foscolo, *Opere*, vol. 1, *Poesie e tragedie*, 788–96. See also
 Paolo Bosisio, "La rappresentazione dell'*Ajace* e la tecnica teatrale foscoliana," *Belfagor* 35 (1980): 149.

44 "Sometimes you could hear clapping hands at some phrases, at some well-
 coloured images, and for worthy verses of poetry." [S'udì talvolta batter le
 mani ad alcune sentenze, a qualche immagine ben colorita, e a certi squarci di poesia che il meritavano.] Pezzi, 1179.

45 "But two minutes later, many of those spectators who had remained began
 to clap their hands, and it was then that you heard some indiscreet and
 even unjust whistles mixed in with the applause. But these last ones were

victorious." [Ma due minuti dopo, parecchi di quegli spettatori ch'erano rimasti, si mossero a batter le mani, e fu allora che s' intese qualche indiscreto ed anco ingiusto fischio mescolarsi coi plausi. Ma quest'ultimi furono vittoriosi.] Pezzi, 1180.

46 Lattanzi, *Corriere delle Dame*, 14 December 1811, 425–6.

47 Each edition of the *Corriere delle Dame* contained short stories, theatrical and poetry reviews as well as tips for women regarding manners and child-rearing. In addition to reports on fashion, the *Corriere delle Dame* also contained weekly news and political updates in a section entitled *Termometro politico*.

48 "cui niuno contrasta veracità d'ingegno, e dignità di stile." Lattanzi, 425.

49 "riescirà difficile il credere che il Sig. Foscolo non otenesse pieni, e generali applause." Lattanzi, 425.

50 "Per quanto egli abbia ben sostenuta la dignità di carattere in Agamennone, ed in Ajace, altrettanto l'ha avvilita in Ulisse, ed in Calcante: il primo lo fa comparire un basso intricante da commedia, ed il secondo, nell'atto quinto principalmente, lo trasforma da Sacerdote in Telegrafo, facendogli narrare dall'alto di una collina alla moglie di Ajace, che trovarsi nella pianura." Lattanzi, 426. Clearly the author was comparing Calcante's presence on stage to the arms set in motion on Claude Chappe's 1792 invention, the optical telegraph.

51 "Queste mie ingenue avvertenze nulla tolgono al merito poetico del Sig. Foscolo, sia per la elocuzione, che per le sentenze ed immagini di che ha dato nuovo e luminoso saggio in questa tragedia." Lattanzi, 426.

52 "lo spirito pubblico di una nazione," as cited in Capra, 498. "Varietà," *Giornale Italiano* 349, 15 December 1811, 1392–6.

53 "Questa tragedia non fu accolta con quegli applausi che sembrava doversi aspettare." "Varietà," 1396.

54 "Forse non mai fu questo Teatro si ridondante di spettatori, nè mai sì grande fu la pubblica aspettazione … questa tragedia ottenuto non abbia l'effetto che ne attendevamo; e ciò faremo noi tanto più volontieri, quanto che le nostre osservazioni servire potranno di avvertimento all'autore nella tragica carriera, per la quale sembra che voglia incamminarsi." "Varietà," 1395.

55 "Ma non mai scuotere e commovere altamente il cuore, unico scopo della tragica poesia." "Varietà," 1395.

56 "La sua tragedia però non riscosse quella corona, a cui sembrava di dover aspirare, e malgrado alcuni pregi che in essa risplendono, lasciò o freddo, o indifferente il cuore degli affollati spettatori." "Varietà," 1395.

57 "Come difettoso venne pure censurato il lungo e freddo soliloquio di Ajace allorchè sta per uccidersi, ed il prolisso dialogo in cui egli ha parte dopo d'essersi ferito. Pare che la disperazione non debba dar luogo a tanti

riflessi, nè a tante apostrofi quante sono quivi in bocca di Ajace furioso." "Varietà," 1396.

58 "Nella tragedia del sig. Foscolo, Ulisse non è più il saggio figlio di Laerte, ma un vile adulatore del Retagemmi, uno scellerato che nulla tralascia per ottenere il suo intento. D'Agammenone poi ha voluto il nostro autore un ambizioso politico modellato più sui precetti di Machiavelli e di Hobbes, che sull'archetipo che viene da Omero presentato." "Varietà," 1396.

59 "Maggior campo di gloria si apirirà forse il nostro autore, se abbandonando i mitologici argomenti rivolgerà il suo ingegno a quelli che trarre si possono dalla storia." "Varietà," 1396.

60 "Pertanto se il Poeta non disegna e non conduce bene la sua azione, talchè sia verosimile nella sua totalità, e ben connessa nelle sue parti, se ne' suoi personaggi non si vedono quei caratteri, e nelle loro parlate quella scelta di pensieri, che convengono all'azione stessa, e che la fanno procedere al suo fine per passioni successivamente destate, se in una parola parla il Poeta, e non l'Attore, allora non vi ha più illusione, l'azione illanguidisce, e l'anima dello Spettatore non si occupa più, e si annoja; allora finalmente non si sa perchè Ajace sia morto." Lampredi, "AJACE, Tragedia nuovissima del sig. Ugo Foscolo," *Il Poligrafo*, 15 December 1811, 590.

61 "Gl'inconvenienti, e gli sbagli di questa Tragedia compariranno in più chiara luce, quando esamineremo i caratteri o falsi o grotteschi che U.F. ha dati agli Eroi d'Omero. Anzi siccome è stato detto, che questo soggetto non è suscettivo d'esser posto in azione Tragica, noi speriamo di potere dimostrare il contrario, delineando un disegno, sopra il quale si può fare, a parer nostro, una buona Tragedia d'Ajace. Noi lo metteremo nel venturo Poligrafo sotto gli occhj de' nostri Leggitori, e del Pubblico. Ci sembra, che dopo aver veduto come questa Tragedia non deve farsi, abbiamo potuto immaginare come debba farsi." Lampredi, ibid., 591–92.

62 "diamo un'occhiata al disegno e economia della Tragedia del sig. U. F. ed ai caratteri de' suoi personaggi." Lampredi, ibid., 590.

63 "Ora io domando, con questo disegno di scene bizzarre, slegate, si può egli fare una vera e buona Tragedia?" Lampredi, ibid., 591.

64 "il disegno di questa Tragedia sia stato mal concepito." Lampredi, ibid., 592.

65 "abbiamo già dimostrato che la Tragedia dell'*Ajace* è un vero mostro per rispetto al disegno." Lampredi, *Il Poligrafo*, 22 December 1811, 594.

66 "il quale difetto si deve attribuire all'ignoranza o la disprezzo dei buoni precetti dell'arte." Lampredi, ibid., 594.

67 Lampredi wrote, "Ma se l'Ajace è un vero mostro, quanto al disegno, esso non lo è punto meno per rispetto ai caratteri dei principali personaggi." Lampredi, ibid., 595.

68 "E da questo lato ancora qualche studio sull'arte avrebbe giovato al poeta
per insegnargli, che i caratteri degli Eroi famosi si debbono rappresentare,
quali le storie, o le tradizioni degli Autori più riputati, ce gli [*sic*] hanno
costantemente dipinti." Lampredi, ibid., 595.

69 "Dimmi ripeto, avresti tu riconosciuto te stesso, se fossi venuto a vedere la
nuova Tragedia, che s'intitola del tuo gran nome? Ohimè! ohimè! tu avresti sicuramente rinnovato la strage delle pecore, e la flagellazione dell'irco,
e ti sarestj ammazzato la seconda volta, vedendoti effigiato in sì strana caricatura, e rappresentato ora come un furioso, che imbestialisce senza motivo, ed ora come un timido novizietto, che consapevole di sue mancanze
palpita e trema al cospetto del P. Abate Calcante?" Lampredi, ibid., 597.

70 "Cotesta non è Tragedia affatto, ma una miserabile parodia di un pezzo
di Storia Eroica, nella quale Agamemnone è trasformato nel Capitan
Covriello, Ulisse in Brighella, Teucro in Arlecchino, Calcante in Pantalone,
Tecmessa in Rosaura, ad Ajace in Meneghino Pecenna." Lampredi, ibid.,
598.

71 "Per rispetto al disegno, all'azione, alla peripezia, ai caratteri, alla mancanza di esposizione nel principio, e di ogni buon fine morale nella conclusione." Lampredi, *Il Poligrafo*, 29 December 1811, 612.

72 "Pochi e radi difetti non distruggeranno mai il valore di un componimento, che sia veramente buono nelle parti essenziali; ma un componimento
cattivo nella sua totalità, rimarrà pur sempre cattivo, a malgrado di qualche bellezza che vi risplenda." Lampredi, ibid., 613.

73 "il soggetto non è *tragediabile*." Lampredi, "Letteratura," *Il Poligrafo*, 5
January 1812, 3.

74 Lampredi, ibid., 6.

75 *E.N.*, 19: 245. Quirina Mocenni Magiotti ran a modest literary salon in
Florence. In 1812, while in Florence, Foscolo had an affair with Mocenni
Magiotti, which ended in 1814 with Foscolo's departure, though they reg-
ularly corresponded with each other until Foscolo's death. As mentioned
in chapter 2, Foscolo rarely wrote about an event at the time it actually
happened. He instead would wait, reflect, and then reconstruct the story
after the fact. For more of Foscolo's epistolary style, and the important relationship between Foscolo and Magiotti, see Parmegiani, chapter 1.

76 Foscolo's complete account of *Ajace*'s demise reads: "But I hear the
Florentine whistles against poor *Ajace*; and they pass over the Apennines,
the Po, the lakes, the frost, and the Alps; so much do they seem to me hor-
ribly resounding! Never mind that Fabbrichesi had lost the best of his actors, the ones who played the best characters of *Ajace*, for despite my
severe paternal guidance, those remaining were scared; the capital truth is
that *Ajace* agitates passions that are now dead and mocked in Italy; … but

today the hearts are dead to those passions; it is better, I will not deny, it is considerably better for Italians; but the tragedy becomes cold." [Intendo bensì le fischiate fiorentine contra al povero *Aiace*; e le passano Appennino, e Po, e laghi, e gelo, ed Alpi; tanto le mi paiono orrendamente sonore! Lascio stare che il Fabbrichesi ha perduto i migliori de' suoi attori, e che a que' migliori i caratteri dell'*Ajace*, malgrado la mia paterna e severa assistenza, erano spavento; la verità capitale si è, che l'*Ajace* agita passioni che ora in Italia sono morte e derise; … ma i cuori sono oggimai incadaveriti per quelle passioni; è meglio, non lo negherò, è assai meglio per gl'Italiani; ma la tragedia diventa fredda.] *E.N.*, 19: 245.

77 For detailed explanation of the division of Italy following the fall of Napoleon, see Alain Pillepich, *Napoléon et les Italiens: République italienne et Royaume d'Italie* (Paris: Nouveau Monde, 2003), 190–8.

78 *E.N.*, 19: 245.

79 See Foscolo's letter, *E.N.*, 17: 214–26.

80 *E.N.*, 8: 367–71.

81 *E.N.*, 17: 214.

82 Ibid., 218.

83 Ibid., 218.

84 Ibid., 215.

85 Ibid., 215.

86 Ibid., 215.

87 Ibid., 215–16.

88 This notion of *discordia armonica* appears again in Foscolo's rarely studied first published lecture "Principles of Poetical Criticism, as Applicable, more Especially, to Italian Literature" (hereafter "Principles," 1824) from the series of lectures entitled *Epoche della lingua italiana* or *Epochs of the Italian Language* (1823–4); *E.N.*, 11.1: 25–36. "Principles" was originally published in July 1824 as "Principles of Poetical Criticism, as Applicable, more Especially, to Italian Literature," *European Review* 1, no. 2: 258–64.

89 This precise sentiment was expressed in 1776 by Samuel Johnson in his biography of Cowley in *Lives of Poets*. Johnson explained, "But wit, abstracted from its effects upon the hearer, may be more rigorously and philosophically considered as a kind of 'discordia concors'; a combination of dissimilar images, or discovery of occult resemblances in things apparently unlike." Samuel Johnson, "Cowley," in *Lives of the Poets*, vol. 1 (London, 1896), 13. Ovid also used the phrase *discors concordia* when referring to the creation of the universe in his *Metamorphoses*, writing "… vapor unidus omnes / Res creat et discors concordia fetibus apta est." *Metamorphoses*, 1: 432–3.

90 *E.N.*, 17: 216.

91 Ibid., 216–17.

92 Ibid., 217.

93 Ibid., 215.

94 Ibid., 217–18.

95 Ibid., 217–18.

96 See note 71.

97 *E.N.*, 17: 218.

98 See Foscolo's own account of his travels in his letter to the Countess of Albany from 4 September 1813, where he explained, "Today marks fifteen days since I went to visit the Prince of Belgioioso; he received me most happily; and while they called us to dinner, he was hit with apoplectic attack, from which he died shortly after; and there I am a guest in a house of mourning; and so as not to be intrusive or bothersome (expecially since there was no person to console), I immediately climbed into the carriage and headed towards Como." [Oggi sono quindici giorni, andai a visitare il Principe di Belgioioso; m'accolse lietissimo; e mentre chiamano a tavola, lo colse l'apoplessia di cui morì poco dopo; ed eccomi ospite nella casa del lutto; e per non essere importuno ed importunante (tanto più che non v'era persona da consolare) montai subitamente in calesse, e pigliai la volta di Como.] *E.N.*, 17: 333.

99 The article appears in issue number 30 of the journal. *E.N.*, 8: 367–71.

100 See Luigi Fassò's introduction in *E.N.*, 8: cxxii–cxxiii.

101 The letter reads, "You write to Venice, and I meanwhile, wanting to or not, went wandering around from Milan up around all the lakes that border with the Swiss. Now I return, tired, exhausted and with eyes full of sleepiness and sun, because believing I would be outside only one day, I had left my blue glasses in Milan … I will tell you the unforeseen reasons for my eleven-day-long pilgrimage." [Tu scrivi a Venezia, ed io frattanto volere e non volere andai ramingando da Milano su per tutti i laghi che confinano con gli Svizzeri. Ritorno ora, stanco, sfinito, e con gli occhi afflitti dal sonno e dal sole, perché credendo di star fuori un dì solo, io aveva lasciati a Milano i miei occhiali azzurri … ti dirò le ragioni non prevedute di questo mio pellegrinaggio d'undici lunghi giorni.] *E.N.*, 17: 329.

102 Ibid., 327–30.

103 Ibid., 332.

104 "They [the people of Como] built a beautiful theatre; and it opened precisely on the day that I arrived there; but the master builders, the impresario, the singers and a thousand other inconveniences prolonged the

opening day in and day out until the 28th of August; and I, day in and day out, … remained there, wanting and not wanting, for more than eight days." [Fabricarono (i comaschi) un bel teatro; e s'apriva appunto nel giorno ch'io v'arrivava: ma i capomaestri, l'impresario, i cantanti, e mille altri inconvenienti protrassero l'apertura di giorno in giorno sino a' 28 d'agosto; ed io di giorno in giorno … mi fermai volendo e non volendo per più d'otto giorni.] Ibid., 333–4.

105 "Meanwhile, as the admirers observe with the telescope wanting to enlarge the object, and the critics abuse the microscope to dissect, or as they say, analyse the defects, I am here observing with the naked eye; and if I come across the truth, I am absolutely certain not to hide my true feelings, and not to arm myself with *abstract* principles, useful more to the fame of the authors of treatises than to the progress of the arts, since the authors of treatises do not want to observe that every work is subject to circumstances, to obstacles and to very complicated concerns: but human attempts in the execution of intellectual design succeed very little" [Frattanto, mentre i lodatori osservano col telescopio volendo ingrandire l'oggetto, e i critici abusano del microscopio per notomizzare, o, com'essi dicono, analizzare i difetti, io mi sto qui osservando a occhio nudo; e se travedo la verità, sono, se non altro, certissimo di non dissimularvi i veri miei sentimenti, e di non armarmi di principj *astratti*, utili più alla fama dei trattatisti che al progresso delle arti, dacchè i trattatisti non vogliono osservare che ogni lavoro è soggetto a circostanze, ad ostacoli ed a riguardi complicatissimi: però gli umani tentativi nell'esecuzione riescono minori assai del disegno intellettuale.] (author's emphasis). *E.N.*, 8: 367–8.

106 "I obtained his design, and comparing it with the finished product …" [Ottenni il suo disegno, e paragonandolo colla fabbrica …]. Ibid., 368.

107 Ibid., 368.

108 Ibid., 369.

109 Ibid., 368.

110 "I saw that the majority of the faults one must ascribe not so much to the men, as *to the problems, to the circumstances, to the obstacles* that, as I told you, luck perpetually interposes between the firmest resolutions and the universal rules of art" [Vidi che la maggior parte delle colpe si dovrà ascrivere non tanto agli uomini, quanto *a' riguardi, alle circostanze, agli ostacoli* che, come vi dissi, la fortuna interpone perpetuamente a' più saldi proponimenti e alle regole universali dell'arte.] (Foscolo's emphasis). Ibid., 368.

111 Ibid., 369.

112 Ibid., 369.

113 Ibid., 370.
114 Ibid., 370.
115 Ibid., 369.
116 Ibid., 369.
117 Ibid., 371.
118 Ibid., 371.
119 See Giuseppe Nicoletti's apt description of Didimo Chierico in relation to Jacopo Ortis in *Foscolo* (Rome: Salerno, 2006), 216–20. See also Joseph Luzzi's nuanced analysis of the duo in his discussion of Foscolo's developing views on Giuseppe Parini at the end of his chapter, "The Body of Parini," in *Romantic Europe and the Ghost of Italy* (New Haven: Yale University Press, 2008), 210–12. Sandra Parmegiani went so far as to claim that "the Didimo/Yorick alter ego remains Foscolo's most authentic self-representation"; Parmegiani, 13.
120 "Invenit enim Didymus nescio in quorum monachorum bibliotheca acroama vetustum de *Eunuchomachia*, id est, de rixantis et lucrosae philologiae usu." *E.N.*, 8: 70. Foscolo's intention with this work was to lash out at his Milanese enemies, and as an 1832 article in the *Foreign Quarterly Review* remarks, "He printed a few copies, to some of which he added a Key. The principal persons alluded to were then fallen, and in disgrace. This was a piece of puerile and paltrey revenge, quite unworthy of him." André Vieusseux, "Foscolo and His Times," *Foreign Quarterly Review* 9, no. 18 (May 1832), 339. Foscolo proposed years later, in a letter to his friend Silvio Pellico, that literary journalism was biased and bent only on praising friends and putting down enemies. *E.N.*, 20: 394. Foscolo continued his letter by remarking that *Il Poligrafo* was the worst and most despicable, most venomous journal of them all. *E.N.*, 20: 394.
121 *E.N.*, 17: 283–90.

Chapter Four

1 "Faccia il cielo, ch'io possa tornare a Venezia sano, nitido, forte; e allora vi leggerò una nuova tragedia *tutta amore*, ch'io aveva incominciata con moltissima vocazione, ma che ho lasciata stare perchè ho mille cose nel cuore, ma nulla nulla dentro il cervello." *E.N.*, 17: 68.
2 "La mia povera *Ricciarda* ch'era la più bella, la più innamorata, e la più disgraziata tra le principesse, mi aspetta." Ibid., 148–9.
3 "Dio sa! Quando potrò vederne la fine?" Ibid., 164.
4 Ibid., 168.

 5 For a complete account of the manuscripts of the tragedy, see Guido
   Bézzola's introduction to *Ricciarda*, *E.N.*, 2: xxxviii–l.
 6 *E.N.*, 17: 217.
 7 Foscolo's continued emphasis on certain elements of the tragedy related to
   graves (i.e., the tomb, an urn, shadows) can be traced to his 1807 poem *Dei
   sepolcri*, as well as to *Ajace*, *Ultime lettere di Jacopo Ortis*, and the sonnet "In
   morte del fratello Giovanni." In act 1, scene 1, ll. 33–4, Corrado warns
   Guido that if he is caught, he could be killed and buried, in the same grave
   with his brother, without dignity: "Nè ti scampava in tempo, or giaceresti
   / Compagno alle insepolte ossa fraterne," *E.N.*, 2: 144. Foscolo expresses a
   similar concern with individual tombstones in *Dei sepolcri*, ll. 13–15: "what
   solace for days lost would be a stone / made to distinguish mine from
   other, countless / bones which Death scatters over land and sea?" [qual fia
   ristoro a' dì perduti un sasso / che distingua le mie dalle infinite / ossa
   che in terra e in mar semina morte?] *E.N.*, 1: 128.
 8 In all three of Foscolo's tragedies, he is concerned with representations of
   his characters' love of power.
 9 Giorgio Pullini, *Teatro italiano dell'Ottocento* (Milan: Vallardi, 1981), 49.
10 Roberto Alonge, *Struttura e ideologia nel teatro italiano fra '500 e '900* (Turin:
   Stampatori Università, 1978), 194.
11 Guidi Di Pino, "La 'Ricciarda,'" in *Atti dei convegni foscoliani* (Rome:
   Istituto Poligrafico e Zecca dello Stato, 1988), 3: 271–83.
12 *E.N.*, 2: 161.
13 See the first novella of the fourth day; Giovanni Boccaccio, *Decameron*,
   ed. Vittore Branca (Milan: Mondadori Editore, 1985), 1: 337–48.
14 The earlier French tragedy tells the story of two young lovers, Tancrède
   and Amenaide, who struggle to realize their affections against a backdrop
   of political and family conflict.
15 An interesting comparison also exists between Foscolo's *Ricciarda* and
   Shakespeare's *Romeo and Juliet*. Although there is no evidence supporting
   the notion that Foscolo relied on Shakespeare when writing his own tragedy, both stories are concerned with the forbidden love of the children of
   two warring families. Moreover, by 1823, the popularity of the story of
   Romeo and Juliet spiked a rise in tourism to Verona, with tourists visiting
   the famed tomb of the two lovers. For more on the cult of *Romeo and Juliet*
   in early-nineteenth-century Italy, see Francesco Bruni's introduction to
   L'Italia e la formazione della civiltà europea: Letteratura e vita intellettuale, ed.
   Francesco Bruni (Turin: UTET, 1994), xiv.
16 "Frammenti su Machiavelli," in *E.N.*, 8: 1–63. Foscolo intended to publish
   "Dello scopo di Gregorio VII" in volume 7 of the *Annali di scienze e lettere*;

however, the piece was sequestered by the censors, who prohibited its publication. *E.N.*, 7: 381–401.

17 See Maria Maddalena Lombardi, "Scheda introduttiva" and "Note" to *Ricciarda* in Foscolo, *Opere*, 1 (Turin: Einaudi-Gallimard, 1994), 876–84; 884–941. For more on the costume connection see Lombardi, 882–3.

18 Giorgio Pullini characterized *Ricciarda* as pre-resorgimental on account of the themes of patriotic love (as portrayed by Averardo) and anti-tyrannical sentiment (as portrayed by Corrado). Pullini, 50.

19 See Pullini's characterization of Guelfo as the "true prototype of dark romanticism." Pullini, 46. See also Ettore Catalano's 2002 book *Le trame occulte*, in which he discussed Foscolo's new-found tendency to prioritize the psychological development of both the male and the female characters. He argued that, unlike Erope and Tecmessa, Ricciarda is a complex character who takes centre stage and dominates the spotlight. Catalano, *Le trame occulte*, 96–7.

20 Alfieri based his 1781 tragedy *Rosmunda* on Rucellai's 1515 tragedy *Rosmunda*.

21 Eugenio Donadoni, *Ugo Foscolo: Pensatore, critico, poeta*, 3rd ed. (Florence: Edizioni Remo Sandron, 1964), 409.

22 Giuseppe Nicoletti recently remarked on how Foscolo's strict adherence to the unity of place did not actually garner favour with contemporary audiences. *E.N.*, Appendix 2, 320.

23 For "are," see *Ricciarda*, act 1, scene 2, v. 111 in *E.N.*, 2: 147 and *Dei sepolcri*, vv. 91, 98, and 184 in *E.N.*, 1: 130 and 131. For "avelli," see *Ricciarda*, act 1, scene 4, v. 269 in *E.N.*, 2: 154; act 4, scene 4, v. 215 in *E.N.*, 2: 187 and *Dei sepolcri*, vv. 131 and 282 in *E.N.*, 1: 130 and 131.

24 *E.N.*, 2: 183.

25 Ibid., 183.

26 Ibid., 184.

27 "Ma ad ogni modo pel giorno 12 dovrò trovarmi a Bologna dove la Ricciarda farà la sua prima comparsa; e non posso lasciarla abbandonata agli attori." *E.N.*, 8: 369.

28 See *E.N.*, 2: 215–25.

29 "La Tragedia fu pessimamente recitata." See *E.N.*, 17: 349.

30 "*Guelfo* avrebbe fatto eccellentemente se non avesse voluto far troppo; *Ricciarda* pareva una ragazza *sentimentale*, anzichè una principessa innamorata altamente; piacque nondimeno al pubblico; a me spiacque moltissimo. *Averardo* fu sostenuto ragionevolmente. Ma *Guido* fu recitato in modo ch'io stesso che lo aveva meditato e scritto e riletto non intendeva ciò che quel disgraziato fantoccio vestito in scena da Eroe volesse mai dire

… Guido, ho paura, sarà carattere Don-Chisciottescamente petrarchesco: ridicolo insomma." *E.N.*, 17: 350.

31 "Dopo il primo atto il pubblico picchiava le mani; ed io nel mio cuore avrei picchiate tutte quelle testacce di corno, le quali non sapevano che il migliore regalo che si possa fare a un autore è il silenzio." *E.N.*, 17: 350.

32 See chapter 2 and Foscolo's letter to Cesarotti, *E.N.*, 14: 39.

33 "Ma la benevolenza pubblica m'irritava ancor più dopo il secondo atto; si chiamava l'autore a battimani, si urlava il mio nome; si tempestava rompendo le sedie perch'io venissi a ricevere le congratulazioni del *popolo-giudice*, il quale intanto guastava la tragedia: uscivano gli attori a incominciare il terz'atto, ed erano rispinti dal *popolo-sovrano* che voleva *fuori* l'Autore. Ma l'Autore che fa lo scrittore, e non già il ciarlatano; … fece il sordo per più di mezz'ora … – Ma la mia modestia fu dall'uditorio ascritta a superbia" (Foscolo's emphasis). *E.N.*, 17: 350–1.

34 See Cesarotti, "Ragionamento," 35.

35 *E.N.*, 17: 351.

36 "Ma quanto all'ultima scena, nè il popolo, nè i comici stessi sanno come la sia finita; perchè il Diavolo ci ha messo nuovamente la coda. Avvenne che, mentre Averardo e Corrado prorompevano su la scena con armati e con fiaccole – io ne rido, ed ella riderà certamente leggendo – avvenne che una di quelle torce diè fuoco alla barba di crino d'una comparsa … e il fuoco da una barba s'appicciò alle altre; e al ridere successe il terrore, perchè l'acquarasa [essential oil] delle fiaccole, cadendo su le assi della scena, le ardeva; e frattanto gli spettatori erano divisi con l'attenzione all'accidente funestamente ridicolo ma reale, ed alla catastrofe immaginaria dell'infelice Ricciarda." *E.N.*, 17: 351.

37 "Io frattanto rimasi incantucciato nel mio palchetto e imperterrito, come quel Turco fatalista che mentre gli crollava addosso la casa continuava a fumar la sua pipa e a sorseggiare il caffè." *E.N.*, 17: 352.

38 "Whoever praises or faults it after this performance would be unjust or a fraud." [Chi la lodasse o la biasimasse dopo questa recita, sarebbe ingiusto o impostore.] *E.N.*, 17: 351–2.

39 See *E.N.*, 8: 374–6.

40 "If the great Alfieri repeated so many times that he himself would have needed three or four diligently executed performances in order to judge his own tragedies, it will not seem strange if we, from one troubled performance alone with several disturbing accidents, cannot give an exact or precise briefing." [Se il grande Alfieri ripetè tante volte che egli medesimo per giudicare delle proprie tragedie avrebbe avuto bisogno di tre o quattro recite diligentemente eseguite, non parrà strano se noi da una sola recita e

con molti estranei accidenti turbata, non possiamo dare un ragguaglio esatto e preciso.] *E.N.*, 8: 374. See chapter 1 for more on Alfieri's "Parere."

41 "If we had been allowed to read the tragedy, you would perhaps hear much rightful praise in the midst of some criticisms made without bitterness or bias." [Se ci fosse stato conceduto di leggere la tragedia, si udirebbero forse molte lodi giustissime in mezzo ad alcune critiche fatte senza amarezza e senza prevenzione.] *E.N.*, 8: 376.

42 "The author no longer obtained that deepest and solemn silence." [L'autore non ottenne più quel profondissimo e solenne silenzio.] *E.N.*, 8: 374.

43 Ibid.

44 See, for example, remarks that accuse the actors of exaggerating and not seeming sure of themselves: "We will say, frankly, that Mr Tessari exaggerated his part ... Mrs Cavalletti, who played Ricciarda, frequently got applause, but even she did not seem sure of herself." [Diremo francamente che il sig. *Tessari* esagerò la sua parte ... La signora *Cavalletti* che recitava la Ricciarda ottenne frequenti applausi, ma anch'ella non parve sicura di sè.] *E.N.*, 8: 375.

45 Ibid.

46 "The characters (and in this part, the author takes greater credit) are different, decisive, and original; it seems that he searches and finds in the darkness of the human heart, some lights in order to show man in a natural and the most original aspect." [I caratteri (e in questa parte l'autore ha il maggior merito) sono vari, decisi, ed originali; pare ch'egli cerchi e trovi nelle tenebre del cuore umano dei lumi per mostrare l'uomo in un aspetto naturale e novissimo.] *E.N.*, 8: 376.

47 "Striking, concise, fleet of judgments; his [Foscolo's] style is both rich and original. Will he be denied a seat among Alfieri and Monti, as Voltaire was among Corneille and Crébillon?" [Vibrato, conciso, parco di sentenze; ricco insieme, ed originale è il suo stile. Gli sarà negato di sedere tra Alfieri e Monti, come Voltaire tra Corneille e Crébillon?] *E.N.*, 8: 376.

48 "Notizie storico-critico sul *Tieste*" first appeared in volume 10 of the *Teatro moderno applaudito*, *E.N.*, 2: 203–8. See chapter 2.

49 "Ho ritirata ... la mia *Ricciarda*; non è paese nè tempo da tragedie." *E.N.*, 17: 441.

50 *E.N.*, 8: 315–20.

51 According to Foscolo, these errors "ruined up until today the attempts of others." [rovinarono fino ad oggi i tentativi degli altri.] Ibid., 315.

52 Ibid., 315–16.

53 "può farsi mediatrice fra la ragione di stato e le passioni del popolo." Ibid., 316.

54 "Procura di dimostrare al pubblico che gli estensori del tuo giornale scriv-
ano per utilità de' loro concittadini, e per desiderio di fama anzi che per
mercantile speculazione ...; Comproverai al pubblico di avere per collabo-
ratori i letterati più dotti ...; Mostra l'intento di scrivere non tanto ai contemporanei quanto alla posterità, quasi che la storia letteraria e la verità
morale e politica trovassero rifugio negli archivi del tuo giornale per
trasmettersi alla cognizione di chi vorrà un giorno conoscerle." Ibid.,
317–18.

55 Said explained, "It must also be recognized that the defensive nationalism
of exiles often fosters self-awareness much as it does the less attractive
forms of self-assertion. Such reconstitutive projects as assembling a nation
out of exile ... involve constructing a national history, reviving an ancient
language, founding national institutions like libraries and universities."
Edward Said, "Reflections on Exile," in *Reflections on Exile and Other Essays*
(Cambridge, MA: Harvard University Press, 2000), 184. Similarly, Glauco
Cambon speculated that England's geography stirred up nostalgic sentiments of Venice in Foscolo: "London would also secretly conjure ... the
image of Ugo's intermediate insular homeland, Venice – seafaring, busy,
lately free Venice. Thus the traumatic, if exciting, experience of finding
himself abroad would be compounded with the strange vibration of a
half-realized recognition, the familiar being mirrored in the alien and
new." Glauco Cambon, *Ugo Foscolo, Poet of Exile* (Princeton: Princeton
University Press, 1980), 306.

56 D. Keith Simonton, *Greatness: Who Makes History and Why* (New York: The
Guilford Press, 1994). For more on an author's quest for fame, see David
Giles, *Illusions of Immortality: A Psychology of Fame and Celebrity* (New York:
St Martin's Press, 2000). For a historical analysis of fame in Western histo-
ry, see Leo Braudy, *The Frenzy of Renown: Fame and Its History* (London:
Oxford University Press, 1986).

57 See *E.N.*, 8: 119–50. Foscolo only published three copies of the *Vestigi*. He
dedicated each of these copies to three separate female acquaintances:
Quirina Mocenni Magiotti, Susetta Füssili, and Metilde Viscontini
Dembowski (1790–1825).

58 The poets Foscolo chose to include in the anthology were Guittone
d'Arezzo (1235–94), Guido Cavalcanti (1258–1300), Dante Alighieri (1265–
1321), Cino da Pistoia (1270–1336/7), Francesco Petrarca (1304–74), Giusto
de' Conti (1390–1449), Leonello d'Este (1407–50), Lorenzo de' Medici
(1449–92), Pietro Bembo (1470–1547), Vittoria Colonna (1490–1547),
Veronica Gambara (1485–1550), Galeazzo di Tarsia (1520–53), Giovanni
della Casa (1503–56), Angelo di Costanzo (1507–91), Torquato Tasso

(1544–95), Alessandro Tassoni (1565–1635), Francesco Redi (1696–1760), Benedetto Menzini (1646–1704), Alessandro Guidi (1650–1712), Giovanni Battista Felice Zappi (1667–1719), Cornelio Bentivoglio (1668–1732), Quirico Rossi (1696–1760), Onofrio Minzoni (1734–1817), Giuseppe Parini (1729–99), Vittorio Alfieri, and himself.

59 Maria Antonietta Terzoli, *I "Vestigi della storia del sonetto italiano" di Ugo Foscolo* (Rome: Salerno Editrice, 1993).

60 Holland House was the residence of the English politician Lord Henry Vassall-Fox, 3rd Baron Holland (1773–1840). The home served as the intellectual headquarters for English liberals and other distinguished men.

61 Foscolo published many articles on Italian literature in London, including his "Articles on Dante," *Edinburgh Review*, 1818; "Essay on the Present Literature of Italy," John Murray, 1818; "Narrative and Romantic Poems of the Italians," *Quarterly Review*, 1819; and the "Italian Poets" series ("Frederick the Second and Pietro delle Vigne," "Guido Cavalcanti," "Michel Angelo," and "The Lyric Poetry of Tasso"), *New Monthly Magazine*, 1822.

62 Joseph Luzzi, *Romantic Europe and the Ghost of Italy* (New Haven: Yale University Press, 2008), 212. See also Maurizio Isabella's 2009 study *Risorgimento in Exile* for more on the roles Italian exiles played in the Risorgimento movement and how they facilitated transnational cultural exchange. Isabella, *Risorgimento in Exile: Italian Émigrés and the Liberal International in the Post-Napoleonic Era* (Oxford: Oxford University Press, 2009).

63 *E.N.*, 11.2: 399–490.

64 See Eric Reginald Vincent, *Byron, Hobhouse and Foscolo: New Documents in the History of a Collaboration* (Cambridge: Cambridge University Press, 1949).

65 *E.N.*, 20: 298–301. The letter is undated. According to the editor of this volume of the *Edizione nazionale*, Mario Scotti, this letter can be placed between 24 and 26 March 1818.

66 "These authors will be the poets who are selected: first, because the verse of every country is the depository of the language, the taste, and the manners of the times; second, because this is found more particularly the case in those nations whose imagination is their predominant faculty; and, in the third place, because the writers chosen on this occasion are in part distinguished for their compositions in prose." *E.N.*, 11.2: 400.

67 Ibid., 486.

68 Ibid., 433.

69 "Criticized" here means "was evaluated and studied by critics" and does not imply a negative connotation. See the Italian version of the "Essay" – "le sue tragedie vagliate da critici d'ogni lingua d'Europa." Ibid., 513.

70 Ibid., 431, 450.

71 Foscolo mentioned by name a few of Alfieri's great tragedies only when
he discussed the Astian's autobiographical sonnet. In the final tercet,
Alfieri compared himself to both the heroic Achilles and the vile Thersites:
"Per lo più mesto, e talor lieto assai, / Or stimandomi Achille, ed or
Tersite. / Uom, sei tu grande, o vil? Mori e il saprai." Foscolo explained,
"Compare the *Orestes*, the *Virginia*, the *Myrrha*, the *Saul*, and some other of
his tragic masterpieces, with his comedies and his *Misogallo*, and we shall
almost think it was the voice of conscience that told him he was some-
times the Achilles, sometimes the Thersites of authors." Ibid., 440.

72 Ibid., 435.

73 "This composition has some brilliant passages; but is, on the whole, devoid of interest. As an experiment it would perhaps be unproducible on
the Italian stage, where the opera has formally excluded all display of
ideas or sentiments, and almost of words, and is solely devoted to the mu-
sician and the ballet master." Ibid., 435.

74 Ibid., lxxxvi.

75 Ibid., 441. In his 1994 article "The Italian Romantic Drama in Its European
Context," Marvin Carlson described the infamous Pepoli and his innovative approach to the theatre, writing: "Only one Alfierian openly broke
with this tradition, primarily under the influence of Shakespeare. This was
the rather eccentric Count Alessandro Pepoli, who after a series of
Arcadian tragedies issued a sort of pre-Romantic manifesto in the *Mercurio
d'Italia* in 1796 entitled 'Sull'utilità, sull'invenzione, e sulle regole di un nuovo genere di somponimento [*sic*] teatrale da lui chiamato fisedia.' In the
name of Shakespeare and looking to the recent popular success of the sentimental comedy as a 'mixed' form, Pepoli proposed seventeen rules for
the *fisedia*, which rejected unity of time and place, allowed the use of both
kings and peasants, prose and verse, and comic and tragic elements, provided that the former did not take precedence." Carlson, "The Italian
Romantic Drama," 239.

76 *E.N.*, 11.2: 441.

77 Ibid., 442–3.

78 Ibid., 443.

79 Ibid., 443.

80 "Per la tragedia [Ippolito] non è nato ché eleganza e nerbo, affetto e passione sono cose diverse." *E.N.*, 15: 115.

81 In a 16 June 1807 letter to Albrizzi, Pindemonte wrote that Foscolo had
stopped writing to him and that he was worried that Foscolo was dis-
pleased with him. Pindemonte guessed that his sincere comments on

Foscolo's poetry were to blame. See Ippolito Pindemonte, *Lettere a Isabella (1784–1828)*, ed. Gilberto Pizzamiglio (Florence: Leo S. Olschki Editore, 2000), 170–1.

82 "The style of this piece is much applauded; the plan of it is on the model of Shakespeare, without, however, a total abandonment of those ancient rules which the Italians will allow no writer to violate with impunity. He [Pindemonte] has introduced choruses sung by young warriors and maidens, and has thus combined, with some success, the English, the Greek, and the Italian drama." *E.N.*, 11.2: 443. For more on Ippolito Pindemonte's *Arminio*, see Pullini, 8–9 and 50–2.

83 Foscolo began his discussion of Ippolito's *Arminio* with the following pointed observation: "It is, however, a fact which any one will verify by a careful enquiry, that the poetry of Hippolitus Pindemonte is not relished by the generality of readers, who are nevertheless obliged to repeat his praises, having been taught that lesson by the learned distributors of literary fame [literary journalists], and by those who are by tacit consent allowed to possess the most cultivated taste." *E.N.*, 11.2: 443.

84 Ibid., 443.

85 For a thorough discussion of the Foscolo–Monti relationship, see Claudio Varese, *Vita interiore di Ugo Foscolo* (Rocca San Casciano: Cappelli Editore, 1966), 19.

86 See, for example, Walter Binni, *Monti poeta del consenso* (Florence: Sansoni, 1981).

87 "The dialogue was found to have more warmth, and colouring, and energy, than that of Metastasio, who was then in possession of the stage; and the audience were not terrified even by the shadow of that harshness, and violence, and obscurity, which characterized the tragedies of Alfieri, who was just emerging into notice, and regarded as a wild irregular genius, scarcely within the pale of literary civilizations. Monti then was the tragic writer of Italy, and was confidently hailed as the successful candidate for an eminence as yet never occupied." *E.N.*, 11.2: 451. For more on Vincenzo Monti's *Aristodemo*, see Pullini, 46–8 and Carlson, 238.

88 For more on Vincenzo Monti's *Galeotto Manfredi* and his *Caio Gracco*, see Pullini, 48–9, 42–4 and Carlson, 238.

89 *E.N.*, 11.2: 452.

90 "*Galeotto Manfredi* ... is not only far below his *Aristodemo*, but beneath the talents of the author." Ibid., 451–2.

91 Ibid., 452.

92 Ibid., 487.

93 Ibid., 468.

94 Nicola Mangini states that Pepoli's "final opera to appear in this period on the Venetian stages was *Ladislao* during carnival of the previous year, at the theatre of San Luca, where it had a good 26 performances." Mangini, 254.

95 With the statement "never sat to the poet for their likeness," Foscolo was unequivocally denying that he modelled any of his characters on contemporary politicians.

96 *E.N.*, 11.2: 484.

97 "Thus, Venice! if no stronger claim were thine,/ Were all thy proud historic deeds forgot, / Thy choral memory of the Bard divine, / Thy love of Tasso, should have cut the knot / Which ties thee to thy tyrants; and thy lot / Is shameful to the nations – most of all, / Albion, to thee: the Ocean queen should not / Abandon Ocean's children; in the fall / Of Venice think of thine, despite thy watery wall." Byron, *The Complete Poetical Works*, ed. Jerome McGann (Oxford: Oxford University Press, 1980), 2: 130.

98 *E.N.*, 11.2: 489. Hobhouse most likely translated this from Foscolo's original Italian for the "Essay." Foscolo's original Italian article is found in *E.N.*, 13: 314–15.

99 Foscolo's friends and family were quite pleased with the "Essay" and the manner in which Foscolo was portrayed. On 18 January 1819, Quirina Mocenni Magiotti wrote, "The book [*Historical Illustrations of the Fourth Canto of Childe Harold*] that you sent me for Marzocchi is so dear to me – slowly but surely I am having it translated in order to also have it in Italian. The article that pertains to you was the first to be translated and you can find comfort in how much Mr Hobhouse gained in my gratitude for having restored the justice that was due to you by your contemporaries." [Il libro (*Historical Illustrations of the Fourth Canto of Childe Harold*) che mi mandaste per Marzocchi mi è carissimo – lo faccio a poco a poco tradurre, per averlo anche Italiano. L'articolo che ti concerne fu il primo a tradursi e puoi supporti quanto il sig. Hobhouse ha acquistato nella mia riconoscenza per averti resa quella giustizia che ti era dovuta da' tuoi contemporanei.] *E.N.*, 21: 11.

100 Pindemonte explained his position that a monument not be erected in honour of Byron in a letter to Isabella Teotochi Albrizzi from October 1826. Pindemonte, *Lettere a Isabella*, 318–19. Hobhouse discussed Pindemonte's displeasure in his book *Italy: Remarks Made in Several Visits from the Year 1816–1854*: "All the praises [in the "Essay"] so justly bestowed upon the verses of Pindemonti [*sic*] did not reconcile the poet to the gentle reproof of those 'spiritual exercises which occupied a considerable portion of his time, and plunged him into that absorbing solitude

which a more rational religion would have taught him to exchange for the active duties and social amusements of life.' That he was offended I had subsequently a painful proof; for when I requested the co-operation of several distinguished contemporaries of Lord Byron towards erecting a monument to his [Byron's] memory, Pindemonti [*sic*] was the only man who not only gave me a refusal, but replied to me in terms deficient in courtesy and Christian candor. He forgot that if any blame was to be attached to the request, I was the culprit, and not Lord Byron." John Cam Hobhouse, *Italy: Remarks Made in Several Visits from the Year 1816–1854* (London: John Murray, 1859), 3: 378 – as quoted in Vincent, 122.

101 Hobhouse, *Italy, Remarks made in Several Visits*, 3: 378 – as quoted in Vincent, 122.

102 Vincent, 19.

103 Carlson, "The Italian Romantic Drama," 243.

104 Lord Byron, *Byron's Letters and Journals*, ed. L.A. Marchand (Cambridge, MA: Belknap Press, 1974–82), 8: 152.

105 For more on Byron's Venetian tragedies and their connection to Foscolo, see Loretta Innocenti, "Le tragedie veneziane di Byron," in *La maschera e il volto: Il teatro in Italia*, ed. Francesco Bruni (Venice: Fondazione Giorgio Cini, 2002), 257–74.

106 See Foscolo's 24 June 1819 letter to Hobhouse, *E.N.*, 21: 62.

107 Given Foscolo's own hand in its editing and reworking, Guido Bézzola considered the 1820 London edition of *Ricciarda* the definitive one. See Bézzola's introduction to *Ricciarda*, *E.N.*, 2: xxxviii–l.

108 "Qui ne dicono meraviglie, e Murray ne vende a dozzine." *E.N.*, 21: 186. There was also an 1830 London edition and a total of nine editions of *Ricciarda* printed in Italy between 1820 and 1837.

109 *E.N.*, 21: 181.

110 *Biblioteca italiana* 5, no. 20 (October–December, 1820): 308–21.

111 "in una parola la tragedia è tale da far onore all'Italia." Ibid., 320.

112 James Atkinson published his translation of *Ricciarda* in 1823 (Calcutta, India: W.M. Thacker & Co).

113 *E.N.*, 22: 313. As Mario Scotti explained in his notes to this letter, we do not know what happened to the translation, nor Foscolo's opinion of it, as we do not have a response to this letter. See *E.N.*, 22: 303, n.1.

114 Ugo Foscolo, "Learned Ladies," *New Monthly Magazine* 1 (January 1821): 223–30; *E.N.*, 10: 203–18.

115 Foscolo, "On Hamlet," *New Monthly Magazine*, 1.4 (April 1821): 462–67; *E.N.*, 10: 583–9. Foscolo also published four articles in the *NMM*'s "Italian Poets" series: "Michel Angelo," *E.N.*, 10: 447–60; "Frederick the Second

and Pietro delle Vigne," *E.N.*, 10: 399–412; "Guido Cavalcanti," *E.N.*, 10: 423–36; and "The Lyric Poetry of Tasso," *E.N.*, 10: 509–20.

116 Foscolo's and Roscoe's plans for this journal, tentatively entitled the *Quarterly Review of Foreign Literature*, were never realized. Foscolo did, however, memorialize his ideas for this new journal in a document entitled *Plan for a Periodical Work on Foreign Literature*, which he appended to a 30 October 1824 letter to Campbell. See *E.N.*, 22: 518–21.

117 Thomas Roscoe, "Remarks on the Life and Works of Ugo Foscolo," *New Monthly Magazine* 1 (January 1821): 76–85.

118 "Biographical Particulars of Celebrated Persons Lately Deceased," *New Monthly Magazine* 21 (October 1827): 440.

119 Thomas Roscoe, "The Works of Ugo Foscolo," *Foreign Quarterly Review* 2 (September 1828): 428.

Chapter Five

1 For an overview of British interest in Italian theatre, see Diego Saglia's "'Freedom alone is wanting': British Views of Contemporary Italian Drama, 1820–1830," in *British Romanticism and Italian Literature: Translating, Reviewing, Rewriting* (Amsterdam: Rodopi, 2005), 238–55.

2 Henry Hart Milman, "Italian Tragedy," *Quarterly Review*, October 1820: 72–102.

3 Foscolo respectfully requested that Teotochi Albrizzi warmly welcome Milman, who was travelling through Italy, to Venice and into Italian literary society in the letter. *E.N.*, 20: 476–7. Maria Graham asked Foscolo in a 28 January 1821 letter how he liked Milman's article, its portrayal of the exile, and Milman's opinions on *Ricciarda*; *E.N.*, 21: 237–8. Douglas Radcliff-Umstead described the close relationship between Foscolo and Milman in his 1965 article "Foscolo and the Early Italian Romantics," *Italica* 42, no. 3 (September 1965): 231–46. He wrote: "Foscolo and Milman were close acquaintances; doubtless, Milman's negative opinions were in part influenced by Foscolo's attitude toward [Alessandro] Manzoni" (241). For more on Foscolo, Milman, and the "Italian Tragedy" article, see also Beatrice Corrigan, "Pellico's *Francesca da Rimini*: The First English Translation," *Italica* 31, no. 4 (December 1954): 215–24.

4 Relying on Joseph Cooper Walker's 1805 history of Italian tragedies, *An Historical and Critical Essay on the Revival of the Drama in Italy* (Edinburgh: Mundell and Son), Milman highlighted the major, and even the minor, tragedians of early Italian history: Gian Giorgio Trissino (1478–1550), Giovanni Rucellai (1475–1617), Ludovico Dolce (1508–68), Luigi

Alamanni (1495–1556), Sperone Speroni (1500–88), Giraldi Cinthio (a.k.a. Giovanni Battista Giraldi, 1504–73), and Antonio Decio (1560–1617). He succinctly described the defects of these early tragedies. See Milman, 81.

5 Ibid., 72.

6 Ibid., 74–5.

7 "The modern Italians, with a language equally capable of expressing the most violent and tumultuous agitation of the soul, or of melting to the most luxurious softness – have nevertheless abandoned those sources of interest and excitement, which almost forced themselves upon them; have neglected a history tragic in every page, and abounding in terrific crime and generous virtue; and have wasted their skill and power on subjects alien to their genius and national character." Milman, 73–4.

8 Ibid., 81–2.

9 "We should have expected from the vehement and impetuous Alfieri, passion violating every rule, and lawless energy trampling upon the established canons of his art; we find him cool, and enslaved to artificial laws. We should have expected at one moment a passage of careless vigour, at another, of deep and soul-felt tenderness; we find the whole laboured into a calm and uniform dignity. We should have expected to shudder and weep; but Alfieri excites neither terror nor tears. We should have guarded against errors of excess and exaggeration, but his love has not much fire, nor his ambition much turbulence … His tragedy, therefore, has neither the simplicity of the Greek, nor the rich variety of the Shakespearian drama: his characters have neither the high ideal grandeur of the former, nor the distinct identity and perfect nature of the latter … His style also bears evident marks of the toilsome process with which he wrought his works. We want the ease, the sudden flow, the heat of inspiration … Still the tragedies of Alfieri are noble poems. He displays consummate skill in unfolding and conducting his plots; he is always eloquent, always able to keep the imagination alive; and the uniform dignity of his manner is in the highest degree imposing: he reconciles us to his want of passionate flights, and the ardent and exalting raptures of poetry, by never deviating into the low or the ludicrous – and if Italy may still hope to possess a greater tragic poet, let her recollect that Alfieri was the first splendidly to vindicate her from the disgrace of entire barrenness." Milman, 82–3.

10 "While Alfieri, in the words of Mr. Hobhouse, 'was regarded as a wild irregular genius, scarcely within the pale of literary civilization, Monti was the tragic writer of Italy, and was confidently hailed as the successful candidate for an eminence as yet never occupied.'" Ibid., 83.

11 "The faults of Aristodemo are an insufficiency of plot for the length of five acts, and an apparent feebleness in the working up of the last scene." Ibid., 83. Following a detailed discussion of a scene, Milman continued, "If Monti had continued to write thus, the high expectations of Italy would not have been disappointed. But the tragediografo of the Cisalpine republic, (for to that office he was appointed,) after having in turn virulently libeled and basely flattered every predominant power, offers a striking instance of the deterioration of talent in proportion to the abandonment of high and generous principle ... Galeotto Manfredi of the same writer aspires not, excepting in a scene or two translated from Shakespeare, above a tame and insipid mediocrity." Ibid., 86. Three years earlier, Foscolo described Monti's *Galeotto Manfredi* in the "Essay" as follows: "Some fine passages constitute the sole merit of the last tragedy [*Caio Gracco*], into which he has introduced some scenes that the Italians are pleased to call *by far too natural – assai troppo naturali*. These scenes were expressly imitated from Shakespeare, and succeeded at first – nobody, however, dared to applaud them in the subsequent representation." *E.N.*, 11.2: 452.

12 "The total failure indeed of Monti, when employed upon the annals of his country, and the flatness of the tragedies written on subjects of the same nature, by Giovanni Pindemonte, and Count Pepoli, might make us tremble for our theory, could we not appeal to a splendid confirmation of it in the works of Foscolo and Pellico now before us." Milman, 86–7.

13 Ibid., 90.

14 See Foscolo's 24 June 1819 letter to Hobhouse, *E.N.*, 21: 62.

15 Corrigan, "Pellico's *Francesca da Rimini*," 220–1.

16 Milman wrote: "The 'Francesca da Rimini,' of Silvio Pellico, is the poem of ardent and unstudied feeling. There is a natural ease in every expression and the artifice of the plot seems to originate rather in the instinctive delicacy of the poet's mind, which shrunk from the undisguised relation of an incestuous passion, and felt intuitively the right way of securing the reader's commiseration for the unhappy pair," Milman, 97.

17 Ibid., 101.

18 "Our terror is so often appealed to, lest the father should slay his child, that we become in some degree familiarised with the danger, and are of course less moved by it." Ibid., 97.

19 "[Foscolo] displays indeed great mastery over the language, to comprise so many ideas in so few words; but when our feelings are addressed, we like not the having to dwell on sentences, the antithetical force and fullness of which occasionally remind us of Tacitus." Ibid., 9

20 Ibid., 97.

21 Ibid.

22 *E.N.*, 8: 376, as discussed in chapter 4.

23 "Signor Foscolo's dramatic career was opened by the tragedy of 'Thyeste,' of which Alfieri is reported to have said, 'if the author be only nineteen he will surpass me.' A tragedy written at that age might naturally expect the indulgence of criticism, and Thyeste, in fact, is the work of a youth, but still that of a young poet." Milman, 90.

24 "The courage and the *youth* of the author enabled him to triumph over his rivals, and his *Thyestes* received more applause than perhaps it deserved" (author's emphasis, "Essay," 468); "il primo saggio d'un giovanetto che non ha ancora compiuto il diciannovesim'anno dell'età sua" ("Notizie," 203); and "il nostro giovine autore" ("Notizie," 207).

25 Milman, 101.

26 *E.N.*, 11.2: 486.

27 "Let him [Foscolo] rest assured, that whatever may be the destiny of his beloved Italy, whether to repose under the leaden scepter of Austria, or to pass through the fiery ordeal of revolution, he deserves well of that country, who makes her feel that, but for her own intestine discords, she might have been one among the nations." Milman, 101–2. Milman's final remarks on Italy, that "she might have been one *among the nations*," clearly were inspired by the "Essay's" inclusion of an excerpt of one of Foscolo's earlier articles, entitled "Senza querele impotenti, né recriminazioni da servi," which was published in the *Lugano Gazette* on 14 April 1815: "We were in want of arms; they were given to us by France, and Italy had again a name *amongst the nations*" (my emphasis). *E.N.*, 11. 2: 489.

28 Alessandro Manzoni, *Il Conte di Carmagnola*, in *Opere*, ed. Lanfranco Caretti (Milan: Mursia, 1974), 763–854.

29 Foscolo described Manzoni as a "young genius born to letters and ardent with patriotic love" [giovine ingegno nato alle lettere e caldo d'amor patrio]. *E.N.*, 1:140. For more on Foscolo's description of Manzoni, see Eugenio Donadoni, *Ugo Foscolo: Pensatore, critico, poeta*, 315.

30 "We fear, however, that the Italians will require a more splendid violation of their old established laws, before they are led to abandon them. Carmagnola wants poetry; the parting scene between the unhappy Count and his family, is indeed affecting, but with this praise and that of occasional simple and manly eloquence the drama itself might be dismissed." Milman, 87.

31 Ibid.

32 "We cannot, however, refrain from making known to our readers the most noble piece of Italian lyric poetry which the present day has produced,

and which occurs as a chorus at the end of the second act of his drama."
Ibid.

33 Alessandro Manzoni, *The Count of Carmagnola and Adelchis*, intro. and
trans. Federica Brunori Deigan (Baltimore: Johns Hopkins University
Press, 2004), 19.

34 "Il Coro è da riguardarsi come la personificazione de' pensieri morali che
l'azione ispira, come l'organo dei sentimenti del poeta che parla in nome
dell'intera umanità." Manzoni, *Opere*, 769. August von Schlegel's series of
lectures, *Über dramatische Kunst und Literatur*, were held in Vienna in 1808–
9, published 1809–11, and translated into French in 1814. Schlegel, *Course
of Lectures on Dramatic Arts and Literature*, trans. J. Black (London: Henry G.
Bohn, 1846).

35 Milman and Chauvet's negative reviews were not the only serious criticisms of Manzoni. His own countrymen also harshly critiqued him, and
the Italian neoclassicists quickly responded with their own reviews in literary journals. For example, in January 1820, Francesco Pezzi published a
review of Manzoni's *Il Conte* in the *Gazzetta di Milano* in which he attacked
Manzoni for blatantly disregarding the unities of time and place, for his
long dialogues, and for the lack of tragic spirit. For more on Pezzi's review, see Brunori Deigan in Manzoni, *The Count*, 23. The *Biblioteca italiana*
also assailed Manzoni's tragedy based on its *triviale* (humble or vulgar)
language, unjustified episodes (*episodi inutili*), and the work's flawed
structure. "*Il Conte di Carmagnola*, tragedia di Alessandro Manzoni," in
Biblioteca italiana 17 (January–March 1820): 232–44.

36 Manzoni, *Lettre à Monsieur Chauvet sur l'unté de temps et de lieu dans la tragédie*, in *Opere*, 855–912. Manzoni reiterated his argument that French tragedy, by adhering to the unities, violated the fundamental principle of
classicism, namely, verisimilitude.

37 In *A History of Modern Criticism: 1750–1950* (New Haven: Yale University
Press, 1955), René Wellek succinctly summarized Manzoni's historical approach to poetry: "The question of the unities is not, however, Manzoni's
central concern. It is merely one instance of his interest in truth. The essence of poetry, he argues, is not invention of fact. All great works of art
are based on events of history or on national traditions considered true in
their time. Poetry is thus not in the events but only in the sentiments and
discourses, which the poet creates by entering sympathetically into their
minds. Dramatic poetry aims at explaining what men have felt, willed and
suffered because of their actions. The poet is, we might draw the conclusion, a historian who, like Thucydides or Plutarch, invents the appropriate

speeches and details for the events supplied by medieval chronicles." Wellek, 262.

38 Manzoni further echoed Schlegel by writing a historical tragedy as prescribed by the German authority. Along these lines, from 1808–9, Schlegel delivered his lectures *Über dramatische Kunst und Literatur* (*Course of Lectures on Dramatic Art and Literature*) in Vienna. He harshly reviewed Alfieri, criticizing his disregard for historical sources as the most egregious of his errors. According to Schlegel, the attempts of Racine and Alfieri to restore the ancient stage were dead ends in literary history. He believed that dramatic art of the present age needed to rediscover the Romantic via national history. He writes: "We have lately endeavored in many ways to revive the remains of our old national poetry. These may afford the poet a foundation for the wonderful festival-play; but the most dignified species of the romantic is the historical. In this field, the most glorious laurels may yet be reaped by dramatic poets who are willing to emulate Goethe and Schiller. Only let our historical drama be in reality and thoroughly national; let it not attach itself to the life and adventures of single knights and petty princes, who exercised no influence on the fortunes of the whole nation. Let it, at the same time, be truly historical, drawn from a profound knowledge, and transporting us back to the great olden time. In this mirror let the poet enable us to see, while we take deep shame to ourselves for what we are, what the Germans were in former times, and what they must again be." Schlegel, 222.

39 "Classiker und Romantiker in Italien, sich heftig bekämpfend," written in 1818 and published in 1820 in *Über Kunst und Althertum*, 6 vols. (Stuttgart, 1816–32). Goethe demonstrated his detailed knowledge of the contemporary Milanese literary scene and the new Italian Romantic school in the article. He notably praised the "clarity of thought" and "profound knowledge of the ancients and moderns" shown by Ermes Visconti (1784–1841) in his 1819 dialogue on the dramatic unities, which was published in *Il Conciliatore*. Goethe wrote that a Classicist, by "clinging" to the "inimitable works" of antiquity, risked ending in "a form of fixity and pedantry." He concluded, "Whoever is preoccupied with the past is only in danger of pressing to his heart as dried up that which has died and has become mummy-like for us." Goethe, *Sämtliche Werke* (Munich: Carl Hanser Verlag, 1986), 11.2: 259.

40 Goethe, "On Criticism," in *Literary Essays*, trans. J.E. Spingarn (New York: Frederick Ungar Publishing Co., 1921), 140–2.

41 Federica Brunori Deigan aptly summarized Goethe's praise for Manzoni in the introduction to her translations of *Il Conte di Carmagnola* and *Adelchi*.

She observed: "The Italian poet and dramatist was, in Goethe's view, the true heir of the historical drama that he and Schiller had initiated in Germany. Goethe had words of admiration for all aspects of Manzoni's tragedy: its structure was devoid of the useless unities; the characters were nuanced, even the secondary parts; the wording was so concise it was impossible 'to detect whether a redundant or a missing word'; the meter, 'whose alternating caesuras and numerous enjambments make it sound like a freely versified recitative, suitable to be passionately declaimed by the intelligent actor and accompanied by music.'" Brunori Deigan, in Manzoni, *The Count*, 23–4.

42 "Criticism is either destructive or constructive. The former is very easy; for one need only set up some imaginary standard, some model or other, however foolish this may be, and then boldly assert that the work of art under consideration does not measure up to that standard, and therefore is of no value. That settles the matter, and one can without any more ado declare that the poet has not come up to one's requirements. In this way the critic frees himself of all obligations of gratitude toward the artist." Goethe, "On Criticism," 140.

43 Ibid.

44 Manzoni, *Opere*, 763.

45 The first issue of the *Biblioteca italiana* featured a letter, entitled "Sulla maniera e l'utilità delle traduzioni," written by Anne-Louise-Germaine Necker, commonly known as Madame de Staël.

46 *E.N.*, 11.2: 490. "It would not be very difficult to state the true merits of this idle enquiry, on the decision of which may, however, depend the turn taken by the literature of the next half century. But this also must be left for another opportunity." *E.N.*, 11.2: 490.

47 *E.N.*, 22: 346. Russell was referring to the poet-critic and editor of the *New Monthly Magazine*, Thomas Campbell and the writer and cleric Sydney Smith (1771–1845).

48 The lectures were the following: (1) "On the origin and object of poetry"; (2) "On the origin, progress, vicissitudes and present state of the Italian Language"; (3) "On the Italian Literature from the Emperor Frederick II to the death of Guido Cavalcanti (from the year 1200 to the year 1300)"; (4) "On the life, the poem and the age of Dante (from year 1300 to year 1330)"; (5) "On the works of Petrarch, Boccaccio and their contemporaries (from year 1330 to year 1390)"; (6) "On the Literary History of Italy from the death of Petrarch and Boccaccio to the death of Lorenzo de' Medici (from year 1390 to 1490)"; (7) "On the age of Leo X and the Literature of the first fifty years of the sixteenth century, in Italy"; (8) "On the Genius and works

of Ariosto and the other Romantic poets"; (9) "On the Poem of Tasso: on his contemporaries, and the change effected by the Jesuits on the literary character of that and the following ages (from year 1550 to year 1600)"; (10) "On the state of Poetry and Literature in Italy and the political domination of the Spaniards, and the literary influence of the Era of Louis the XIVth (from year 1600 to year 1700)"; (11) "On the Institution of the Arcadia, on the Genius and Poetry of Metastasio: and on the state of Literature and the Canons of criticism in Italy in the eighteenth century to the Revolution (from year 1700 to year 1790)"; and (12) "On the Poetry of Italy during the years of the Revolution to the present day (from year 1790 to year 1823)." See Cesare Foligno's introduction for more on the genesis of the project. *E.N.*, 11.1: ix–xlii.

49 "The poets and critics of Italy have been, during the last six or seven years, divided into two irreconcilable and distinct factions, one being named the *Classicisti*, and the other the *Romantici*. It appears to the *Classicisti* that the Italians, as the direct descendants and legitimate successors to the literary reputation of the Greeks and Romans, aught not to depart from the ancient principles of poetry that have been followed from Homer downwards. On the other hand the *Romantici* affirm 'that the Italians as Europeans, ought to feel, and to think, and to write like other living nations; and that the advances of science, of literature, and the arts, require more modern theories of criticism'" (Foscolo's emphasis). *E.N.*, 11.1: 26.

50 Foscolo laments the Di Breme attack in a 16 March 1819 letter to Quirina Mocenni Magiotti. See *E.N.*, 21: 24.

51 "After a thousand grave treatises, and lighter tracts, and satires, and epigrams that have been published upon this controversy, we remain, in spite of ourselves, convinced, that we cannot possibly adhere either to the one party or the other, and that we must either preserve a silent neutrality, or speak at the risk of provoking the two armies to combat against us, who stand alone." *E.N.*, 11.1: 26–7.

52 Foscolo wrote, "It is to be observed, that both these parties concur in affirming, 'that poetry ought to imitate nature.' Thus, therefore, the *Classicisti*, who profess themselves worshippers of the hallowed rules of antiquity, and the *Romantici*, who deride every sort of theory that is not modern, adopt, on this point, one common doctrine … We shall then examine in what it is that this imitation of nature consists." Ibid., 27.

53 "The poet, the painter, and the sculptor, do not imitate by mere copying, but they select, combine, and imagine, as perfected and united in that which they represent, many new and beautiful varieties which do really exist in the creation of nature, but are, however, frequently invisible,

because they are minute, scattered, and confused among a thousand common or disagreeable varieties, so that the only beautiful varieties of creation are never seen so united together and harmonized in nature as to form a perfection equal to that which man is capable of imagining, and which the poet represents by means of his art." Ibid., 28.

54 "Art, perpetually imitating nature, represents truth; but genius, devising, assembling, and distributing upon a single object, with the same laws and spontaneity that are exercised by nature, the variety which she has dispersed over different objects, creates the ideal. Consequently, the ideal, unaccompanied by truth, is either strangely fantastical, or metaphysically refined; but without the ideal, every imitation of truth will always turn out to be vulgar." Ibid., 29.

55 "Poetry, therefore, creates for us other objects and different worlds. And if it too faithfully imitated existing things and the world which is, it would cease to be poetry; because it would bring before our eyes the cold, sad, monotonous reality." Ibid., 30.

56 Ibid., 34–5. For Dante's story of Count Ugolino, see *Inferno*, 33, 67–75.

57 "There exists in the world an universal secret harmony, which man pants to discover as necessary to solace the toils and the sorrows of his existence; and in proportion as he finds the harmony in question, – in proportion as he feels and rejoices in it, so will his passions subside to exalt and purify him; and then, consequently, his reason will perfect itself. This harmony, however, of which the existence is so evident, and the necessity has been so powerfully experienced more or less by all mankind, we see (as is the case with every thing that nature presents to man) commixed with a discord of things; and so they reciprocally thwart and frequently destroy one another." *E.N.*, 11.1: 30.

58 "And here we may conclude our illustrations and reasonings, by declaring, that whatever judgment it may be ours to offer with respect to poetry, we shall proceed upon the opinion, that all works of imagination proceed from the necessity and the faculty which man has, of embellishing and enlarging, by ideal separations and additions, the natural reality of all things; and that, in fact, every representation of life, despoiled of those illusions which adorn and enrich it, would become insupportably tedious." Ibid., 35.

59 This citation is from Foscolo's 1826 article "The Women of Italy," *London Magazine* 6: 22 (October): 204–19.

60 "On Hamlet," *New Monthly Magazine* 1, no. 4 (April 1821): 462–7. *E.N.*, 10: 583–9.

61 The English playwright was only one of four tragedians throughout history whom Foscolo deems worthy of study in his 1796 *Piano di studi*. *E.N.*, 6: 7. Foscolo's high esteem for Shakespeare is also evidenced by his numerous citations of Shakespeare's tragedies in his other critical articles. For example, Foscolo quoted from *Measure for Measure* in the French version of his 1819 article "Narrative and Romantic Poems of the Italians." He compared lines from Giambattista Casti's poem *Tartaro* with Shakespeare's: "Ces deux lignes: 'Han gli stessi delitti un vario fato; / Questi diventa re, quegli è impiccato': experiment précisément la meme idée que ces deux de Shakespeare – *Measure for Measure*: 'Well, Heaven forgive him! and forgive us all! / Some rise by sin, and some by virtue fall.'" *E.N.*, 11.2: 16. Foscolo quoted from act 2, scene 3 in *Measure for Measure* in his 1822 article "Learned Ladies": "Shakespeare assures us, that 'Love talks with better knowledge, and knowledge with dearer love"; *E.N.*, 11.2: 210. Foscolo quoted from *Othello* act 2, scene 1, in his article "An Essay on the Love of Petrarch" – "He [Petrarch] endured for twenty-one years the misery of adoring at once and suspecting the human being that he believed to be the only one that was essential to his happiness – a perplexity which wears to death, and humbles before his own eyes every man who 'Is of a constant, loving, noble nature'"; *E.N.*, 10: 31. Foscolo also cited two lines from *Measure for Measure* in this essay, "Shall we desire to raise the sanctuary, / And pitch our evils there?" *E.N.*, 10: 20.

62 The translated passage can be found in *Wilhelm Meisters Wandeljahre*, 1, book 4, in *Goethes sämtliche Werke* (Stuttgart and Berlin: J.G. Cotta, 1902–7), 17: 284. Foscolo discussed his upcoming work for the *New Monthly Magazine* in a 2 January 1821 letter to Talbot (*E.N.*, 21: 232–3); he did not mention "On Hamlet." The exile had already composed his article "On Hamlet" according to a February 1821 letter from Cyrus Redding to Foscolo. Due to an abundance of contributions to the journal, there was not enough room to publish it at that time. Redding explained, "I am indeed sorry to hear that our miserable climate affects your health and trust that the attack of rheumatism you have suffered will be transient and leave no other effects than delight experienced in changing from a state of suffering to health and vigor. We have had such a press of matter for the magazine this month that we did not most fortunately need your second article ["On Hamlet"] and therefore we have found no inconvenience – The first on justice ["Learned Ladies"] was partly composed but will not be in the magazine this month as it was not perfected and Mr. Campbell thought it better that it should lie over. I called on you to get the other

sheet and speak about it but as you are aware did not see you. The Hamlet Mr. C. has read over he says [*sic*] in a little slip of paper enclosed his ideas upon it." *E.N.*, 21: 248.

63 "It is clear to me that Shakespeare's intention was to exhibit the effects of a great action, imposed as a duty upon a mind too feeble for its accomplishment; in which sense I find the character consistent throughout." *E.N.*, 10: 585.

64 The complete citation reads, "Here is an oak tree planted in a china vase, proper only to receive the most delicate flowers. The roots strike out, and the vessel flies to pieces." Ibid.

65 Samuel Johnson, *Johnson's Preface to Shakespeare*, ed. P.J. Smallwood (Bristol: Bristol Classical Press, 1985), 4–5.

66 *E.N.*, 10: 589.

67 Ibid., 585.

68 Vittorio Cian, "Un articolo shakespeariano di Ugo Foscolo," in *Giornale storico della letteratura italiana* 91: 273 (April–June 1928): 349. The following texts were available to Foscolo at the British Museum: *Les années d'apprentissage de Guillaume Meister. Roman traduit de l'allemand.* 2 vols. (Coblence, 1800–1); and *Alfred, ou les l'Années d'Apprentissage de Wilhelm Meister. Traduit de l'Allemand par C.L. Sevelinges*, 3 vols. (Paris, 1802).

69 Alessandro Manzoni, *Tragedie: Il Conte di Carmagnola e L'Adelchi, aggiuntevi le poesie varie dello stesso, ed aclune prose sulla teoria del dramma tragico* (Florence: Giuseppe Molini, 1825).

70 *E.N.*, 11.2: 557–618. "Della nuova scuola drammatica italiana" was to have been a review of the 1825 Florence edition of Manzoni's tragedies, Camillo Ugoni's 1826 commentary of Manzoni and the new Romantic school of tragedy, *Sur les tragédies de Manzoni et la nouvelle école dramatique en Italie* (Paris, 1826), Carlo Tedaldi Fores's 1825 historical tragedy *Beatrice Tenda* (Milan), and Eduardo Fabbri's *Francesca da Rimini* (written 1802, published 1822).

71 Wellek, "The Italian Critics," in *A History of Modern Criticism*, 2: 266.

72 "Some of them move freely through the brand-new transcendental regions of the Sublime, of the Great, and of the Ideal Beauty; others are crouched and motionless in the shadow of antiquity listening to bits of the oracles called Aristotle's *Poetics*, and explaining them and instilling them in a thousand ways. Nevertheless, they all agree to begin and conclude with the sentence: *that poetry must be the imitation of nature* (Foscolo's emphasis). [Gli uni spaziando nelle regioni nuovissime trascendentali del Sublime, del Grande, e del Bello Ideale; gli altri accosciati ed immobili sotto l'ombra dell'antichità ad ascoltare que'frammenti d'oracoli chiamati *Poetica*

d'Aristotile, e spiegarli e inculcarli in mille maniere. Gli uni e gli altri pur nondimeno s'accordano a incominciare e conchiudere con la sentenza: *che la poesia dev'essere imitazione della natura.*] *E.N.*, 11.2: 570.

73　"Or la parola di imitazione fu ella mai ben definita? E quella di natura può ella essere mai definibile?" Ibid., 570.

74　"The secret in any work of the arts of imagination lies completely in incorporating and identifying the reality and the fiction in such a way that one does not dominate the other, that they never split, nor analyse, nor are easily distinguishable one from the other." [Il secreto in qualunque lavoro dell'arti d'immaginazione sta tutto nell'incorporare e identificare la realtà e la finzione in guisa che l'una non predomini sovra l'altra, e che non possano mai dividersi, nè analizzarsi, nè facilmente distinguersi l'una dall'altra.] Ibid., 564.

75　"So the truth in fact, naturally powerful in itself because it is based on what we experience and see every-day and therefore does not provoke wonder or curiosity, is that one finds himself the authoritative author and identified with that which the human imagination wants to create, and with that which does not exist except in the unrestricted circle of possibilities. So our wonder and curiosity are excited in us by the greatness, diversity, and truth with which poetry, sculpture and painting present to our mind the objects that, seeing them before us every day, seemed cold, ordinary, and always the same; and [that,] imagined differently than those we see, seemed hardly possible for us. Our trust in the poet, captivated by the experience we have with the real existence of those objects, and our excited wonder of their novelty, unite in a single sentiment to establish the illusion." [Allora la verità di fatto, naturalmente potente per sè, perchè è fondata su ciò che esperimentiamo e vediamo ogni giorno e perciò non eccita meraviglia nè curiosità, si trova sommista e immedesimata a ciò che la immaginazione umana suole creare, e che non esiste che nell'incircoscritto circolo de' possibili. Allora la curiosità nostra e la meraviglia sono eccitate in noi per la grandezza e diversità e verità con che la poesia, la scultura e la pittura presentano alla nostra mente gli oggetti che vedendoli dinanzi a noi giornalmente ci parevano freddi, ordinari, e sempre i medesimi; e immaginati diversi da quelli che li vediamo, ci parevano appena possibili. La nostra fede al poeta, cattivata dalla esperienza che abbiamo dell'esistenza reale di quegli oggetti, e la nostra meraviglia eccitata dalla lor novità si uniscono in un solo sentimento a costituire l'illusione.] Ibid., 564.

76　"But this habit of historical poets has now degenerated into abuse, intemperance and mania in every country, and Italians justify themselves with the example of the French and German, and even more, the English." [Ma questo vezzo de' poeti storici è ormai degenerato in abuso, in intemperanza, e in mania in ogni paese, e gl'Italiani si giustificano con l'esempio de' Francesi e Tedeschi e ancor più degl'Inglesi.] Ibid., 565.

77 "He [Goethe] has promoted questions of literary criticism, notably of tragic poetry among the Italians; having professed that he does it to promote a system; having illustrated the system with a new tragedy, took me away from the danger, which I would have never confronted, of doing an experiment with the system and rules and theory in a production in another language (from that) which I only seem to know, and to that which I applied so much and which moved me to learn from others." [L'avere egli [Goethe] promosso questioni di critica letteraria segnatamente di poesia tragica fra gl'Italiani, l'aver professato ch'ei lo fa per favorire un sistema, l'aver illustrato il sistema con una nuova tragedia, mi tolgono dal pericolo, che non avrei mai affrontato, di far esperimento di sistema e regole e teoria sovra una produzione in altra lingua (da quella) che sola mi par di sapere, e alla quale ho applicato quel tanto che m'è toccata d'imparare delle altre.] Ibid., 572.

78 "It seems that today the fellow citizens of Alfieri, looking to make better tragedies, or at least ones completely different than his, only keep imitating him and passing him by the critics to discuss around their own works. In so doing, and also by just trying to maintain a different path from his, we praise them, and if they ever succeed in doing better, we will praise them." [Pare che oggi i concittadini dell'Alfieri mirando a far tragedie migliori, o non foss'altro diverse in tutto dalle sue, si riserbino solo a imitarlo e sorpassarlo a discorrere da critici intorno a'loro propri lavori. Del fare e anche del solo tentare di tenere strada diversa dalla sua li lodiamo, e se mai riusciranno a far meglio, li loderemo.] Ibid., 568.

79 "Lo stile in Italia è un oggetto di moda; mutavasi una volta di secolo in secolo, or forse di mese in mese. [. . .] Ora l'idolo è Dante, meritamente dicono, e lo credo; ma quando si pensi agli amori ch'ottenne altra volta Petrarca, non parrà una stranezza il predire che i posteri riguardando alla presente mania di *danteggiare* si faranno beffe di noi, come noi ci facciamo beffe dei Petrarchisti di un altro secolo" (Foscolo's emphasis). Ibid., 587.

Epilogue

1 Foscolo chose to use his characters' names among other aliases, specifically including Jacopo Ortis, Lorenzo Alderani, and Didimo Chierico.

2 See Eric Reginald Vincent's account of Foscolo's final years in *Ugo Foscolo: An Italian in Regency England* (Cambridge: Cambridge University Press, 1953).

3 André Vieusseux, "Foscolo and His Times," *Foreign Quarterly Review*
   9 (May 1832): 336.
4 Shelley, 394.
5 Guerra, "Mary Shelley's Contributions to Lardner's *Cabinet Cyclopaedia:
   Lives of the Most Eminent Literary and Scientific Men of Italy*," in *British
   Romanticism and Italian Literature: Translating, Reviewing, Rewriting*, ed.
   Laura Bandiera and Diego Saglia (Amsterdam: Rodopi, 2005), 231–7.
6 Shelley, 354.
7 Ibid.

Selected Bibliography

Acchiappati, Gianfranco. *Raccolta foscoliana Acchiappati: Edizioni originali e ristampe scritti su riviste letterarie e giornali*, vol. 1. Milan: Distribuzione Edizione il polifilo, 1988.

Alfieri, Vittorio. "Parere sulle tragedie." In *Opere di Vittorio Alfieri da Asti*. Vol. 35, edited by Morena Pagliai, 81–167. Asti: Casa d'Alfieri, 1978.

Alonge, Roberto. *Struttura e ideologia nel teatro italiano fra '500 e '900*. Turin: Stampatori Università, 1978.

Apollonio, Carla. "Foscolo lettore e critico di Shakespeare." *Otto/Novecento* 2, no. 1 (January/February 1978): 29–47.

Aristotle. *Aristotle's Poetics*. Translated by James Hutton. New York: W.W. Norton & Company, 1982.

Barricelli, Franca R. "'Making a People What It Once Was': Regenerating Civic Identity in the Revolutionary Theatre of Venice." *Eighteenth-Century Life* 23, no. 3 (1999): 38–57.

Berchet, Giovanni. *Lettera semiseria: Scritti scelti di critica e di polemica*. Edited by Luigi Reina. Milan: Mursia, 1977.

Bézzola, Guido. "La polemica degli anni 1810–1811: Origini, aspetti letterari e politici." In *Atti dei convegni Foscoliani*, vol. 2, 115–36. Rome: Istituto Poligrafico e Zecca dello Stato, 1988.

Biblioteca italiana. Milan, 1816–40.

Binni, Walter. *Foscolo e la critica: Storia e antologia della critica*. Florence: La Nuova Italia, 1967.

– *Carducci e altri saggi*. Turin: Einaudi, 1972.

– *Monti poeta del consenso*. Florence: Sansoni, 1981.

"Biographical Particulars of Celebrated Persons Lately Deceased." *New Monthly Magazine* 21 (October 1827): 440.

Boccaccio, Giovanni. *Decameron*. Edited by Vittore Branca. 2 vols. Milan: Arnoldo Mondadori Editore, 1985.

Borgese, Giuseppe. *Storia della critica romantica in Italia*. Verona: Mondadori, 1949; reprint of 1920 edition.

Bosisio, Paolo. *La parola e scena: Studi sul teatro italiano tra Settecento e Novecento*. Rome: Bulzoni Editore, 1987.

– "La rappresentazione dell'*Ajace* e la tecnica teatrale foscoliana." *Belfagor* 35 (1980): 139–56.

– *Tra ribellione e utopia: L'esperienza teatrale nell'Italia delle repubbliche napoleoniche (1796–1805)*. Rome: Bulzoni, 1990.

Braudy, Leo. *The Frenzy of Renown: Fame and Its History*. London: Oxford University Press, 1986.

Bruni, Arnaldo. *Foscolo traduttore e poeta: Da Omero ai "Sepolcri."* Bologna: CLUEB, 2007.

Bruni, Francesco. "Dante e Byron: Un incontro ravennate." *Letture classensi* 28 (1999): 95–153.

– *Italia, vita e avventure di un'idea*. Bologna: Il Mulino, 2010.

Bruni, Francesco, ed. Introduction to *L'Italia e la formazione della civiltà europea: Letteratura e vita intelletuale*. Turin: UTET, 1994.

Byron, Lord George Gordon. *Byron's Letters and Journals*. 12 vols. Edited by L.A. Marchand. Cambridge, MA: Belknap Press of Harvard University Press, 1974–82.

– *Childe Harold's Pilgrimage Canto the Fourth*. London: John Murray, 1818.

– *The Complete Poetical Works*. Vol. 2. Edited by Jerome McGann. New York: Oxford University Press, 1980.

Cambon, Glauco. *Ugo Foscolo, Poet of Exile*. Princeton: Princeton University Press, 1980.

Capra, Carlo. "Il giornalismo nell'età rivoluzionaria e napoleonica." In *La stampa italiana dal Cinquecento all'Ottocento*. Vol. 1, edited by Valerio Castronovo, Giuseppe Ricuperati, Carlo Capra, 371–537. Bari: Laterza, 1976.

Carlson, Marvin. "The Italian Romantic Drama in Its European Context." In *Romantic Drama*, edited by Gerald Gillespie, 223–48. Amsterdam, Philadelphia: John Benjamins Publishing Company, 1994.

– *The Italian Stage from Goldoni to D'Annunzio*. London: McFarland & Co., 1981.

Carrer, Luigi. *Vita di Ugo Foscolo*. Edited by Carlo Mariani. Bergamo: Moretti & Vitali, 1995.

Catalano, Ettore. *Foscolo "tragico": Dal Tieste alle Ultime lettere di Jacopo Ortis*. Bari: Laterza, 2001.

– *La spada e le opinioni: Il teatro di Foscolo*. Foggia: Bastogi, 1983.

– *Le trame occulte: L'Ajace e la Ricciarda nel percorso teatrale di Ugo Foscolo*. Bari: Laterza, 2002.

Cesarotti, Melchiorre. *Opere*. Vol. 32, edited by Giuseppe Barbieri. Florence: Presso Molini, Landi & Co., 1800.

– *Poesie di Ossian*. In *Dal Muratori al Cesarotti*, edited by Emilio Bigi, Vol. 4. 87–269. Milan: Riccardo Ricciardi Editore, 1960.

– "Ragionamento sopra il diletto della tragedia." In *Dal Muratori al Cesarotti*, edited by Emilio Bigi, Vol. 4, 27–53. Milan: Riccardo Ricciardi, 1960.

Chauvet, Victor. *Manzoni – Stendhal – Hugo e altri saggi su classici e romantici*. Edited by Carlo Cordié. Catania: Università di Catania, 1958.

Chiarini, Giuseppi. *La vita di Ugo Foscolo*. Edited by Guido Mazzoni. Florence: G. Barbèra, 1927.

Chini, Rita. "Il 'Poligrafo' e l''Antipoligrafo': Polemiche letterarie nella Milan napoleonica." *Giornale storico della letteratura italiana* 149 (1972): 87–105.

Cian, Vittorio. "Un articolo shakepeariano di Ugo Foscolo." *Giornale storico della letteratura italiana* 91 (April–June 1928): 343–64.

Ciccarelli, Andrea. "L'*Ajace* di Foscolo fra azione e inazione: Ovvero il rifiuto della storia." *Quarterly Journal in Modern Foreign Languages* 49, no. 3 (Fall 1995): 203–13.

– *Manzoni: La coscenza della letteratura*. Rome: Bulzoni, 1996.

Ciccone, Stefania De Stefanis. "Per uno studio del linguaggio dei periodici milanesi del primo Ottocento (1800–1847)." *Lingua nostra* 41 (March 1980): 26–33.

Cimmino, Nicola Francesco. *Ippolito Pindemonte e il suo tempo*. 2 vols. Rome: Edizioni Abete, 1968.

Coleridge, Samuel Taylor. "Hamlet." In *Lectures and Notes on Shakspere and Other English Poets*, 342–68. London: George Bell and Sons, 1904.

Il Conciliatore. Edited by Vittore Branca. Florence, 1953–4.

Conti, Antonio. *Giulio Cesare*. Parma: F. Carmignani, 1770.

Corrigan, Beatrice. "Foscolo's Articles on Dante in the *Edinburgh Review*: A Study in Collaboration." In *Collected Essays on Italian Language and Literature Presented to Kathleen Speight*, 211–25. Manchester: Manchester University Press, 1971.

– "Pellico's *Francesca da Rimini*: The First English Translation." *Italica* 31, no. 4 (December 1954): 215–24.

Costelloe, Timothy M. "The Theater of Morals: Culture and Community in Rousseau's *Lettre à M. d'Alembert*." *Eighteenth-Century Life* 27, no. 1 (Winter 2003): 52–71.

Crébillon, Prosper Jolyot de. *Atrée et Thyestes*. In *Oeuvres de Crébillon*, vol. 1, 89–155. Paris: P. Didot, 1802.

Crescimbeni, Giovan Mario. *La bellezza della volgar poesia*. Rome: Buagni, 1700.
– *Storia dell'Accademia degli Arcadi*. London: T. Becket, 1804.
Davis, P.J. *Seneca: Thyestes*. Duckworth Companions to Greek and Roman Tragedy. London: Duckworth, 2003.
Dell'Aquila, Michele. *Foscolo e il romanticismo*. Bari: Adriatica Editrice, 1992.
Del Vento, Christian. *Un allievo della rivoluzione: Ugo Foscolo dal "noviziato letterario" al "nuovo classicismo" (1795–1806)*. Bologna: CLUEB, 2003.
De Michelis, Cesare. "Foscolo e il teatro giacobino veneziano." In *Atti dei convegni Foscoliani*, vol. 1, 127–42. Rome: Istituto poligrafico e Zecco dello Stato, 1988.
De Sanctis, Francesco. *Storia della letteratura italiana*. Edited by Niccolò Gallo. Introduced by Giorgio Ficara. Turin: Einaudi, 1996.
Dionisotti, Carlo. "Venezia e il noviziato di Foscolo." In *Appunti sui moderni: Foscolo, Leopardi, Manzoni e altri*, 33–53. Bologna: Il Mulino, 1998.
Di Pino, Guido. "La 'Ricciarda.'" In *Atti dei convegni Foscoliani*, vol. 3, 271–83. Rome: Istituto Poligrafico e Zecca dello Stato, 1998.
Donadoni, Eugenio. *Ugo Foscolo: Pensatore, critico, poeta*. 3rd edition. Florence: Edizioni Remo Sandron, 1964.
Doni, Carla. *Il mito Greco nelle tragedie di Ugo Foscolo (Tieste-Ajace)*. Rome: Bulzoni Editore, 1997.
Donoghue, Frank. *The Fame Machine: Book-Reviewing and Eighteenth-Century Literary Careers*. Stanford: Stanford University Press, 1996.
Edinburgh Review. Edinburgh and London, 1802–1929.
Favaro, Adriano. *Isabella Teotochi Albrizzi: La sua vita, i suoi amori e i suoi viaggi*. Udine: P. Gaspari, 2003.
Feldman, Martha. "Opera, Festivity and Spectacle in 'Revolutionary' Venice." In *Venice Reconsidered: The History and Civilization of a City State 1297–1797*, edited by John Jeffries Martin and Dennis Romano, 217–62. Baltimore, MD: Johns Hopkins University Press, 2000.
Foligno, Cesare. *Note sul Foscolo critico*. Naples: Libreria Scientifica Editrice, 1945.
Foscolo, Ugo. "Abbozzo dell'*Edippo*." In *Edizione nazionale delle opere di Ugo Foscolo*, vol. 2, *Tragedie e poesie minori*, edited by Guido Bézzola, 227–35. Florence: Felice Le Monnier, 1961.
– "L'addio all'Italia." In *Edizione nazionale delle opere di Ugo Foscolo*, vol. 8, *Prose politiche e letterarie dal 1811 al 1816*, edited by Luigi Fassò, 314. Florence: Felice Le Monnier, 1972.
– *Ajace*. In *Edizione nazionale delle opere di Ugo Foscolo*, vol. 2, *Tragedie e poesie minori*, edited by Guido Bézzola, 59–138. Florence: Felice Le Monnier, 1961.
– "Articolo su Dante." In *Edizione nazionale delle opere di Ugo Foscolo*, vol. 9, *Studi su Dante*, part 1, edited by Giovanni Da Pozzo, 1–55. Florence: Felice Le Monnier, 1979–81.

– "Articolo su Dante 2." In *Edizione nazionale delle opere di Ugo Foscolo*, vol. 9, *Studi su Dante*, part 1, edited by Giovanni Da Pozzo, 57–145. Florence: Felice Le Monnier, 1979–81.

– *Bibliografia foscoliana*. In *Edizione nazionale delle opere di Ugo Foscolo*, Appendix, pt. 1 and 2, edited by Giuseppe Nicoletti. Florence: Felice Le Monnier, 2011.

– *Dei sepolcri*. In *Edizione nazionale delle opere di Ugo Foscolo*, vol. 1, *Poesie e carmi*, edited by Francesco Pagliai, Gianfranco Folena, and Mario Scotti, 128–31. Florence: Felice Le Monnier, 1985.

– "Della nuova scuola drammatica italiana." In *Edizione nazionale delle opere di Ugo Foscolo*, vol. 11, *Saggi di letteratura italiana*, part 2, edited by Cesare Foligno, 557–618. Florence: Felice Le Monnier, 1958.

– "Dell'origine e dell'ufficio della letteratura." In *Edizione nazionale delle opere di Ugo Foscolo*, vol. 7, *Lezioni articoli di critica e di polemica (1809–1811)*, edited by Emilio Santini, 3–37. Florence: Felice Le Monnier, 1967.

– *Edippo tragedia inedita*. Edited by Mario Scotti. Milan: Rizzoli, 1983.

– *Epistolario I (1794–1804)*. In *Edizione nazionale delle opere di Ugo Foscolo*, vol. 14, edited by Plinio Carli. Florence: Felice Le Monnier, 1949.

– *Epistolario II (1804–1808)*. In *Edizione nazionale delle opere di Ugo Foscolo*, vol. 15, edited by Plinio Carli. Florence: Felice Le Monnier, 1952.

– *Epistolario III (1809–1811)*. In *Edizione nazionale delle opere di Ugo Foscolo*, vol. 16, edited by Plinio Carli. Florence: Felice Le Monnier, 1953.

– *Epistolario IV (1812–1813)*. In *Edizione nazionale delle opere di Ugo Foscolo*, vol. 17, edited by Plinio Carli. Florence: Felice Le Monnier, 1954.

– *Epistolario V (1814–1815)*. In *Edizione nazionale delle opere di Ugo Foscolo*, vol. 18, edited by Plinio Carli. Florence: Felice Le Monnier, 1956.

– *Epistolario VI (1815–1816)*. In *Edizione nazionale delle opere di Ugo Foscolo*, vol. 19, edited by Giovanni Gambarin and Francesco Tropeano. Florence: Felice Le Monnier, 1966.

– *Episotolario VII (1816–1818)*. In *Edizione nazionale delle opere di Ugo Foscolo*, vol. 20, edited by Mario Scotti. Florence: Felice Le Monnier, 1970.

– *Epistolario VIII (1819–1821)*. In *Edizione nazionale delle opere di Ugo Foscolo*, vol. 21, edited by Mario Scotti. Florence: Felice Le Monnier, 1974.

– *Epistolario IX (1822–1824)*. In *Edizione nazionale delle opere di Ugo Foscolo*, vol. 22, edited by Mario Scotti. Florence: Felice Le Monnier, 1992.

– *Esperimento di traduzione dell'Iliade di Omero*. In *Edizione nazionale delle opere di Ugo Foscolo*, vol. 3, *Esperimento di traduzione dell'Iliade*, part 1, edited by Gennaro Barbarisi, 4–69. Florence: Felice Le Monnier, 1961.

– "Essay on the Present Literature of Italy." In *Edizione nazionale delle opere di Ugo Foscolo*, vol. 11, *Saggi di letteratura italiana*, part 2, edited by Cesare Foligno, 399–490. Florence: Felice Le Monnier, 1958.

– *I frammenti sul Machiavelli*. In *Edizione nazionale delle opere di Ugo Foscolo*, vol. 8, *Prose politiche e letterarie dal 1811 al 1816*, edited by Luigi Fassò, 1–64. Florence: Felice Le Monnier, 1972.
– "Frederick the Second and Pietro delle Vigne." In *Edizione nazionale delle opere di Ugo Foscolo*, vol. 10, *Saggi e discorsi critici*, edited by Cesare Foligno, 455–62. Florence: Felice Le Monnier, 1953.
– "Guido Cavalcanti." In *Edizione nazionale delle opere di Ugo Foscolo*, vol. 10, *Saggi e discorsi critici*, edited by Cesare Foligno, 423–36. Florence: Felice Le Monnier, 1953.
– "Intorno ad antiquari e critici." In *Edizione nazionale delle opere di Ugo Foscolo*, vol. 11, *Saggi di letteratura italiana*, part 2, edited by Cesare Foligno, 302–24. Florence: Felice Le Monnier, 1958.
– "Italian Periodical Literature." In *Edizione nazionale delle opere di Ugo Foscolo*, vol. 11, *Saggi di letteratura italiana*, part 2, edited by Cesare Foligno, 327–66. Florence: Felice Le Monnier, 1958.
– "Learned Ladies." In *Edizione nazionale delle opere di Ugo Foscolo*, vol. 10, *Saggi e discorsi critici*, edited by Cesare Foligno, 203–18. Florence: Felice Le Monnier, 1953.
– "The Lyric Poetry of Tasso." In *Edizione nazionale delle opere di Ugo Foscolo*, vol. 10, *Saggi e discorsi critici*, edited by Cesare Foligno, 373–80. Florence: Felice Le Monnier, 1953.
– "Michel Angelo." In *Edizione nazionale delle opere di Ugo Foscolo*, vol. 10, *Saggi e discorsi critici*, edited by Cesare Foligno, 447–60. Florence: Felice Le Monnier, 1953.
– "Narrative and Romantic Poems of the Italians." In *Edizione nazionale delle opere di Ugo Foscolo*, vol. 11, *Saggi di letteratura italiana*, part 2, edited by Cesare Foligno, 1–202. Florence: Felice Le Monnier, 1958.
– "On Hamlet." In *Edizione nazionale delle opere di Ugo Foscolo*, vol. 10, *Saggi e discorsi critici*, edited by Cesare Foligno, 583–9. Florence: Felice Le Monnier, 1953.
– *Opere*. Vol. 1, *Poesie e tragedie*. Edited by Franco Gavazzeni, Maria Maddalena Lombardi, and Franco Longoni. Turin: Einaudi-Gallimard, 1994.
– *Parere sulla istituzione di un giornale letterario*. In *Edizione nazionale delle opere di Ugo Foscolo*, vol. 8, *Prose politiche e letterarie dal 1811 al 1816*, edited by Luigi Fassò, 315–19. Florence: Felice Le Monnier, 1972.
– "Per la istituzione di un teatro civico." In *Edizione nazionale delle opere di Ugo Foscolo*, vol. 6, *Scritti letterari e politici dal 1796 al 1808*, edited by Giovanni Gambarin, 717. Florence: Felice Le Monnier, 1972.
– *Piano di studi*. In *Edizione nazionale delle opere di Ugo Foscolo*, vol. 6, *Scritti letterari e politici dal 1796 al 1808*, edited by Giovanni Gambarin, 1–10. Florence: Felice Le Monnier, 1972.

– *Postille a Silvio Pellico.* In *Edizione nazionale delle opere di Ugo Foscolo,* vol. 8, *Prose politiche e letterarie dal 1811 al 1816,* edited by Luigi Fassò, 403–4. Florence: Felice Le Monnier, 1972.
– "Principles of Poetical Criticism, as Applicable, More Especially, to Italian Literature." In *Edizione nazionale delle opere di Ugo Foscolo,* vol. 11, *Saggi di letteratura italiana,* part 1, edited by Cesare Foligno, 25–36. Florence: Felice Le Monnier, 1958.
– *Ricciarda.* In *Edizione nazionale delle opere di Ugo Foscolo,* vol. 2, *Tragedie e poesie minori,* edited by Guido Bézzola, 139–99. Florence: Felice Le Monnier, 1961.
– "Sulla Ricciarda." In *Edizione nazionale delle opere di Ugo Foscolo,* vol. 8, *Prose politiche e letterarie dal 1811 al 1816,* edited by Luigi Fassò, 374–6. Florence: Felice Le Monnier, 1972.
– "Sul nuovo Teatro di Como." In *Edizione nazionale delle opere di Ugo Foscolo,* vol. 8, *Prose politiche e letterarie dal 1811 al 1816,* edited by Luigi Fassò, 367–71. Florence: Felice Le Monnier, 1972.
– *Tieste.* In *Edizione nazionale delle opere di Ugo Foscolo,* vol. 2, *Tragedie e poesie minori,* edited by Guido Bézzola, 3–57. Florence: Felice Le Monnier, 1961.
– *Versi dell'adolescenza.* In *Edizione nazionale delle opere di Ugo Foscolo,* vol. 2, *Tragedie e poesie minori,* edited by Guido Bézzola, 239–84. Florence: Felice Le Monnier, 1961.
– *Vestigi della storia del sonetto italiano.* In *Edizione nazionale delle opere di Ugo Foscolo,* vol. 8, *Prose politiche e letterarie dal 1811 al 1816,* edited by Luigi Fassò, 119–50. Florence: Felice Le Monnier, 1972.
– "Ultimato di Ugo Foscolo nella guerra contro i ciarlatani, gl'impostori letterari ed i pedanti." In *Edizione nazionale delle opere di Ugo Foscolo,* vol. 7, *Lezioni articoli di critica e di polemica (1809–1811),* edited by Emilio Santini, 296–315. Florence: Felice Le Monnier, 1967.
– *Ultime lettere di Jacopo Ortis.* In *Edizione nazionale delle opere di Ugo Foscolo,* vol. 4, *Ultime lettere di Jacopo Ortis,* edited by Giovanni Gambarin. Florence: Felice Le Monnier, 1933.
– "The Women of Italy." In *Edizione nazionale delle opera di Ugo Foscolo,* vol. 12, *Scritti vari di critica storica e letteraria 1817 al 1827,* edited by Urberto Limentani and John Lindon, 418–69. Florence: Felice Le Monnier, 1978.
Franzero, Carlo Maria. *A Life in Exile, Ugo Foscolo in London, 1816–1827.* London: W.H. Allen, 1977.
Frattini, Alberto. *Il neoclassicismo e Ugo Foscolo.* Bologna: Cappelli, 1965.
Fubini, Mario. *Dal Muratori al Baretti: Studi sulla critica e sulla cultura del Settecento.* 2nd ed. Bari: Laterza, 1954.
– *Ugo Foscolo.* Florence: La Nuova Italia, 1962.
Fumaroli, Marc. "Les abeilles et les araignées." In *La querelle des anciens et modernes,* 7–200. Ed. Anne-Marie Lecoq. Paris: Gallimard, 2001.

Galetti, Alfredo. *Le teorie drammatiche e la tragedia in Italia nel secolo XVIII (1700–1750)*. Cremona: Fezzi, 1901.

Gambarin, Giovanni. "Note foscoliane." In *Saggi foscoliani e altri studi*, 165–78. Presented by Mario Fubini. Rome: Bonacci Editore, 1978.

Giles, David. *Illusions of Immortality: A Psychology of Fame and Celebrity*. New York: St Martin's Press, 2000.

Gimma, Giacinto. *L'idea della storia dell'Italia letterata*. Naples: Nella Stamperia di Felice Mosoca, 1723.

Giorgetti, Cinzia. *Ritratto di Isabella: Studi e documenti su Isabella Teotochi Albrizzi*. Florence: Le Lettere, 1992.

Giornale Italiano. 14 December 1811, 1395–6.

Girardi, Enzo Noè, ed. *Goethe e Manzoni, Rapporti tra Italia e Germania intorno al 1800*. Florence: Leo S. Olschki, 1992.

Goethe, Wolfgang von. "Goethe e i romantici italiani." Translated by E. Meyer. *Antologia* 55 (July 1825): 26–7.

– "On Criticism." In *Literary Essays*, translated by J.E. Spingarn, 140–2. New York: Frederick Ungar Publishing Co., 1921.

– *Wilhelm Meisters Wandeljahre*. In *Goethes sämtliche Werke*, vol. 17. Stuttgart and Berlin: J.G. Cotta, 1902–7.

Goffis, Cesare Federico. *La tragedia dall'Alfieri al Manzoni*. 2 vols. Genoa: Tilgher, 1973.

Granese, Alberto. *Ugo Foscolo tra le folgori e la notte*. Salerno: Edisud, 2004.

Gravina, Gian Vincenzo. "Della tragedie." In *Opere italiane: Della ragion poetica e della tragedia*. Cosenza: Walter Brenner Editore, 1992.

Graziosi, Elisabetta. "Arcadia Femminile: Presenze e Modelli." *Filologia e critica* 17 (1992): 321–58.

Guerra, Lia. "Mary Shelley's Contributions to Lardner's *Cabinet Cyclopaedia: Lives of the Most Eminent Literary and Scientific Men of Italy*." In *British Romanticism and Italian Literature: Translating, Reviewing, Rewriting*, 221–36. Amsterdam: Rodopi, 2005.

Hobhouse, John Cam. *Historical Illustrations to the Fourth Canto of Childe Harold*. London: John Murray, 1818.

– *Italy, Remarks Made in Several Visits from the Year 1816–1854*. London: John Murray, 1859.

– *Recollections of a Long Life*. Vol. 3, edited by Lady Dorchester. London: John Murray, 1910.

Horace. *Epistles Book II and Epistle to the Pisones*. Edited by Niall Rudd. Cambridge: Cambridge University Press, 1989.

Innocenti, Loretta. "Le tragedie veneziane di Byron." In *La maschera e il volto: Il teatro in Italia*, edited by Francesco Bruni, 257–74. Venice: Fondazione Giorgio Cini, 2002.

Isabella, Maurizio. *Risorgimento in Exile: Italian Émigrés and the Liberal International in the Post-Napoleonic Era*. Oxford: Oxford University Press, 2009.

Johnson, Samuel. "Cowley." In *Lives of the Poets*, vol. 1. London, 1896.

– *Johnson's Preface to Shakespeare*. Edited by P.J. Smallwood. Bristol: Bristol Classical Press. 1985.

Kruger, Loren. *The National Stage: Theatre and Cultural Legitimation in England, France, and America*. Chicago: University of Chicago Press, 1992.

Lampredi, Urbano. "AJACE, Tragedia nuovissima del sig. Ugo Foscolo." *Il Poligrafo*, 15 December 1811, 589–92.

– "Letteratura." *Il Poligrafo*, 22 December 1811, 594–8.

– "Letteratura." *Il Poligrafo*, 29 December 1811, 610–13.

– "Letteratura." *Il Poligrafo*, 5 January 1812, 3–6.

Lanza, Maria Teresa. *Foscolo*. Storia della critica. Palermo: Palumbo, 1977.

Lattanzi, *Corriere delle Dame*. 14 December 1811, 425–6.

Le Tourneur, Pierre. *Shakespeare traduit de l'Anglois*. 20 vols. Paris: Le veuve Duchesne, 1776–83.

Limentani, Uberto. "Testimonianze inglesi sul Foscolo." *Giornale storico della letteratura italiana* 133 (July–September 1956): 390–409.

Lindon, John. *Studi su Foscolo "inglese."* Pisa: Giardini editori e stampatori, 1987.

Lombardi, Maria Maddalena. "Sull'attribuzione al Foscolo dell'«Edippo», tragedia di Wigberto Rivalta." *Studi di filologia italiana* 54 (1996): 291–309.

Luzzi, Joseph. *Romantic Europe and the Ghost of Italy*. New Haven: Yale University Press, 2008.

Maffei, Scipione. *De' teatri antichi e moderni e altri scritti teatrali*. Edited by Laura Sannia Nowé. Modena: Mucchi Editore, 1988.

– *Merope*. Edited by Celestino Garibotto. Verona: Edizioni di "Vita Veronese," 1954.

Mangini, Nicola. "La vita teatrale nella Venezia del Foscolo." In *Atti dei convegni Foscoliani*, vol. 3, 237–56. Rome: Istituto Poligrafico e Zecca dello Stato, 1988.

– "Venezia il Foscolo e la rappresentazione del 'Tieste.'" *Rivista italiana di drammaturgia* 14 (1979): 37–55.

Manzoni, Alessandro. *Il Conte di Carmagnola*. In *Opere*, edited by Lanfranco Caretti, 763–854. Milan: Mursia, 1974.

– *The Count of Carmagnola and Adelchis*. Introduction and translation by Federica Brunori Deigan. Baltimore: Johns Hopkins University Press, 2004.

– *Lettre à Monsieur Chauvet sur l'unité de temps et de lieu dans la tragédie*. In *Opere*, edited by Lanfranco Caretti, 855–912. Milan: Mursia, 1974.

– *Tragedie: Il conte di Carmagnola e L'Adelchi, aggiuntevi le poesie varie dello stesso, ed aclune prose sulla teoria del dramma tragico*. Florence: Giuseppe Molini, 1825.

Marcazzan, Mario. "La letteratura e il teatro." In *La civiltà veneziana del Settecento*, ed. Diego Valeri. Florence: Sansoni, 1960.

Marchand, Leslie, ed. *Byron's Letters and Journals.* 12 vols. Cambridge, MA: Belknap Press, 1974.

Marseglia, Luigi. *Drammaturgia e romanzo. Primo Ottocento: I generi letterari nel "Conciliatore."* Bari: Palomar, 2004.

Marshall, David. "Rousseau and the State of Theater." *Representation* 13 (1986): 84–114.

Martello, Pier Jacopo. "Del verso tragico." In *Scritti critici e satirici*, edited by Hannibal S. Noce, 151–88. Bari: Laterza & Figli, 1963.

Martinelli, Bortolo. "Ugo Foscolo storico della letteratura italiana." *Otto/Novecento* 4 (1989): 1–29.

Martinetti, G.A. *Delle guerre letterarie contro Ugo Foscolo.* Turin: Paravia, 1881.

– "Sul testo delle tragedie di Ugo Foscolo." In *Giornale storico della letteratura italiana* 23 (1894), 208–31.

Masiello, Vitilio. "Foscolo e Vico: Le fondazioni foscoliane della coscienza tragica." In *Atti dei convegni Foscoliani*, vol. 3, 435–56. Rome: Istituto Poligrafico e Zecca dello Stato, 1988.

Mattioda, Enrico. *Teoria della tragedia nel Settecento I.* Modena: Mucchi Editore, 1994.

– *Tragedie del Settecento.* Vol. 1. Modena: Mucchi Editore, 1999.

May, Frederick. "Calliroe e Ifianeo: Work in Progress on the 'English' Period of Ugo Foscolo." *Italica* 41, no. 1 (March 1964): 63–73.

Mazza, Antonia Tonucci. "Riflessioni foscoliane sulla figura e sui compiti del critico." *Otto/Novecento* 2, no. 1 (January/February 1978): 1–28.

Messbarger, Rebecca. *The Century of Women: Representations of Women in Eighteenth-Century Italian Public Discourse.* Toronto: University of Toronto Press, 2002.

Michieli, Adriano Augusto. *Ugo Foscolo a Venezia.* Venice: Visentini Cav. Federico, 1903.

Milman, Henry Hart. "Italian Tragedy." *Quarterly Review*, October 1820: 72–102.

Monti, Vincenzo. *Aristodemo.* Edited by Arnaldo Bruni. Parma: Ugo Guanda Editore, 1998.

– *Lettere d'affetti e di poesia.* Edited by Angelo Colombo. Rome: Salerno Editrice, 1993.

Muratori, Ludovico Antonio. *Della perfetta poesia italiana.* Edited by Ada Ruschioni. 2 vols. Milan: Marzorati Editore, 1971.

Naselli, Maria. *La fortuna del Foscolo nell'Ottocento.* Genoa: Società Anonima Editrice Francesco Perrella, 1923.

Nicoletti, Giuseppe. "Alfierismo mediato e controcorrente nel *Tieste* foscoliano." *Annali alfieriani* 4 (1985).
– *Foscolo*. Rome: Salerno, 2006.
Parmegiani, Sandra. *Ugo Foscolo and English Culture*. London: Legenda (Modern Humanities Research Association and Maney Publishing), 2011.
Pecchio, Giuseppe. *Vita di Ugo Foscolo*. Edited by G. Nicoletti. Milan: Longanesi, 1974.
Pellico, Silvio. *Tragedie di Silvio Pellico*. Florence: Le Monnier, 1859.
– "Vera idea della tragedia di Vittorio Alfieri, ossia la dissertazione critica dell'avvocato Giovanni Carmignani confutata dall'avv. Gaetano Marrè, professore di dirrito commerciale nella R. Università di Genoa, articolo primo." In *Il Conciliatore*. Edited by Vittorio Branca, vol. 1, 34–8. Florence: Felice Le Monnier, 1953.
– "Vera idea della tragedia di Vittorio Alfieri, ossia la dissertazione critica dell'avvocato Giovanni Carmignani confutata dall'avv. Gaetano Marrè, professore di dirrito commerciale nella R. Università di Genoa, articolo secondo." In *Il Conciliatore*. Edited by Vittorio Branca, vol. 1, 128–35. Florence: Felice Le Monnier, 1953.
Pepoli, Alessandro Ercole. *Tragedie*. Parma: Reale tipografia, 1791–6.
Peterson, Thomas E. *The Revolt of the Scribe in Modern Italian Literature*. Toronto: University of Toronto Press, 2010.
Pezzi, Francesco. "*Il Conte di Carmagnola*, tragedia di Alessandro Manzoni." *Biblioteca italiana* 17 (January–March 1820): 232–44.
– "Notizie interne." *Corriere Milanese*, 10 December 1811, 1179–80.
Pillepich, Alain. *Napoléon et les Italiens: République Italienne et Royaume d'Italie*. Paris: Nouveau Monde, 2003.
Pindemonte, Giovanni. *Poesia e lettere di Giovanni Pindemonte*. Edited by Giuseppe Biadego. Bologna: N. Zanichelli, 1883.
Pindemonte, Ippolito. *Arminio*. Verona: Dalla Società tipografica, 1819.
– *Lettere a Isabella (1784–1828)*. Edited by Gilberto Pizzamiglio. Florence: Leo S. Olschki Editore, 2000.
Praz, Mario. "Foscolo tra romanticismo e neoclassicismo." In *Atti dei convegni Foscoliani*, vol. 1, 17–32. Rome: Istituto Poligrafico e Zecca dello Stato, 1988.
Prospetto delle sessioni della Società d'Istruzione Pubblica di Venezia. Venice: Giovanni Zatta, 1797.
Pullini, Giorgio. *Teatro italiano dell'Ottocento*. Milan: Vallardi, 1981.
Quadrio, Francesco S. *Della storia e della ragione di ogni poesia*. 4 vols. Bologna: F. Pisarri, 1739–49.
Quarterly Review. London: John Murray, 1809–1906.

Raccolta di carte pubbliche, istruzioni, legislazioni e del nuovo governo democratico. Vols. 1–10. Venice: 1797.

Raccolta di tutte le carte pubbliche stampate ad esposte ne' luoghi piu frequentati della citta di Venezia. Vols. 1–10. Venice: 1797.

Radcliff-Umstead, Douglas. "Foscolo and the Early Italian Romantics." *Italica* 42, no. 3 (September 1965): 231–46.

– *Ugo Foscolo.* New York: Twayne Publishers, 1970.

"Remarks on the Life and Writings of Ugo Foscolo." *New Monthly Magazine and Literary Journal* 1 (January 1821): 76–85.

Robertson, J.G. *Studies in the Genesis of Romantic Theory of the 18th Century.* New York: Russell & Russell, 1962.

Rosada, Bruno. "Considerazione sul *Tieste* foscoliano." In *Atti dei convegni Foscoliani*, vol. 3, 451–72. Rome: Istituto Poligrafico e Zecca dello Stato, 1988.

– "Foscolo scolaro a Venezia." *Ateneo veneto* 19, nos. 1–2 (1981): 52–70.

– *Foscolo a Venezia negli ultimi anni della Serenissima.* Treviso: Grafiche San Vito, 2006.

– *La giovinezza poetica di Ugo Foscolo tra Dalmazia e Venezia.* Venice: Alcione editore, 2011.

Roscoe, Thomas. "Remarks on the Life and Works of Ugo Foscolo." *New Monthly Magazine* 1 (January 1821): 76–85.

– "The Works of Ugo Foscolo." *Foreign Quarterly Review* 2 (September 1828): 428.

Saglia, Diego. "'Freedom alone is wanting': British Views of Contemporary Italian Drama, 1820–1830." In *British Romanticism and Italian Literature: Translating, Reviewing, Rewriting*, 238–55. Amsterdam: Rodopi, 2005.

Said, Edward. "Reflections on Exile." In *Reflections on Exile and Other Essays*, 173–86. Cambridge, MA: Harvard University Press, 2000.

Santangelo, Giorgio. *Il dramma romantico in Italia.* 2 vols. Palermo: Manfredi, 1971–2.

Scalvini, Giovita. *Foscolo Manzoni Goethe, Scritti editi e inediti.* Turin: Einaudi, 1948.

Schlegel, August von. *Course of Lectures on Dramatic Arts and Literature.* Translated by J. Black. London: Henry G. Bohn, 1846.

Scotti, Mario. *Foscoliana.* Modena: Mucchi Editore, 1997.

– *Fra erudizione e poesia.* Rome: Bonacci, 1973.

Shelley, Mary. "Ugo Foscolo." In *Lives of the Most Eminent Literary and Scientific Men in Italy, Spain and Portugal*, vol. 2, 353–94. London: Longman, Rees, Orme, Brown, Green & Longman, 1835.

Simonton, D. Keith. *Greatness: Who Makes History and Why.* New York: The Guilford Press, 1994.

Staël, Mme de. *Oeuvres complètes*. 3 vols. Geneva: Slatkine, 1967.

Stocchi, Manilo Pastore. "1792–1797: Ugo Foscolo a Venezia." In *Storia della cultura veneta*, vol. 6, 21–58. Vicenza: Neri Pozza, 1986.

Teatro moderno applaudito, Vol. 13. Venice, 1797.

Il teatro italiano V: La tragedia dell'Ottocento. Edited by Emilio Faccioli. Turin: Einaudi, 1981.

Teatro tragico-italiano. Naples, 1847.

Teatro tragico italiano. Florence: Passigli Borghi & Co., 1830–1.

Teotochi Marin Albrizzi, Isabella. *Ritratti*. Edited by Gino Tellini. Palermo: Sellerio, 1992.

Terzoli, Maria Antonietta. *Foscolo*. Rome: Laterza, 2000.

– I *"Vestigi della storia del sonetto italiano" di Ugo Foscolo*. Rome: Salerno Editrice, 1993.

Tiraboschi, Girolamo. *Storia della letteratura italiana*. 9 vols. Florence: Presso, Molini, Landi e co, 1805–13.

Toffanin, Giuseppe. *L'eredità del Rinascimento in Arcadia*. Bologna: Zanichelli, 1923.

Turchi, Roberta. *Paride Zajotti e la "Biblioteca italiana."* Padua: Liviana editrice in Padova, 1974.

– "Ugo Foscolo e la 'Biblioteca italiana.'" In *Atti dei convegni Foscoliani*, vol. 3, 583–628. Rome: Istituto Poligrafico e Zecca dello Stato, 1988.

Vallone, Aldo. *La polemica Foscolo-Lampredi, con due inediti del L.* Galatina: 1946.

Varese, Claudio. *Vita interiore di Ugo Foscolo*. Rocco San Casciano: Cappelli Editore, 1966.

Vieusseux, André. "Foscolo and His Times." *Foreign Quarterly Review* 9, no. 18 (May 1832): 312–44.

Viglione, Francesco. "Sul teatro di Ugo Foscolo." *Annali della R. Scuola Normale Superiore di Pisa* 18 (1946): 1–152.

– *Ugo Foscolo in Inghilterra*. Catania: Muglia, 1910.

Vincent, Eric Reginald. *Byron, Hobhouse and Foscolo: New Documents in the History of a Collaboration*. Cambridge: Cambridge University Press, 1949.

– *Ugo Foscolo, and Italian in Regency England*. Cambridge: Cambridge University Press, 1953.

Visconti, Ermes. "Dialogo sulle unità drammatiche di luogo e di tempo." *Il Conciliatore* 2 (January–June 1819): 90–117.

Voltaire (F.M. Arouet). *Les Pélopides*. In *Oeuvres complètes de Voltaire*, vol. 2, 176–91. Paris: Chez Fume, 1835.

Waquet, Françoise. *Le modèle français et l'Italie savante. Conscience de soi et perception de l'autre dans la République des Lettres (1660–1750)*. Rome: École française de Rome, 1989.

Walsh, Rachel A. "Difetti di Disegno: *Sul nuovo teatro di Como* di Ugo Foscolo."
  Giornale storico della letteratura italiana 625, no. 1 (2012): 91–109.
– "Making Histories and Defending Reputations: Ludovico Antonio Muratori
  and Ugo Foscolo." *Rassegna Europea di Letteratura Italiana* 36 (December
  2010): 111–28.
– "Theatrical Spinning: *Ricciarda* and Ugo Foscolo's Campaign for Fame."
  MLN 124 (Italian issue, January 2009): 137–57.
Wellek, René. "The Italian Critics." In *A History of Modern Criticism: 1750–1950*,
  vol. 2, 265–72. New Haven: Yale University Press, 1955.
Wicks, M.C.W. *The Italian Exiles in London, 1816–1848*. Manchester: Manchester
  University Press, 1937.
Zajotti, Paride. "*Ricciarda*." *Biblioteca italiana* 5, no. 20 (October–December
  1820): 308–21.

Index

Pezzi, Francesco, 50, 55, 117, 158nn44–5, 180n35
Piano di studi: about, 22–3; major poets, 144nn55–6; major tragedians, 28, 47, 185n61; and Rubbi's *Parnaso*, 22, 144n53; second section, 25
Pignotti, Lorenzo, 144n55
Pindemonte, Giovanni: *Donna Caritea*, 31, 90; in "Essay," 144n57; Foscolo on, 23; literary feuds, 87–8, 89, 90; Milman on, 99, 178n12; omission from *Piano di studi*, 23; spectacles, 27, 87
Pindemonte, Ippolito: Alfieri's influence, 20; *Arminio*, 87–8, 173nn82–3; and Byron, 92, 174n100; in "Essay," 85, 92; and Foscolo, 87–8, 144n57, 172n81, 173nn82–3; Milman on, 99; salons, 22
Pius VII, Pope, 53
playwrights. *See* theatres
Poesie, xiv–xv, 44
Poetics (Aristotle), 11–12, 18, 140n6, 142n30
poetry, Italian: academy treatises on, 11; Foscolo's "Italian Poets" series, xvii, 171n61, 175n115; Foscolo's lectures on, 104, 162n88, 182n48; major poets in *Piano di studi*, 144nn55–6; Muratori's criticism, 14–15; sonnets, 83, 170nn57–8; the sublime, 14–15; Vico's influence, 45. *See also* "Principles of Poetical Criticism"
Il Poligrafo: about, 51, 54–5, 156n26; *Ajace* original reviews, 54–5, 57–8, 61, 121–36, 137nn8, 20; literary feuds, 51, 54–5, 57–8, 70, 82, 156n26, 165n120

Portugal, Antonio Fonseca, 65
Prepiani, Giovanbattista, 125, 156n30
"Principles of Poetical Criticism," xvii–xviii, 104–6, 109, 162n88, 182n48, 183nn49, 52–3, 184nn54–8
publications. *See* journals
public opinion, 106
public theatre. *See* civic theatre
Pullini, Giorgio, 49, 73, 167nn18–19

Quadrio, Francesco S., 45, 153n104

Racine, Jean, 11–12, 181n38
Radcliff-Umstead, Douglas, 176n3
"Ragguaglio d'un'adunanza dell' Accademia de' Pitagorici," xv, 50
"Ragionamento sopra il diletto della tragedia" (Cesarotti), 16–18, 27, 28, 39, 52
Rapin, René, 10
Redding, Cyrus, 95, 185n62
"Reflections on Exile" (Said), 82, 170n55
Reggio Emilia, xiii, 39
"Remarks on the Life and Works of Ugo Foscolo" (Roscoe), 96
Ricciarda, 71–97; about, 4, 8, 72–4; actors, 76–80, 169n44; Alfieri's influences, 73; censorship, 80–1, 91; characters, 72–3, 75, 80, 100, 166n8, 167n19, 169n46; classical unities, 72, 167n22; composition, xvi, 71–2; costume, 74, 167n17; dagger, 75–6; and *Dei sepolcri*, 167n23; dramatist on stage, 17, 77, 79; in "Essay," 90–1; fire on stage, 78–80; Foscolo's criticism, 76–7; Foscolo's response to criticism, 91; graveyard imagery, 72, 75, 166n7, 167n23; harmonious discord,